MEMORIES OF
BRITAIN PAST

MEMORIES OF
BRITAIN PAST

The illustrated story of how we lived, worked and played

Juliet Gardiner

Reader's Digest | gettyimages

CONTENTS

7   Introduction

8   Chapter One   CHILDHOOD DAYS

10   A New Baby
20   Off to School
22   Toy Story
34   Radio and TV Times
36   Learning to Join In
42   Children in Wartime
44   Teenage Dreams

54   Chapter Two   BRITAIN AT WORK

56   Living on the Land
62   Hopping Holidays
66   How We Worked Then
70   Digging for Black Gold
78   Work in Wartime
82   Civil Defence Volunteers
84   New Britain
92   Service with a Smile
94   Part of the Union
98   The Professionals

108   Chapter Three   WHERE WE LIVED

110   Town or Country
120   Street Games
122   Making a Home
128   Staying In

136 A Nation of Gardeners
140 Digging for Victory
144 Feeding the Family
152 A Day Out Shopping
160 Making Christmas Special

162 Chapter Four | OUT AND ABOUT

164 On the Move
174 Picnics and Pitstops
176 Holidays and Days Out
190 Day Trippers
192 Having a Good Time
202 Playing the Game
206 Keeping Fit
212 The Austerity Olympics

214 Chapter Five | BRITAIN CELEBRATES

216 Parties for the Nation
224 The Festival of Britain
228 Life's Special Occasions
230 Wartime Weddings
240 A Calendar of Tradition

256 Index

259 Bibliography

259 Picture Credits & Acknowledgements

INTRODUCTION

Mid century Britain – from about 1930, through the Second World War, up to around 1980 – was a period when Britain changed perhaps more definitively and dramatically than at any other time in its long history. This book will remind you of how life was before many of those changes happened, starting from the very beginning with the birth of a new baby, through school and how people worked, to home and social life and, finally, celebrating our special occasions.

Much of Britain's landscape was transformed in this period: what the Welsh architect Clough Williams-Ellis called the 'harness of the countryside' was pulled tighter as towns were ringed with sprawling housing estates and new roads drove deep into rural enclaves, opening them up to 'incomers' and commuters, to day trippers and holiday makers with the necessary accoutrements of petrol stations, B&Bs and youth hostels. Town and cityscapes were altered too – sometimes almost out of recognition. The combination of slum clearance in the 1930s and aerial bombardment in the Second World War left city centres ripe for redevelopment. Chain stores and boutiques infiltrated the traditional ground of butchers, bakers, greengrocers and ironmongers, but high streets were threatened more by supermarkets and out-of-town shopping.

People's lives changed in these years: infant mortality fell while life expectancy and robust good health increased. Families tended to become smaller and more affluent, childcare became increasingly permissive and children's horizons expanded (as their toy cupboards filled) along with those of their parents. The arrival of the 'consumer society' – exemplified by the emergence of the 'teenager' – the decline of traditional industry and the increase in the number of women working outside the home transformed the way that people lived, worked and spent their leisure time.

Not everything from 1930 was unrecognisable by 1980. The so-called 'social media' was not yet all-pervasive and people still relished the theatre, cinema, music, dancing, and reading books and newspapers. Most cherished their homes, enjoyed days out in the countryside, played and watched sports as ever and delighted in occasions for celebration. The mid 20th century was a challenging, rapidly evolving era, and it was in many ways the crucible of the Britain we inhabit today.

Juliet Gardiner

LET'S DANCE
Five-year-old Carol-Lynn Rawlins, already a champion ballroom dancer, gives a dancing lesson to the boy from next door, Mitchell Edwards, in 1963.

Chapter One | CHILDHOOD DAYS

A NEW BABY

When Florence Rose Endellion Cameron was born in 2010, her photograph featured on the front pages of newspapers the world over. Soft and sweet, her hair little more than a downy tuft, snuggled in a gossamer-fine white shawl in her mother's arms, the baby born to the British Prime Minister and his wife seemed like all such new-borns, and the pictures of her were timeless in their appeal. But gently pull back the shawl and reflect on the changes that pregnancy, childbirth and the care of babies went through in the course of the 20th century.

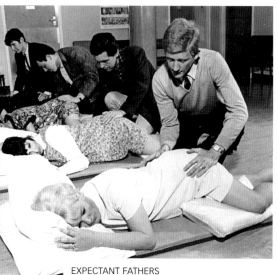

EXPECTANT FATHERS
Childbirth had once been strictly a woman's affair, but by 1968, when this photograph was taken, times were changing. These fathers attending an antenatal class in Margate, Kent, were expected to take an active part in supporting their wives through pregnancy, childbirth – and beyond.

PREVIOUS PAGE
Schoolgirls play netball in a playground on the roof of the Henry Fawcett School in Kennington, South London, in 1938.

In 1900 virtually all women had their babies at home. Well-to-do women would be attended by a doctor who had probably examined them regularly throughout pregnancy. Working-class women might use the services of a midwife, if the family could afford one since it cost around 10 shillings. If a doctor was needed, that might be a financial disaster as he would charge around £2. Otherwise the birth might be overseen by a 'handy' woman, a friend or neighbour whose only qualification was that she had borne children of her own.

Not that all midwives were highly qualified: after 20 years of campaigning by the Midwives Institute, the Midwifes Act for England and Wales was finally passed in 1902. This was the first Act of Parliament to seek to improve standards by requiring a minimum period of training, but it was not until 1936 that another Act established a training course and instituted a salaried scheme for midwives under the control of local government.

A dangerous business

The change was not before time. In 1900 some 3,000 women in Britain died each year in childbirth and by the 1930s the rate had actually risen to around 3,500 deaths each year. The death rate among the better off was as high and sometimes higher than among poorer, less well-nourished women – private fee-paying nursing homes often had the highest rates of mortality. Such facts seem to fly in the face of common sense, since medical advances and higher standards of hygiene might have been expected to make childbirth safer, not more dangerous.

Andrew Topping, Medical Officer of Health in Rochdale in Lancashire, blamed local GPs, calling the way some delivered babies 'little short of murder'. The problem, he thought, lay in the medicalisation of childbirth, since there was every incentive for doctors to intervene. Before the advent of the National Health Service (NHS), doctors were paid more if they used instruments, so forceps were increasingly used and careless or unscrupulous practice could introduce infection that harmed mother and baby. Dr Marie Stopes, the advocate of birth control within marriage, found that many women suffered from the consequences of childbirth for the rest of their lives. In 1931 a leading obstetrician reckoned that 10 per cent of all women were disabled by the experience.

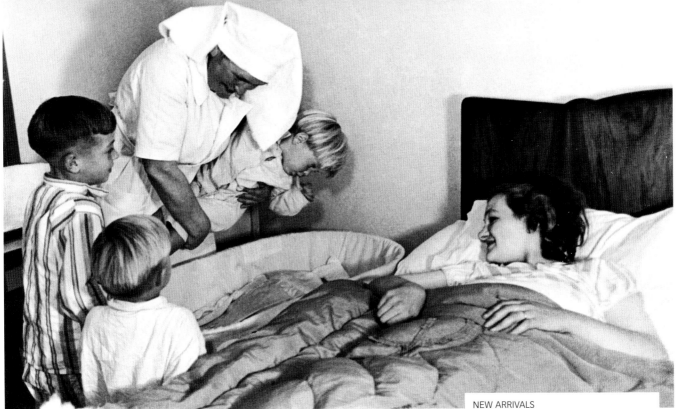

Until 1929, when the old Poor Law was abolished, there were usually maternity wards attached to Poor Law infirmaries, workhouses and charity hospitals, but only the poor and the destitute used them and the death rate was generally higher than for home births. When such hospitals were taken over by local authorities conditions improved and women started to choose to have their babies in hospital, although the better off still tended to favour private nursing homes: in 1933 a quarter of births were in hospital, compared to just 15 per cent in 1927. Gradually the death rate of childbirth fell as penicillin and antibiotics reduced deaths from puerperal sepsis, blood transfusions saved women who haemorrhaged, and safe Caesarean section became routine.

Pioneers of natural birth

Nevertheless, many women still chose to have their babies at home. Perhaps they were put off by all the medical procedures in hospital, or by the regimented day with no time to get to know their baby before it was whipped off to a communal nursery to be returned only at feeding time. A less medicalised approach was advocated by the natural childbirth pioneer Dr Grantly Dick-Reid.

As a young obstetrician attached to the London Hospital in the East End, Dick-Reid had attended a young woman giving birth in a damp, poorly lit room in Whitechapel. He tried 'to persuade my patient to let me put a mask over her face so that she could inhale some chloroform, but the girl refused … saying that she had no need of this help'. As he was preparing to leave Dick-Read asked why she had refused the mask. 'It didn't hurt', the young woman responded. 'It wasn't meant to, was it?' It was an epiphany

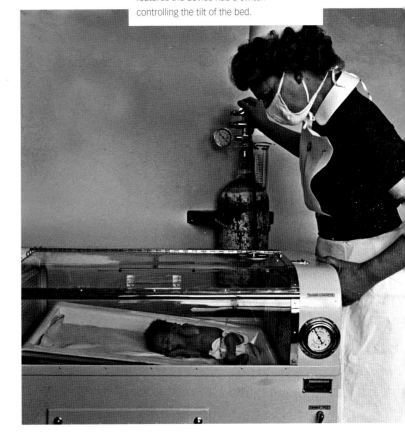

NEW ARRIVALS
Above: Three pyjama-clad boys are introduced by the midwife to their newborn baby sister after a home delivery in Mottingham, Kent, in 1946.
Below: A baby, born two months prematurely, being cared for in the new incubator installed in Wolverhampton's Women's Hospital in 1954. Among other features the device had a switch controlling the tilt of the bed.

moment for the doctor whose first book, *Natural Childbirth*, was published in 1933 and his most popular, *Revelation of Childbirth*, in 1944. His views struck a chord with Prunella Briance, a 30-year-old mother of one child, who blamed a stillbirth on medical intervention. In 1956 she put an advertisement in *The Times* and *Daily Telegraph* announcing the formation of 'a natural childbirth association ... for the promotion and better understanding of the Dick-Read system ...'. A flood of responses confirmed that there was a great desire for a better way of giving birth. Eight months later, the Natural Childbirth Association of Great Britain – later the National Childbirth Trust (NCT) – held its inaugural meeting. 'We knew nothing about having a baby back in the 1950s', Mrs Briance recalled later, and indeed the *Sunday Express Baby Book*, a popular manual at the time, did little to enlighten anyone, devoting just one paragraph to the delivery itself.

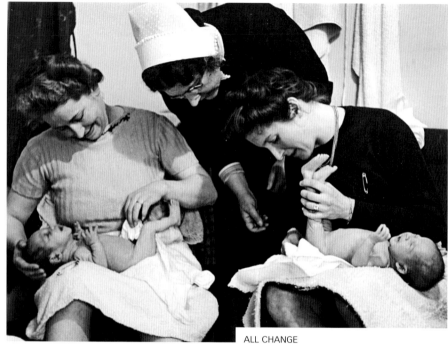

ALL CHANGE
Under a nurse's watchful eye, two new mothers undertake the delicate task of changing their newborn babies' nappies. The photograph was taken at Fircroft postnatal home in Buckinghamshire, in May 1943.

Classes in what to expect in childbirth would surely have been welcome to Ivy Summers back in the 1930s. As she remembered it, 'You had to hold onto a towel when you had your pains to bring on the baby. Well, in them days you had a roller towel. We used to put it on the bed rail and you used to pull on it when the baby was being born ... you didn't make a row because the kids was in the next bedroom ... You didn't want to frighten them ... I don't think with any of my children I ever made a sound ... I just used to have a handkerchief in me hand and I had a towel to pull on ... First thing they heard was the baby crying ... And then you laid in bed for nine days and on the tenth day when you got up you felt ten feet tall. And then you had to start all over again, looking after the kids and that.'

NAPPY SERVICE – Alternatives to washing nappies

Back in 1952, when this van (left) was photographed on delivery duty in Kensington, London, only the wealthy could afford bespoke nappy services, with collection, laundering and return delivery of clean nappies. Other women with babies had the daily chore of soaking and washing terry cloth nappies. But one woman in Britain, mother-of-three Valerie Gordon Hunter, was seeking another solution. In 1948 she and her husband,

Pat Hunter, obtained the first patent for a disposable nappy. Although there was resistance to the idea from many doctors and manufacturers, the next year the couple teamed up with Robinsons of Chesterfield to produce Paddis, the world's first disposable nappy, which they promoted at the Mothercraft Exhibition in London in November 1950. More than a decade would pass before Pampers, a rival, were launched in the USA in 1961.

After the introduction of the NHS in 1948 the number of maternity beds and obstetricians increased considerably, until by the 1960s more than half of all births took place in hospital. By the end of the following decade just 1 per cent of babies were born at home. Medical science took another mighty stride forward in July 1978 with the birth in Oldham of the world's first 'test tube baby', Louise Brown, the first of thousands of IVF conceptions that gave hope to couples who had little chance of having a family of their own without such intervention.

Dads join in

Wherever the birth took place, the NCT regarded childbirth as a joint venture and encouraged fathers to be there. This was a novel idea. As Rosaleen Mansfield, an NCT member since the 1950s, recalled: 'I remember one obstetrician who … considered it almost pornographic to allow husbands into the delivery room. He said it was a dirty business and men shouldn't be subjected to it.' Previously, husbands were despatched – or despatched themselves – to the pub while their

BATH TIME
Olive Burdekin bathes her baby in the washing-up bowl in front of the kitchen range. The kitchen was the warmest room in the remote farmhouse that she and her husband Alan were renovating near Fishguard in Pembrokeshire, Wales, in 1947.

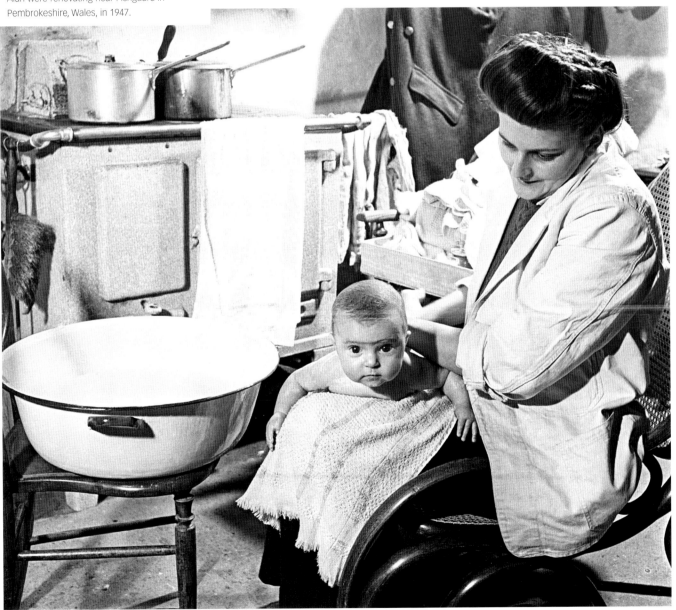

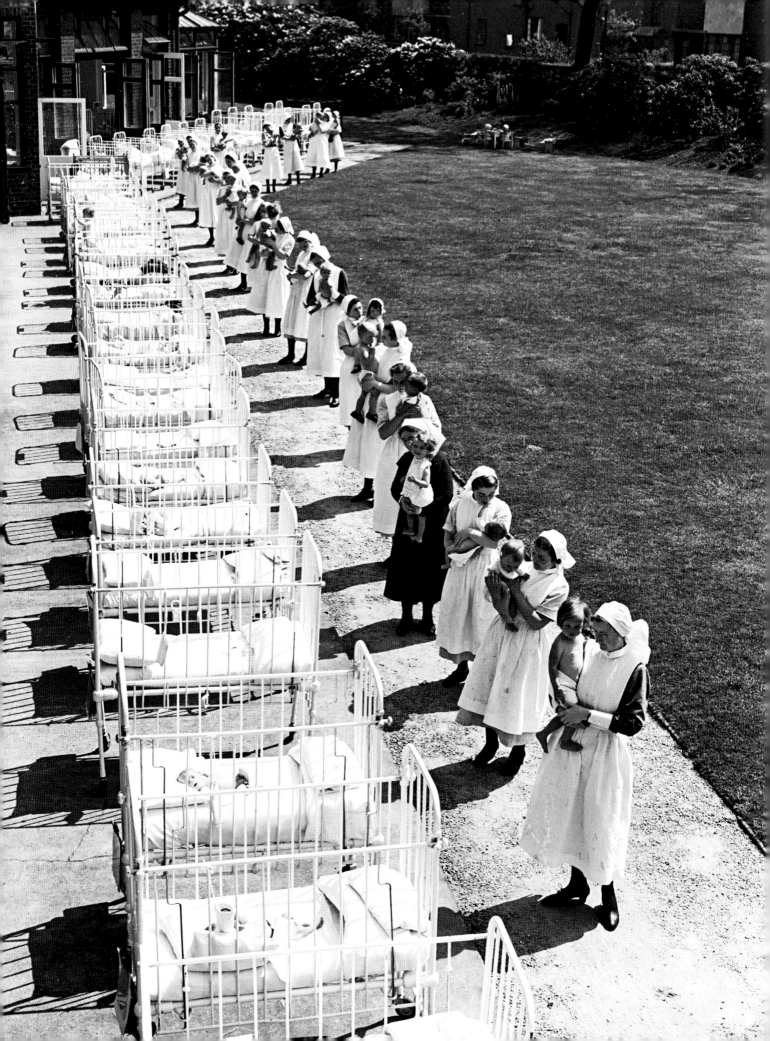

baby was being born. Dr John Gribbins, writing in 1940 on the care of young babies, saw the role of a father as being 'that of an information bureau … it is your proud duty to phone up the relatives and tell them that mother and child are doing well; to send an announcement of the birth to the papers … and to notify the local officer of health.' While in labour, Kathleen Davey was asked by her midwife to put a pillow over her mouth when she screamed 'because the noise might upset your husband in the other room'.

When the baby was born it would be wrapped in a piece of muslin or dressed in a long Viyella nightgown, then placed in a wicker moses masket or a bassinette trimmed with broderie anglaise. If times were hard, a wooden drawer lined with a towel might be a baby's first bed. Older infants slept in a dropsided cot, usually painted in a pastel colour and decorated with some suitable transfer of little lambs or fairies. A Lloyd Loom nursing chair was often abandoned in favour of taking the baby into bed for night-time feeds. Feeding bottles evolved from boat-shaped objects to straight ones plunged nightly into a Milton bottle sterilising unit, and SMA milk formula replaced Cow & Gate powdered milk. A picture by Margaret Tarrant over the cot, often of the baby Jesus surrounded by animals, might be usurped by a mobile of ducks slowly turning to delight the child.

By the 1960s, nightgowns were giving way to the equally unisex babygro, an all-in-one outfit of stretchy towelling with poppers for easy nappy changing. Even nappies evolved from bulky terry towelling, fastened with a single safety pin and washed by hand as a daily chore, to disposables. At first they were a godsend for days out, though considered an extravagance, but soon the only form of protection most mothers were prepared to contemplate.

The first Mothercare shop opened in Kingston upon Thames in 1961 and soon there were more than 100 branches in high streets all over Britain. They sold everything that an expectant mother could need for herself and her baby, and with the growing affluence of the decade many were no longer content to dress their infants in hand-me-downs. By the 1970s, even if fond grandmas and aunts were still knitting shawls, jackets, bootees and mittens, mothers were more likely to buy practical, easy-to-wash outfits to dress their babies, putting them to sleep in zip-up sleeping bags. By now infants were bathed in special baths on stands rather than in the kitchen sink, and were carried around in papoose-like slings until they were old enough to be pushed around in Maclaren buggies. These mini deckchairs on wheels, designed by an aeronautical engineer, were easy to fold up and could be hung over an arm for boarding a bus. It was a far cry from the bulky carriage-built prams that the mothers of the 1970s had probably occupied as babies themselves, with a tray underneath for the daily shopping.

The Truby King way

Along with infant transport, infant rearing changed radically over the decades. The ideas of a New Zealander, Frederick Truby King, came to dominate middle-class childcare in Britain after the First World War. Convinced that infant deaths were largely due to 'irrational feeding', Truby King advocated breastfeeding for the first nine months of life on a strict four-hourly timetable. He also advocated 'as much fresh air and sunshine as possible' to establish 'good habits'. The baby would be

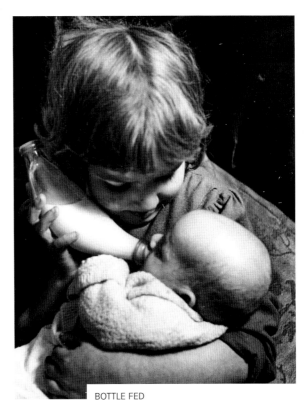

BOTTLE FED
Above: Ivy Bourne from Bloxwich, near Walsall, gave birth to triplets, then twins. Here, one of Ivy's older daughters feeds her young sibling with a bottle in 1953.
Below: A Ministry of Food poster from 1951 promotes the health benefits to children of drinking milk.

HOSPITAL HELIOTHERAPY
Left: In keeping with the 1930s obsession with the health-giving properties of fresh air, nurses took babies and toddlers outdoors to soak up the sun. This row of cots was lined up in the garden of the Duchess of York's Hospital for Babies at Burnage, Manchester.

TEETHING TROUBLES
Two disconsolate infants take part in the Workington and District Agricultural Society 7th Annual Baby Show, which attracted 130 entries. The photograph illustrated an article in *Picture Post* magazine in 1952 asking 'Are Baby Shows Necessary?'

LEARNING TO BE A DAD
Fathers attending a class organised by the Mothercraft Training Society, at their centre in Kingston upon Thames in Surrey in July 1939.

decanted into a pram after the morning feed, then put outdoors in all weathers to sleep (at least in theory) until the next feed was due. 'You fed your baby, changed her, winded her and put her in her pram and wheeled her to the end of the garden, and that was that. And you didn't really give her the cuddles and the love and the affection.'

This strict regime caused many mothers a great deal of anxiety. Listening to their crying baby but forbidden to pick it up, they would wonder where exactly they were going wrong. In working-class homes, Truby King probably had less impact. Rearing children in the 1930s, Ivy Summers never left her babies to cry: 'I used to pick 'em up and do my work when they were asleep.' They were fed pretty much on demand, and 'all had a bone dummy from when they were born to about three years old and I never took it off them until they gave it up themselves … They didn't believe in that at the [baby] clinics though … I was always in their black books.'

In contrast, upper-class Rose Luttrell, who had two children in the 1920s, had a nurse when they were tiny, later replaced by a nanny. 'In those days mothers never looked after their own babies … [My baby] used to be brought down after tea, and I used to go and watch Nanny put him to bed … My bedroom was quite a long way from the nursery, so I wouldn't hear them crying at all.'

'Enjoy your baby'

Truby King recommended that a baby should sleep for 21 hours a day. In fact most babies did not sleep anything like that much: 14.9 hours was the average recorded in 1963 by psychologists John and Elizabeth Newsom. By then, though, Truby King's rigid theories were being ousted by a more baby-centered approach. *The Common Sense Book of Baby and Child Care*, published in 1946 by an American doctor, Benjamin Spock, became most new mothers' bible by the 1960s – indeed it almost outsold the Bible itself. The book's appeal was not just that it was comprehensive – the index listed every conceivable subject from temper tantrums to itchy toes – but also lay in its suggestion that, on the whole, a mother's instincts could be trusted, that babies often knew best when it came to what they wanted, and that babies could and should be fun, not mini-strangers to be brought to heel by firm handling. Spock was followed by British experts, such as Dr Hugh Jolly and Penelope Leach, offering much the same message – 'Enjoy your baby'.

MOTHER'S HELP
A nanny takes her two young charges to the beach at Bournemouth to make the most of a rare sunny day during the family's summer holiday in August 1954.

Going potty

If baby care was exhausting, child development brought a new set of challenges. When your baby reached toddlerhood, at somewhere around a year or 18 months, home could become a battleground as the previously compliant infant developed a will of its own. In her *Mothercraft Manual* of 1948, Mabel Liddiard drew up a daunting chart of 'milestones' by which parents should measure the development of their child. By a year not only should the unfortunate infant weigh precisely 22lb, it should also be able to have its 'napkin left off during the day', have cut six teeth and say 'a single word clearly'. It could also 'have a cold bath', although why was not made clear. Truby King would have thought this timetable pretty slack: he believed education began in the first week of life and a baby should be 'held out' over a chamber pot after a feed from birth. Even this was an improvement on the advice of the American psychologist turned advertising executive John B. Watson, who in 1912 had advocated strapping an infant onto a special toilet seat, alone, with the bathroom door closed and no toys for distraction, until after some 20 minutes it would have 'performed'.

'I had access to the nursery whenever I wanted but you didn't do anything actually with the baby – Nanny did everything ... You didn't interfere with Nanny.'

ROSE LUTTRELL, AN UPPER-CLASS MOTHER IN THE 1920S

Despite misgivings, Margaret Swanton bought her first baby up the Truby King way in the 1940s. 'I was told to hold him over the pot after every feed when he was only a few months old. The rim of the pot just had to barely touch his

bottom, meaning that the poor little baby could feel the
chill underneath him and presumably, if he didn't perform
he'd get a really cold bottom ... Well, of course he never
did anything at all ... but they kept saying, "No, you must
get him potty trained ... otherwise you'll have a little boy
who's still dirtying his pants until he's five or six."
I got the impression that he would turn into some sort of
sexual deviant. I think that was basically what it was all
about, and that potty training engendered self-control.'

Dr Spock was much more relaxed about toilet training.
In 1946 he wrote: 'I think that the best method ... is to
leave [it] almost entirely up to your baby ... Be friendly
and easygoing about the bathroom ... All you can work
with is his willingness.' But even Spock began to have
doubts: by the 1960 edition of his book, he had decided

ALL TOGETHER NOW
Toddlers obediently undergo communal potty training in a Brixton nursery in 1955. The effectiveness of early regimentation would be queried in the next decade.

SLEEPING ON THE STREET
Left: A child peers out of the window of a ground-floor tenement flat in the Gorbals, Glasgow, in about 1960, while a baby sleeps peacefully in its little pram outside.

that 'By the time a child is 18 months old, I think you should begin his training even if there is no readiness', though 'training' consisted of lavish praise – and probably treats – for 'performance' rather than punishment for 'accidents'.

One small but significant change in the world of the toddler concerned household arrangements. In the pre- and post-Second World War years, the house itself was largely left the same and it was the small person who was constrained – in a wooden playpen, by reins when taken out, in a high-sided cot at night. By the more permissive Sixties, it was the house that was rearranged around the child: ornaments were put on high shelves, furniture corners padded, childproof catches installed on cupboards, guards put round cooker hobs, gates installed at the bottom of the stairs. The focus had swung: no longer was a child expected to fit in with an adult agenda; he or she was now at the centre of family life.

OFF TO SCHOOL

'A good nursery school doesn't take the place of home; it adds to it', pronounced Dr Spock. Compared to some countries, Britain was slow to get the nursery school habit. In Germany kindergartens, or children's gardens, had been started in 1837 by Friedrich Froebel, who originally called his initiative a 'care, playing and activity institute for small children'.

Nursery schools, kindergartens, playgroups, pre-schools – all are names for establishments that care for children, usually from three years old, supervising educational play and generally socialising small people before they go to 'proper school' at the age of five. Their practice and provision has been as varied as their name. The 1918 Education Act had empowered local authorities to set up nursery schools in an attempt to compensate in some way for the tragedy of the First World War 'by the creation of a system of education', to quote the President of the Board of Education, H.A.L. Fisher, '[that] will increase the value of every human unit in the whole of society'. But although a few local authorities did make provision for the under-fives – and growing understanding of child psychology began to show that nursery schools offered real benefits – economic restraints held most back.

By 1931 only about 2,000 children in Britain were receiving nursery education, either in one of the 44 local authority nurseries open at the time or in others run by voluntary bodies aided by grants. By 1939 the number of nurseries had increased to 114 and those fortunate enough to attend one had a fairly structured day. There would typically have been 25 to 30 in a class, with plenty of outdoor play on seesaws, slides and climbing frames. After a rest on a folding canvas bed at lunchtime, there were indoor activities each afternoon that included stories, singing nursery rhymes and playing percussion instruments.

During the war, nurseries were opened to allow mothers to do essential war work – 12 per cent of those with young children worked full-time, and many more undertook voluntary duties. Most of these closed after the war, and the number of children in nursery schools barely increased at all between 1930 and 1960, a year in which local authorities were actually discouraged from spending their limited educational resources on nursery places. By the mid 1960s pressure for the provision of nursery school places was growing both from working mothers (often teachers themselves) and from people aware that children in deprived areas needed the opportunities to socialise that the schools provided.

THE VIEW AHEAD
Children at a Port of London day nursery in Wapping, near the Tower of London, queue up to look through a telescope over the River Thames in 1933.

TOY STORY

A child with no toys will invent them by wrapping a hairbrush in a tea towel and carrying it around as if it were a baby doll, or sitting in a cardboard box making noises like a car, or banging a saucepan with a wooden spoon in the absence of a drum. Play often mimics the adult world: children come home from school to play 'teachers', push a teddy bear in a doll's pram to the 'shop', or pour water from a teapot and offer round 'cups of tea' to guests. Toys enable all of this: miniaturised versions of the things that adults use, they allow children to play at being mothers and fathers, doctors and nurses, firefighters, soldiers and, of

OUTDOOR FUN

Top left: Children's games often involve role-play, like these young boys pretending to be 'Red Indians' with the help of home-made costumes and a bit of war paint in summer 1967.

Top centre: One little boy acts as a traffic policeman to help his pedal-powered friends across the road in February 1941.

Bottom left: Boys in an East London school playground in 1931 playing football with the added twist of being on roller skates.

course, cowboys and indians. Toys socialise children and teach them to interpret the world they inhabit. In wartime Britain, 'cops and robbers' morphed into 'Nazis and Allies'.

Many toys seems eternal, although their forms may have changed: dolls that a century ago were fragile porcelain or wax evolved into sturdy, undressable, bathable plastic. Barbie introduced the new concept of the adult 'fashion' doll. Balls, bicycles, scooters, roller skates, kites – all moved on as new materials and technologies made more sophisticated products possible. Toys have fashions, too: hula hoops in the Fifties, space hoppers in the Seventies, Ninja Turtles and Cabbage Patch dolls are all of their era. The plain, unpainted 'educational toys' of the Sixties seem to hail from a different planet than the plastic robots of a decade or so later.

The best toys have always encouraged children's imagination and developed their skills of co-ordination, agility and perception. The child

developmental psychologist Friedrich Froebel believed that children could be taught the principles of mathematics by playing with wooden shapes. The instinct to build seems innate, whether it is with simple wooden blocks, the once ubiquitous Meccano and later Lego, or authentic construction kits.

Children never seem to tire of some types of toys and play. Miniature cars have been popular from Dinky toys in the Thirties, to racing cars on Scalextric tracks from the Fifties, to modern remote-operated vehicles. And children always love dressing up, whether in mother's cast-off dresses, jewellery, hats and shoes, or in later decades in ready-made outfits that transform a child into a pirate, a princess, or a witch.

LEARNING BY DOING

Top right: Play often has practical, educational value, as suggested by these two girls, dressing their dolls in hand-knitted clothes in 1944.
Centre right: A boy plays an early video game of noughts and crosses, a forerunner of computer games, in 1975.
Bottom right: A little boy has his sights set on Lego in the toy department of Bentalls department store in Kingston, Surrey, in 1969.

Children in Gordonbush in the Scottish Highlands make their way to school in 1956, where a single teacher taught them all, aged from five to eleven, in one classroom.

'Most children would benefit from a good nursery school' Dr Spock claimed in 1960. 'Every young child by the age of three needs other young children … not only to play with but also to learn how to get along with. This is the most important job in his life. He also needs space to run and shout in, apparatus to climb on, bricks and boxes and boards to build with, trains and dolls to play with. He needs to learn how to get along with other grown-ups besides his parents. Few children nowadays have these advantages in their own home …'

In 1964 a survey by the National Union of Teachers (NUT) found two-year waiting lists for a third of nursery schools. The overwhelming majority of middle-class mothers would have sent their children to nursery school if they could, but instead they were having to use childminders or au pairs – not always satisfactory and unregulated until legislation in 1948. Almost three-quarters of working-class mothers felt the same, with the added concern that, as terraced slums on friendly streets were demolished and families were rehoused in high-rise blocks, there was a lack of space for their children to play. In 1967 the Plowden Committee recommended 'a large expansion of nursery education', but this advice was largely ignored. In 1969 the Labour government launched an Urban Aid programme offering grants to local authorities to provide nursery classes for more than 10,000 children in areas of greatest need. But it was not until the Conservative government's White Paper on education in late 1972 that the systematic development of pre-school education really started to move forward. Funds were then allocated and premises acquired so that an increasing number of children had the opportunity of a nursery school place.

The playgroup alternative

There were many establishments outside the control of local authorities that offered nursery or playschool facilities for those who were prepared to pay. Some, such as Froebel and Montessori nurseries (the latter inspired by Maria Montessori's *Casa di Bambino* in a poor district of Rome), had a strong educational philosophy and were staffed by trained teachers, or 'leaders', promoting learning through play. Then there were pre-school playgroups. The first was started by a Mrs Belle Tutaev in Marylebone in 1961; ten years later, there were around 600 catering for some 170,000 children, mainly in London and the Home Counties, and an active Pre-school Playgroups Association had been started.

Although many playgroups were run by qualified supervisors, they were not nursery schools but rather assemblies of 'six to 30 children aged between two-and-a-half to five years who play together daily or several sessions weekly'. Held in church or village halls, or even in someone's front room, with mothers encouraged to help, the playgroups provided opportunities for art activities and stories, with water and sand play in the garden if the weather was good. With names like 'Lollipop', 'Jelly Tots', 'Little Buds' and 'Peter Pan', they aimed to teach social skills such as sharing as well as concentration, hand-eye coordination and how to tell the time. For children in areas with few pre-school facilities, the Save the Children Fund set up playgroups – 120 by 1971 – and parents or carers could bring their pre-schoolers to free 'one o'clock clubs' organised by local authorities in parks and areas around tower blocks. These provided an afternoon's play, orange juice and biscuits for children who might otherwise have been cooped up all day.

The changing face of the primary school

Until the 1960s most children in primary schools were taught in large classes by one teacher, typically in a school originally commissioned by a Victorian school board. There were rarely 'subject teachers' at primary schools. Pupils sat at individual desks, put their hands up to answer questions and tried not to bang their desk lids too hard as they got their books out. They learned to do arithmetic and joined-up writing, practising carefully in lined paper exercise books and

FIRST DAY TEARS
A five-year-old boy on his first day at St Nicholas County Primary in Loughton, Essex, in 1952.

ARTISTIC LICENCE
Two girls painting pictures at Bousfield, a newly built primary in Kensington, London, where 'progressive' ideas of light and a more relaxed approach to education seem in evidence in 1957.

On a pavement in a busy London street in October 1959, a nun from Tyburn School teaches her pupils to skip. The school had no playground, so the children had to spend playtimes indoors. Then local shopkeepers gave the school permission to use five square yards of pavement. Sister May Philippa, the head mistress, was delighted, saying 'Perhaps one day we will have a real playground'.

drawing their 'pot hooks' in pencil or with a nibbed pen dipped into an inkwell set into a hole in the desk. The end of lessons was marked by the ringing of a brass hand bell in the corridor. Children jostled to be 'blackboard monitor', cleaning off the teacher's chalk writing at the end of lessons, or 'milk monitor', handing out third-of-a-pint bottles with a straw stuck through the top to each pupil at playtime (before Margaret Thatcher, as Minister of Education, 'snatched' the free milk away in 1971). Playtime usually meant going out into a concrete or asphalt playground, with no play equipment other than hopscotch squares chalked on the ground or a long skipping rope brought to school in a girl's brown leather satchel.

Belief in the importance of 'child-centred' learning was becoming educational orthodoxy as early as the 1930s, but it was slow to permeate most schools. It was hard to be flexible in the atmosphere of a Victorian board school, which were 'bleak, unwelcoming, gaunt', as the director of an educational project in Liverpool wrote. 'There was no central heating in the school', remembers Roland Thomas of his 1930s school days in Wales. 'Each of the three classrooms had an open fire and it was the duty of the strongest boys to fill buckets of coal from the cellar.' But with the school building boom of the 1960s – in 1968, for example, £16 million was allocated to Educational Priority Areas – newly completed light and airy buildings began to invite experimentation. Rows of desks and benches were replaced with pint-sized tables and chairs, the children's own paintings adorned the walls, creative writing was encouraged, measuring jugs and scales helped children to find out about weights and measures for themselves, while the

'Wendy House' and 'shop' became as ubiquitous in classrooms as the blackboard had been. The struggle throughout the post-war years was to reduce class sizes – 50 or more in a class was common until the late 1960s, when the goal of a maximum of 40 children per class was finally achieved in almost all primary schools. With the reduction in pupil numbers and the re-styling of classrooms, teachers could wander round encouraging and guiding as the children worked on projects, instead of merely standing in front of a quiescent class in rows. Some schools tried teaching in 'family groups' of children, while specialist teachers might visit on a regular basis to teach music or introduce the children to French.

The composition of the classes was also changing. By 1966 there were more than 100,000 immigrant children in primary schools: by 1971 that number had more than doubled, with most living in urban areas. A substantial number of these children spoke little or no English. By the start of the 1970s an additional 3,000 teachers had been appointed to work in areas with a high concentration of immigrants. Gradually, what started as a language learning initiative would evolve into a cultural exchange, with native British-born children finding their curriculum enriched with knowledge of other cultures and celebrations, such as the festivals of Diwali and Eid alongside that of Christmas.

Secondary education

The 1918 Education Act raised the school leaving age from 12 to 14, then in 1926 the Haddow Committee recommended that elementary schooling be split into 'primary' (up to age 11) and 'post primary' or secondary stages. But local

SPORTING COMPETITION
Sports Day was an annual ritual at most primary schools, giving proud parents a chance to see their children in action. Above: Eight year-old Stephen Hosgood wins the sack race at Ravenor School in Middlesex in June 1962. Below: Girls aged 10 and 11 compete in the 80 yard dash at London's White City stadium in 1954.

authorities received no financial incentive to reorganise educational provision, and at first few did so. As late as 1938, only 64 per cent of schoolchildren were being educated in separated primary and secondary schools: the remainder – some 600,000 children across the country – still attended elementary schools on the old model. 'The top few pupils were intelligent and could mop up facts like blotting paper, but we had to wait for the rest of the huge classes', recalled the Labour MP Ellen Wilkinson of her school days. It was not until the 1944 Education Act introduced by R.A. Butler that the old elementary system was finally abolished.

Enter the 11-plus

The school leaving age was raised to 15 in 1947, then to 16 in 1972. In England and Wales the externally examined General Certificate of Education (GCE) replaced the old school certificate in 1951, and grammar school pupils sat Ordinary level GCEs at 16 and Advanced level at 18, a required qualification for those who wanted to go on to university or professional training. Entry to grammar schools was highly selective: in the final year of primary school, at the age of 11 – the age at which it was considered that 'general intelligence' was best measured – pupils sat the

'There is, on the whole, nothing on earth intended for innocent people so horrible as a school. To begin with, it is a prison ...'

GEORGE BERNARD SHAW

grading exam or 'I1-plus'. Those who passed, and only about a fifth did, had the opportunity to go to grammar school. Technical schools never materialised in sufficient numbers to realise the hopes of the reformers who recommended them, so most of the rest went to 'secondary moderns' to be taught domestic science and other practical subjects. In practice, the lack of further educational qualifications usually condemned them to a life in low-paid, low-status jobs.

For working-class children who passed the 11-plus but could not afford to pay fees, a number of 'special' (means-tested) and free school places were on offer by the 1930s, holding out a rickety ladder to educational achievement. Even so, many struggled to pay for the uniform and 'extras', such as hockey sticks and games kits, that grammar schools demanded. Twice a year, when the sales were on in the shops, Joan Moody was taken by her mother to buy her school uniform. 'Father came, too, complete with cheque book … to Daniel Neal's [in Kensington High Street] for shoes and clothes; our feet were measured by X-ray machines to make sure we had the right size. I remember having a navy blue blazer bought for me in the Harrods' sale, which I loathed. My Mother said it was much better quality than the regulation school blazer, but it had square corners instead of round and I hated it!'

In the 1930s not only were many working-class parents suspicious of 'book learning' but the wages of older children were often needed to supplement the family income. By the late 1950s, growing affluence provided more incentive to stay on at school to get qualifications that would lead to a better job. The number of those opting to remain in education beyond the statutory leaving age increased steadily year on year. At the same time the margin of error in 11-plus exam results began to cause unease. Were intelligence tests really the neutral instrument that

SCIENTIFIC SLIDE SHOW
Above: A master at Manchester Grammar School oversees a group of sixth form pupils working with microscopes during a biology lesson in 1950.
Below: A chemistry class at Sedgehill Comprehensive School, London, in 1960. The photograph was used to illustrate an article about the merits of co-education, which argued that the presence of girls in the classroom had a 'steadying effect' on the boys, though that was not necessarily to the advantage of the girls.

had been believed, or did they disadvantage working-class children? Was the system deeply divisive, preordaining a child's future at too tender an age? For newsreader Peter Sissons, looking back on hearing the results of the 11-plus in the 1950s at a primary school in Liverpool (the same one attended by John Lennon and Jimmy Tarbuck), there was little doubt it was unfair. 'The school was gathered together and those who had passed were called up to the podium one at a time with their own round of applause. The poor sods who had failed were left sitting in the hall – they only realised they had failed because they had not been called up.'

Towards the comprehensive system

The Newsom Report, published in 1963, spoke of 'reserves of ability that can be tapped'. By then Kidbrooke school in southeast London, the first comprehensive to offer entry across the ability range without selective examination, had been open for nine years. In 1962 Anglesey had introduced a fully comprehensive system, and across the country there were 106 'comps', some of them educating as many as 2,000 pupils. In 1965 the Labour government announced plans to 'end selection at 11-plus and to eliminate separatism in secondary schools'. Although the Conservative government, elected in 1970, withdrew the instruction, the march towards comprehensive education was inexorable – by 1971 there were some 1,300 such schools, educating around a third of the secondary-school age group. A few local authorities reorganised their school provision in other ways, introducing 'middle schools' for pupils aged 9 to 13 that combined features from both primary and secondary schools. A few grammar schools clung on, fiercely defended by those who thought they offered the finest tradition of academic education available. Few mourned the demise of the 'secondary mod'.

The hard life of the privileged pupil

The poet Hugo Williams recalled: 'I was eight when I set out into the world/Wearing a grey flannel suit'. He was on his way to a prep school, Lockers Park, in Hertfordshire. Such fee-paying schools, which were entirely or mainly boarding, were preparatory to entry (by entrance exam) to public school.

'Down With Skool' wrote Ronald Searle's Molesworth of St Custard's, and not many children had happy memories of their prep school days. It does seem a peculiar idiosyncrasy of the British to send children as young as seven away from home. Lord Montagu of Beaulieu recalled his years at St Peter's Court School in Kent. 'I was educated as a child to being away from home, cut off from family and close friends; I was used to an all-male society disciplined by routine and the clock; I was already hardened by indifferent food and a degree of physical discomfort.' Thus when he was imprisoned in Wakefield jail for homosexual offences in 1954, he found himself well prepared.

PRESENT AND CORRECT
Pupils of Harrow School file past their headmaster, Dr J.L. James, on Founders Day in 1954. 'Call-over' required the boys to doff their straw hats as their names were called out.

Well into the 1960s conditions in prep schools were often primitive, with no heating in dormitories, cold baths and highly competitive games, including all-weather cross-country runs. There were endless petty rules in a life governed by the bell, bullying by other pupils and frequent use of the cane or slipper – or, in the case of one headmaster, a butter pat, with the smooth side for minor offences and the ridged for more serious misdemeanours. Punishments were sometimes sadistically administered by 'the beak', and unless a school was blessed with a kind matron, life could indeed be bleak in a place where, like below-stairs servants, children were called by their surnames and encouraged to 'forget home'.

HEIGHTENED PROSPECTS – From public school to parliament

Writing in 1972, George MacDonald Fraser, author of the 'Flashman' series, was in no doubt about the benefits of a public school education. For close on two centuries, he claimed, 'they have influenced virtually everything about our country – and, through the old Empire and the remaining Commonwealth, a sizeable part of the world as well'. The figures backed him up. In the early 1960s, no fewer than 87 per cent of the Conservative government's cabinet ministers and 64 per cent of executives in Britain's top 100 firms were public-school educated. Figures from the 1950s showed 70 per cent of army officers of the rank of Lieutenant-General and above, 66 per cent of bishops and 59 per cent of civil servants above Assistant Secretary level also fitted the bill. More than a third of the 1961 edition of *Who's Who* were public-school educated and Eton claimed a sixth of the entire total. The advantages of a public school education stretched across party lines. Almost one in four of Labour MPs elected in 1945 had been to public schools – including the Prime Minister, Clement Attlee (Haileybury) – and 35 per cent of ministers in the Labour cabinet of 1964 had too.

UNCONVENTIONAL PLAYGROUND
During a break in 1959, pupils at Barnham village primary school in West Sussex revel in the challenges presented by an assemblage of old tyres, rope ladders and ropes slung between trees.

Over all loomed the 'common entrance exam' at 13 to public school, so called because they were open to pupils outside the aristocracy, often founded with charitable endowments for poor students, although fees soon eclipsed any original charitable income. In 1861 the Clarendon Commission began an investigation of the 'great schools' of England – the boarding schools of Eton, Harrow, Winchester, Rugby, Shrewsbury, Charterhouse and Westminster, plus two 'day' schools, St Paul's and Merchant Taylors', which formed the core of what were defined as public schools. Since then the number of public schools had not increased significantly but the definition had and in 1968 the Public Schools Commission confirmed that public schools, as distinguished from private schools, could be designated as those that were members of the Headmasters' Conference or Governing Bodies Association, which included some schools for girls.

What public school offered

Throughout the 20th century between 5 and 8 per cent of British children went to fee-paying or 'independent' schools – at a considerable cost. Average fees per year at major boarding schools rose from £545 in 1966 to £2,744 in 1980. So what did parents get for their money? For themselves there was the prospect of a quieter life, with their offspring looked after for long stretches of the year and few requirements except to send a weekly letter and a few treats for the tuck box now and then, and to show up at sports day without wearing an embarrassing hat.

For the children there were smaller classes, a curriculum based on the classics (although science was making increasing inroads by the 1960s), better and more varied facilities for sport – lacrosse more often than hockey for girls, rugby rather than soccer for boys. And, of course, the improved chance of good qualifications and a place at a 'good' university – for every child leaving state schools in 1961 with three or more 'A' levels, there were six from public and private schools. Two decades later this ratio was almost unchanged, but the proportion of public school pupils achieving those results had more than doubled from 20 to 45 per cent. Public schools even beat the remaining grammar schools, with a third of their pupils going on to university compared to 27 per cent from the grammars.

But what about the boys and girls themselves? Boarding school might mean Angela Brazil or Enid Blytonish fun, with pranks and japes, midnight feasts in the dorm and slang incomprehensible to anyone outside the closed world of the school. Or it could be endless weeks of homesickness and being bullied, with little privacy and intense pressure to conform, all in Spartan surroundings. 'The floors were bare and the bathroom had just two tiny tubs for 20 boys', recalled a pupil at Wellingborough, who slept in an iron bed in a dormitory with the 19 others.

Above all, though, public schools were influential because so many former pupils occupied leading positions in the nation, and that made them controversial. Writing in 1956, the socialist politician Anthony Crosland hoped to see the 'gradual closure' of prep and public schools because they were an 'early and influential source of class insemination'. Yet no Labour government called for their abolition, although they did encourage more integration between public and state school systems. In 1944 a report had recommended that public schools make up to a quarter of their places available to children on scholarships paid for by local authorities. But local authorities preferred to spend their money on improving provision for state pupils. Meanwhile, the independent schools, and the prep schools that fed them, enjoyed a recovery from the relative doldrums into which many had fallen during the Depression of the 1930s.

RADIO AND TV TIMES

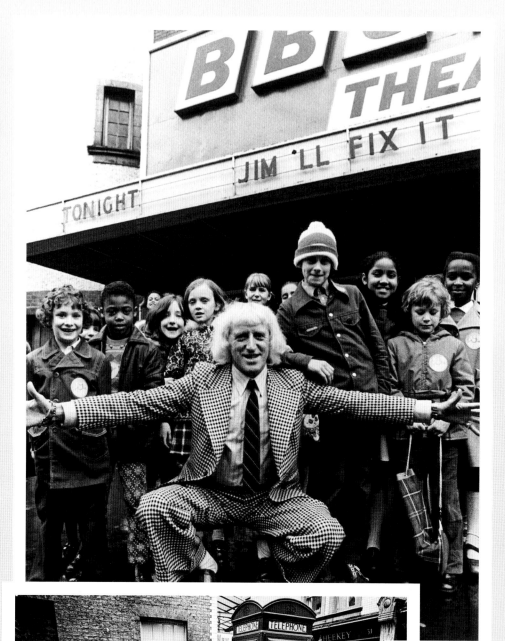

After lunch, thousands of pre-school British children in the 1950s and 60s would settle down to hear *Listen With Mother* on the radio. 'Are you sitting comfortably?' they would be asked, then as small heads nodded the voice would continue 'Then I'll begin'. When older brothers and sisters came in from school, they were most likely to have tea while listening to Uncle Mac (Derek McCulloch) on Children's Hour, which had started as far back as 1922 and was broadcast between 5 and 6 o'clock. Delights included *Toytown* featuring Larry the Lamb, Denis the Dachshund and Mr Growser, a grocer.

As children grew older, favourites might include *Dan Dare*, *Dick Barton – Special Agent* and comedy shows such as ventriloquist Peter Brough's *Educating Archie* or *The Clitheroe Kid* with Jimmy Clitheroe (born in 1921, he was no kid by 1956 when the show started). Teenage listeners would endlessly imitate the surreal voices of *The Goons* – Spike Milligan, Peter Sellers, Harry Secombe and Michael Bentine – first broadcast in 1951.

CHILDHOOD MEMORIES
Millions of British children have grown up with memories of Jimmy Savile's *Jim'll Fix It* (top left), the menacing Daleks on *Dr Who* (bottom left) and *Watch With Mother* represented here (below) by the toytown world of Trumpton, narrated by Brian Cant and first shown in November 1966.

In 1953, the year of Queen Elizabeth II's coronation, some 100,000 television sets were bought across Britain, so many more children started to watch programmes made specially for them. Early stars of children's TV were Annette Mills and Muffin the Mule, first broadcast in 1952. BBC transmission began at 3.00pm on weekdays, 5.00pm on Sundays, and until 1957 the BBC kept the toddlers' truce, going off-air from 6.00 to 7.00pm to make it easier for parents to get their children to bed.

Watch With Mother, like its radio equivalent, was specially made for pre-school children. First there was *Andy Pandy*, with his friends Teddy and Looby Loo, then later *The Flowerpot Men* (Bill, Ben and Little Weed), *Rag, Tag and Bobtail* and *The Woodentops*. Pinky and Perky, two puppet pigs, made their TV debut in 1957, the same year that Sweep joined Sooty – already an established star – on the hands of Harry Corbett. Sooty got his first regular television spot on *Saturday Special*, which alternated with *Whirligig* on a Saturday afternoon. Other favourites included Richard Hearne as Mr Pastry and, from 1955, *Crackerjack*, with hectic games and quizzes – and a cabbage for a wrong answer. In 1958 *Blue Peter* arrived, presented by Lelia Williams, a former Miss England. Its mix of guests, documentary reports, pets and endless things to do with egg boxes, washing-up bottles and sticky-back plastic made it a huge success.

The year 1964 saw the start of *Play School* ('Here's a window, here's a door'), which evolved first into *Playbus*, then *Playdays*. From 1965 on, *Jackanory* offered the simple joys of storytelling, with an actor in an armchair reading a book. *Watch with Mother* moved on with *Camberwick Green* and *Trumpton* ('Pugh! Pugh! Barney McGrew! Cuthbert! Dibble! and Grubb!'), *Tales from the Riverbank* and *Mary, Mungo and Midge*. Parents often enjoyed watching with their children, particularly such series as *Captain Pugwash*, the cartoon pirate, the *Magic Roundabout* with Florence, Dougal, Zebedee and Brian the Snail, and Oliver Postgate's charming *Noggin the Nog*, *Bagpuss* and *The Clangers*. For older children, 1963 brought the weekly excitement of *Dr Who*, with William Hartnell as the very first Doctor in the Tardis time machine.

One drawback of black and white television was that it could be hard to tell who was who. Pinky and Perky, for example, had different coloured waistcoats, but who could tell? So Perky wore a hat as well. Colour arrived in 1967. Another milestone in children's TV came in 1978 with Phil Redmond's *Grange Hill*, a gritty drama about life in a secondary school. Despite occasional complaints, the programme would run for 30 years and feed the debate about whether television was a good thing or a bad thing for children.

FINDING OUT
Blue Peter has become the world's longest-running children's show, having first aired in 1958. The presenters pictured with canine guests in 1968 are (left to right) John Noakes, Valerie Singleton and Peter Purves. An ITV entrant in the educational programme stakes was *How*, presented here by Jill Graham (left) and Fred Dinenage.

LEARNING TO JOIN IN

One of the most vital lessons of childhood is learning how to get along with others. In the first half of the 20th century, the Scout movement became the most important organisation outside school to promote the development of children. Founded first for boys, with the Girl Guides following a few years later, the movement gave many young people their first taste of the outdoor life and a valuable lesson in self-reliance.

BRASS SECTION
Members of a school band pose with their instruments – a tuba and two cornets – in front of the Queen's Hall in London, where they were taking part in a schools competition in 1932.

The Labour Prime Minister Harold Wilson was an enthusiastic boy scout in his youth: at the age of 12, he won a competition in the *Yorkshire Post* with an essay about his hero Robert Baden-Powell, founder of the Scout movement. As Labour leader in the 1960s, Wilson recalled the scout's fourth law: 'a scout is a friend to all, and a brother to every other scout, no matter of what country, class or creed'. But when the Boy Scout movement was founded it was propelled not only by a socialist impulse but by an imperialist one too.

As a colonel, later major-general, in the British army during the Second Boer War in South Africa, Baden-Powell had been appalled at the poor physical specimens he had come across among the recruits. He was also impressed by the way in which the army served, in his view, as 'a university for the working-classes'. After the war he felt there must be no more 'sinking back into our easy chair'. Rather, boys should be offered an active and adventurous outdoor life in a movement that provided the opportunity to 'promote the development of young people in achieving their full physical, intellectual, social and spiritual potential'.

B-P, as he was known, was convinced that offering lads a chance to taste the outdoor life would stop them hanging about aimlessly on street corners and turn them into 'good citizens'. In 1907 he published *Scouting for Boys* to promote his vision; it became an international bestseller, revised and updated throughout the 20th century and outsold only by the Bible, the Qur'an and Mao Zedong's *Little Red Book*. The Boy Scout Movement rapidly became the largest youth organisation in the world, while membership in Britain rose from 343,000 in 1940 to 588,396 in 1960.

A good scout

'A true scout,' wrote B-P in a foreword to a new edition published in 1932, 'is looked up to by other boys and by grown-ups as a fellow who can be trusted, a fellow who will not fail to do his duty however risky and dangerous it will be.'

Dressed in a uniform based on that of the South African police — khaki shirt, 'lemon squeezer' Stetson hat, knee-length shorts and a neckerchief with a horn or leather woggle — most boy scouts faced no challenge bigger than the annual camp. There they slept under canvas in bell or ridge tents and dug their own latrines; they cooked — or more likely burned — meals such as corned beef hash, or potatoes baked in the smouldering ash of a campfire; they tracked wild animals, played ritualistic games, sang songs such as 'The Day Is What You Make It' and 'Crest of a Wave' and spun yarns around the campfire as they whittled sticks. They were awarded proficiency badges for mastering skills such as tying knots, building bridges and chopping wood, which their mothers sewed onto their uniform — unless the badge was for sewing, in which case a boy would presumably do it himself.

'We never fail when we try to do our duty, we always fail when we neglect to do it.'

ROBERT BADEN-POWELL

'There is no room for the shirker or grouser' in the Scout Movement, said B-P. As well as obeying his parents and the King (after 1952, the Queen) the good scout was expected above all to 'Be Prepared'. Not everyone was sure what for – 'I promised to "Be Prepared" as a scout (for what? against whom?)', wondered Paul Vaughan. In 'Bob a Job'

'I PROMISE TO DO MY BEST'
On 2 September, 1939 – the day before Britain declared war on Germany – Girl Guides pour out strong tea made over a camp fire at Cudham, near Bromley in Kent

week it meant being ready to knock on the neighbours' doors offering to mow the lawn, sweep up leaves, or take the dog for a walk, all to earn a shilling to contribute to the costs of an organisation that was staffed entirely by volunteers.

To join the Scouts, boys had to be at least 11 years old. Since many scouts had brothers younger than this who were eager to join in the fun, a junior league called the Wolf Cubs, later shortened to Cubs, was founded for boys aged eight to eleven. They wore bottle-green caps, and in addition to doing many of the things that the scouts did, they also played a lot of games based on Rudyard Kipling's *Jungle Book*, following a pack leader named Akela. Pack activities often involved 'a grand howl' of 'Dyb, dyb, dyb' and 'Dob, dob, dob', acronyms for the injunctions 'Do Your Best' and 'We'll Do Our Best'.

Something for the girls

A sister organisation for girls, known as the Girl Guides, was started by B-P's sister Agnes in 1910; she was later succeeded as head of the girls' organisation by B-P's wife, Olave. In *How Girls Can Help to Build Up the Empire*, Agnes wrote that the aim of the guides was 'character training much on the lines of Boy Scouts', since, as B-P himself insisted, 'girls must be partners and comrades'. Dressed in marine blue shirts and navy serge skirts, guides could win badges for stalking, mechanics and carpentry, and later poultry farming, interpreting, astronomy and bee-keeping, as well as more traditional feminine pursuits such as massage, lacemaking, nursing, childcare, housekeeping and floristry. The Guides enjoyed similar popularity to the Scouts, with numbers rising from 400,236 to 594,491 in the two decades to 1960. 'My friends at school and in the Guides meant almost more to me than my family', remembered Joan Moody. They also had a cadet branch, the Brownies, led by a 'Brown Owl' and a 'Tawny Owl'. Divided into packs with names like Pixies (charged to help 'those in fixes') and Elves, they danced round a pâpier maché toadstool at the start of every meeting.

Changing times

The 'youthquake' of the 1960s inevitably affected the movement. While membership of the brownies and cubs held steady, that of scouts and guides was in decline. In 1967, after an internal review, 'boy' was dropped from the name 'boy scout', and the lemon-squeezer hat and shorts became a thing of the past, replaced by green berets and fawn-coloured trousers. The proficiencies to aim for were also rethought in line with a new age, to include such new challenges as parachute-jumping. By the 1970s the cover of the magazine *The Guider* was more likely to depict a girl guide playing a guitar than cooking sausages over a campfire. There was even an apostate who ventured to suggest that maybe Crimplene, the new miracle fabric, would be a suitable material for guides' uniforms.

The Boys' Brigades

Another organisation that sported a uniform and offered working-class boys opportunities for active and profitable leisure in the open air was the Boys' Brigade (BB), which had been set up in Glasgow in 1883 with the aim of promoting 'Christian manliness'. Under the motto 'Steadfast and Sure', the Brigade combined a commitment to God and religion with gritty opposition to the temptations of the modern world such as cinemas, drinking and gambling. It flourished in the 1930s, particularly in areas of high unemployment

ON PARADE
Above: Girls show off Brownie uniforms – new on the left, old on the right – at the Girl Guide headquarters in London in 1967.
Below: A leader, taking the part of the Duke of York, inspects Boys' Brigade sections from London at rehearsals for the organisation's 50th Jubilee Celebrations in 1933.

PRACTISING TOGETHER

Many children, especially girls, learnt to socialise as they learnt to dance.
Above: A yawning five-year-old gives less than her full attention during a class at the Ballet Rambert School, Notting Hill Gate, London, in 1967.
Left: Schoolgirls give a display of country dancing in Findhorn, Scotland, to the accompaniment of an accordion.

(although less so in Wales with its strong anti-militarist tradition). The BB's military-style uniform included a pillbox hat until as late as 1971, long after it had been abandoned by the army. Boys also sported a haversack and a leather 'Sam Browne' belt over their ordinary clothes as they marched up and down in church parades most Sundays, beating drums, twirling sticks, blowing bugles and sometimes presenting arms with dummy rifles.

In September 1933, the 'BB' held its 50th Jubilee Conventicle in Hampden Park Football Stadium in Glasgow. With 130,000 'brigadiers' packed into the stadium, and 100,000 boys unable to gain entry, it was the largest open-air service ever held in Scotland. Five years later at a Festival of Youth held at the Albert Hall in London, the BB gave the largest massed physical training display ever seen in Britain – perfectly in line with government efforts at the time to get the British fit. The Brigade spawned several imitators, all religious and all military – the Jewish Lads' Brigade, the Catholic Boys' Brigade and the Church Lads' Brigade, the latter an offshoot of the Band of Hope, the children's wing of the temperance movement. The Boys' Brigade continued to be active during the Second World War, despite the severe disruption caused by evacuation and war work. Its membership increased slightly immediately after the war, but declined thereafter. By 1979 it had lost a third of its members in spite of – or more likely because of – 'the discipline and spiritual values [it] had upheld in the face of changing attitudes and shifting moral standards'.

Alternatives and rivals

From its very early days the Scouting movement had its critics. John Hargreaves, who was Scout HQ Commissioner for Woodcraft, became increasingly disillusioned with what he saw as its patriotic jingoism. In 1920 he set up a breakaway group called the Kibbo Kift Kindred – 'kibbo kift' being a dialect term for 'proof of great strength' – which attracted other disenchanted scout masters. The movement, which was strongly tinged by aspects of occultism, was devoted to strenuous hiking, camping and other outdoor activities; its members wore a green and brown uniform modelled on a Saxon cowl and jerkin.

Kibbo Kift never attracted a large following, and soon it split, too, when in 1925 a 19-year-old member named Leslie Paul started a rival organisation for young people, the Woodcraft Folk. This new group had links with the German *volk* movement, rejecting industrialisation, capitalism and everything urban in pursuit of an ambitious aim – nothing less than 'the rebirth of the human race'. The Woodcraft pledge was to develop 'communal responsibility' in young people by living close to nature: the name 'Woodcraft' was intended to refer to the skills needed to live in the open air, rather than making things from wood. Groups camped out, went hiking, learned to follow animal tracks and light fires. Members took Woodcraft names on joining (Leslie Paul's was 'Little Otter') and each new recruit's birth name was inscribed on a piece of bark which was ceremoniously burned. Despite the mystical – and to a degree supremacist – overtones in this 'blood brotherhood of the campfire', the Woodcraft Folk are still going today.

TEAM WORK
Eight-year-old Tony Kelly is given a drink between rounds by his second, Brian King, at the Leyton Boxing Club in East London in 1956.

CHILDREN IN WARTIME

Children were in the front line from the beginning in the Second World War. On 1 September, 1939, two days before war was declared, Operation 'Pied Piper' started to evacuate children from urban areas where bombing was expected. It was not compulsory, but leaflets urged parents to send their children to safety. Mothers were evacuated with babies and pre-school children, while older children went with their school with teachers in charge (in Scotland all children were evacuated with their mothers). The children mustered in school playgrounds as early as 6.30am, clutching a small suitcase (or pillow case, or even a brown paper parcel), a gas mask in its cardboard box and perhaps a favourite toy. The case contained a change of underwear, night clothes, plimsolls or slippers for indoors, socks, a toothbrush, comb, soap, towel and face cloth. Even these basics were beyond some in the inner cities, where many of the evacuees came from. 'Being poor, we only had one tube of toothpaste between four of us', remembers Irene Weller. 'My mother kept saying, "I don't know how you are going to manage if you get split up".'

It was a heart-rending time for parents, watching their children being marched off, unsure if they were doing the right thing. How would they be treated by their 'foster parents'? And when they would see them again? As one headmistress recalled: 'We had their children in trust, and to keep life as normal and safe and happy for them as possible was our task. As we went, the balloon barrages were slowly rising all round us – a strangely beautiful sight, and a dramatic reminder of the reason for our going.'

GOING AWAY
Top: Children being evacuated out of London at the outbreak of the war in September 1939.
Above: London evacuees, billeted on a Sussex farm, are enchanted by the first lambs of the year in 1940.

STAYING PUT
Right: Children in a South London street collect up fragments of anti-aircraft shells in September 1940.
Centre right: Children wearing tin hats hitch a ride on a carriage during April 1941.
Far right: A little girl holds tightly onto her doll in the rubble of her bomb-damaged home in 1940.

It had been expected that 3.5 million children would be evacuated. The actual figure was nearer 1.9 million, but even so when they arrived at their destinations there was considerable confusion. Many evacuees ended up in the wrong place – Anglesey expected 624 elementary school children, but they got 2,468 and somehow billets had to be found. For some children evacuation proved a happy experience in the countryside. For others it was a nightmare in unsympathetic homes, where they were barely fed but expected to work hard in the house or on the farm. Some were desperately homesick, but never told their parents. Education suffered on the whole since schools in the danger zones were closed and the influx of evacuees in reception areas meant that classes had to double up. Teachers had to come out of retirement to replace those called up into the services or war industries.

By December 1939 some 60 per cent of evacuees had returned home and despite the dangers few fled again when bombs began to fall. Of 60,595 civilians killed on the Home Front, 7,736 were under 16 – around one in every eight deaths. And thousands of children grew up without their father and sometimes without their mother.

Whether evacuated or not, children played an active part in the war effort. They collected salvage – jam jars, rags, cardboard, newspapers, bones, string – filled pigs' bins with vegetable peelings, helped 'dig for victory' in gardens and allotments, collected rose hips for vitamins and helped to 'make do and mend'. Boys became expert plane spotters and shrapnel collectors.

From the age of 14, when children left school, they really were in the front line, acting as messengers during air raids or helping St John's Ambulance and the Red Cross. Some joined up as military cadets or the Home Guard.

REUNION
Evacuee children rush to greet their parents on 4 December, 1939 (below). The parents had travelled in special trains from London for a visit to their children in the provincial town where the children were billeted.

TEENAGE DREAMS

In 1959 the magazine *Queen* proclaimed it to be a 'bad year for dodos'. The 'old firm' in politics, music, design, clothes and class consciousness was about to be confined to the dustbin of history. There would be a new morality, new ways of living and loving, even a new language.

It was the dawn of the Sixties. Almost 40 per cent of the population was under 25, and a glad confidence in youth was a new phenomenon. The very word 'teenager' was a recent import into English. Back in 1943 another magazine, *Housewife*, had referred to the teen years as 'the awkward age', poised uncomfortably between childhood and adulthood. Not sure what to wear, girls were either gawky in ankle socks and sandals, or they dressed like their mothers and looked prematurely middle-aged. For boys, in angst about the transition from short to long trousers, it was clearly apprentice time. The word 'adolescent' said it all; derived from the Latin *adolescere*, meaning to grow up, it reflected a time of transition, to be hurried through not celebrated – until the Sixties arrived.

Growing up fast in pre-war Britain

Up until 1918, children aged 12 who had passed the Education Code's Fifth Standard, or attended school for a minimum of 300 sessions over the previous five years, were eligible to begin work half-time – thousands did, particularly in the textile mills of the industrial north. They would either spend alternate days at school and work, or else work in the mills from early in the morning and attend school from 2.00 to 4.30pm. Such children put their childhood prematurely behind them. A report at the time concluded that the child 'does not know whether he is boy at school or a man', and although the practice was by then dying out, it was not completely eradicated until the 1920s.

After 1918 most children left school at 14. Boys entered an apprenticeship, or more likely took whatever unskilled or semi-skilled job they could find. They lived at home, handing most of their wages to their mother for bed and board. For working-class girls the most usual occupation before the First World War was live-in domestic service, but after the war girls were increasingly reluctant to take such jobs. Instead, they might go to work in a factory on leaving school, or perhaps a shop where they could be required to live in and work as many as 80 hours a week. The more fortunate found clerical jobs. Like her brothers, an office worker would live at home, handing most of her earnings to her mother. There would be outings to friends' houses, the cinema or a dance hall, but most girls saved what was left of their earnings for their 'bottom drawer' and the day they got married.

HARD BOYS – AND GIRLS
Skinheads, wearing a 'uniform' of Doc Martens boots, jeans and braces, pose for the camera in 1983. One wears a Union Jack tee-shirt, a fashion originally popularised by Carnaby Street retailers in the Mod era 20 years earlier.

TEENAGE ROMANCE?
Two teenagers talk in the grounds of Holt Hall in Norfolk, where the Norfolk Education Committee organised a social experiment in April 1951 designed to ease the transition from school to adult life.

In the 1930s, job prospects could be bleak for the young. Employers would often take on school leavers only to dispense with their services when they reached 16, the age when National Insurance contributions fell due. It could then be hard to find another job. 'There are scores of young men in the Valley who have never worked since the age of 16', said one Welsh miner. 'At 16 they become insurable, and the employers sack them rather than face the extra expense. So we have young men who have never had a day's work since. They have nothing to hope for but an aimless drift. I'm glad no son of mine is in that position.' The Second World War brought independence to a lot of young people, but they still had to grow up fast. Many were evacuated away from home, others moved away to work and got used to having a regular wage. A lot of young people did responsible, sometimes harrowing, work in the Civil Defence services – and waited to be called up.

Birth of the teenager

The school-leaving age was raised to 15 in 1947, and for the first time there seemed to be a distinct category of working-class youth who were no longer children but as yet had no desire to 'settle down' and embrace the conventions of adulthood. 'Teddy Boys', the first manifestation of this phenomenon, got their name from their distinctive Edwardian-style jackets. From Jermyn Street and Savile Row, the fashion spread south past the Elephant and Castle and on to Catford, Lewisham and Penge, then out to the provinces, growing more extreme as it went. Hair was long(ish), greased and combed back to form a quiff at the front and a 'DA' (duck's arse) at the rear – a comb was among a Teddy Boy's most valued possessions. Jackets were draped and long, with a velvet collar, and worn with narrow 'boot lace' tie, drainpipe trousers and crepe-soled 'brothel creeper' shoes.

RIVER SERENADE
A group of Cambridge undergraduates take a break from punting on the River Cam to enjoy a riverbank singsong in April 1957. Folk music had a growing following in the Fifties. The folk revival gathered pace at folk clubs up and down the country in the Sixties, but suffered a serious blow when even Dylan went electric in 1965.

'Of course there are "Teddy Boys" with evil ways,' wrote journalist Hilde
Marchant in May 1954, 'but the vast majority of young men merely wish to wear
Edwardian suits as a change from boiler suits and factory overalls.' Nevertheless,
the 'Teds' were demonised by their elders. They were banned from dance halls,
thrown out of pubs, turned down for employment and blamed for gang violence.
There were reports of fights between rival gangs armed with bicycle chains and
knuckle-dusters. Most were just scuffles among lads with few opportunities for
fun, but some incidents were more serious. Teddy Boys, excluded from 'table-
tennis-playing youth clubs', attacked those inside. Then, in the summer of 1955,
Rock Around the Clock reached British cinemas. During screenings at the Trocadero
in Elephant and Castle and the Prince of Wales cinema in Harrow Road,
Paddington, riots erupted as 'Teds' ripped out seats so they
could jive to Bill Haley and the Comets. The pattern was
repeated in cinemas up and down the country.

*'I expect I'll be dead by the time
I'm 30. We all will.'*

A 'TYPICAL TEENAGER' INTERVIEWED BY *QUEEN* MAGAZINE IN 1959

National service

But for young men in the 1950s, there was a salutary rite of
passage to be got through: national service. The Labour
Party had opposed conscription when it was introduced for the first time shortly
before the war started in 1939, and when the war was finally over, after the
surrender of Japan in August 1945, it might have been imagined that under a
Labour government wartime uniforms would be folded away for good. But the
world was still a turbulent place, with unrest in the Far East, the Middle East and
India, while Europe now felt threatened by the USSR. Britain might have ceded its

YOUNG MILITARY MEN
National service soldiers on their way to a camp in Purfleet, Essex, where they were on standby to take over from striking gas workers in the East End of London in October 1950.

role as a superpower, but it still had one as an international policeman, and its regular army was desperately overstretched. There were also those who argued that a spell of military discipline had proved beneficial in wartime, bringing men of all classes together, and that it would do no harm to extend the practice into peacetime, perhaps helping to stem the tide of juvenile delinquency.

In May 1947, despite a Labour rebellion, the National Service Act became law: all men other than the blind and the mentally and physically unfit were liable for call-up at 18. The clergy, miners, sea fishermen, merchant seamen and some agricultural workers were exempt, and if a youth was doing an apprenticeship, gaining professional qualification or studying at university he could defer his national service (although not usually at Oxford or Cambridge, which preferred undergraduates to have had two maturing years in the military).

As in wartime, the impression that young men could choose which branch of the forces to serve in proved to be an illusion – 72 out of every 100 ended up in army khaki. There was also little choice about where they were sent. In the early days, one in every two conscripts was dispatched, usually by troopship, to one of the world's trouble spots – Korea, Cyprus, Kenya. Nearly three-quarters of British men in the Korean War, which broke out in 1950, were on national service. No one was sent to fight in Korea under the age of 19, but they were shipped out to Hong Kong ready to be transferred the day after their 19th birthday. More than 200 national servicemen died in Korea, more than 100 in Malaya and probably more in accidents.

NATIONAL SERVICE – Daily life in the army

Conscripts first faced a medical, which was something of a lottery – flat feet might mean rejection or acceptance, depending on the attitude of the doctor involved. For those who passed – the vast majority – a brown OHMS envelope would arrive a couple of weeks later containing a third-class rail warrant and a postal order for the first day's pay – 4 shillings until 1950, then 5 shillings and sixpence.

Life in the army was harsh for those who had never left home before: reveille was at 6.15am, but some masochistic NCOs would start bellowing as early as 5 o'clock. The uniform was itchy and uncomfortable and rarely fitted well, while wearing hobnail boots for hours on the parade ground blistered the rookies' tender feet. Days consisted of 'square-bashing' – marching back and forth and presenting arms – along with polishing boots and brass buttons, cleaning billets and washrooms, and standing for bedside inspections with all possessions neatly folded while an eagle-eyed officer checked that everything was in order. This time-consuming procedure was relaxed in the mid 1950s. Food was usually 'stodgy but adequate' – rationing remained in force until 1954 in Britain, so there were often shortages of eggs, sugar and meat. Worse still, the haircuts administered by barbers who would have done a good job shearing sheep were deeply mortifying for young men who had so carefully cultivated their quiffs in civilian life.

During the 13 years that national service lasted, as many as 2.3 million young men served king or queen and country for little more than pocket money. They were paid £1 8s a week – in 1951 the average wage was £8 8s 6d – which rose to £1 18s for the last batch called up (but deferred) in 1962, when the average wage had surged to £15 7s. An official army guide, published in 1953, claimed that the national service experience was 'an education in itself – the finest in the world: quite apart from the training and instruction the national serviceman will receive, he will meet and live with men drawn from all classes of society, of all trades, of all standards of education, and of various religious and political faiths …'. There was some truth in this: many young men were given a leg-up in life by national service. But by the mid 1950s, with the Korean War over, the mood had changed. By that time films such as *Carry On Sergeant* (1958) and the Boulting Brothers' *Private's Progress* (1956) – in which Terry-Thomas as Major Hitchcock barked 'You're an absolute shower', giving the nation a new catchphrase – were poking fun at the military in a way that would have been unthinkable ten years earlier. In 1956, *Brassey's Annual* reported from an army survey that '15 per cent like the life, 10 per cent hate it … and the remaining 75 per cent do their best and long for the day when it will be over'. Which it finally was, for everyone, in 1962.

BAN THE BOMB
Pupils from Parliament Hill School for Girls in north London gather in Trafalgar Square for a Campaign for Nuclear Disarmament (CND) march to the Atomic Weapons Research Establishment at Aldermaston in Berkshire at Easter 1958. The demonstrators were protesting against the H-bomb.

The young go their own way

Maybe the regimentation of national service partly fed the anarchism of the young in the late 1950s and 60s. Long before London had been recognised as 'swinging' in an article in the American magazine *Time* in 1966, there had been an underground culture in the capital. Soho was at its heart, with jazz venues such as Ronnie Scott's putting on all-night sessions of American trad and modern jazz, played by homegrown talent such as George Melly and John Chiltern and the Feetwarmers. New Italian espresso bars had taken over from the Thirties trend for milk bars, serving frothy coffee and with a juke box in the corner that was sometimes replaced by live music.

Most famous of the coffee bars was the Two I's, which launched the careers of Tommy Steele (real name Tommy Hicks) and Cliff Richard (formerly Harry Webb). Many of their customers were art school students, or those who would like to be, influenced both by the American 'beat generation' of Jack Kerouac and Allen Ginsburg and the Paris left-bank existentialists personified by Juliette Greco. The women wore black polo-necked sweaters, their hair long and straight, eyes heavily made up, lips pale; the men sported beards and wore corduroy trousers, sandals and duffle coats.

It was not just style: there was a political edge, too, as it was young people like these who joined the Campaign for Nuclear Disarmament (CND). In February 1958 some 5,000 people crammed into Westminster Hall for the first meeting of CND, with Canon Collins, a former wartime RAF chaplain now at St Paul's Cathedral, in the chair and the philosopher Bertrand Russell as president. On Good Friday that year hundreds marched from Trafalgar Square to the atomic research establishment at Aldermaston in Berkshire, their ranks swelling along the way to an estimated 8,000, who trudged along in the rain singing 'Ban, ban, ban the bloody bomb' to the tune of 'When the Saints go Marching in'. The *New Statesman* reported, with some glee, that 'official circles are confused and alarmed about the Campaign for Nuclear Disarmament'. To the young the campaign was compelling – it was action instead of generalisations.

The growing student body

Being a student was an enviable thing to be in the 1960s. Tuition was free and most students had scholarships or local authority grants. They might work in the vacations – maybe helping out with the Christmas post, or selling tickets for deckchairs in summer – but almost none had to work during term

STRUMMING TO A NEW BEAT
Christopher Radmall playing the guitar to an attentive audience at a venue known as Brad's Club in London in the early 1960s.

TRADITIONAL TASTES
Young lads queue up for fish and chips, Britain's perennial takeaway, in a shop in Handsworth, Birmingham, in about 1978.

time and so could devote themselves wholeheartedly to study and the pursuit of pleasure. Moreover, there were more places to study. In 1939 there had been 50,000 full-time students, but this number had doubled by 1958.

The post-war mantra was that Britain needed more vocational training if it was to compete with Germany, Japan and the USA. In 1963 this was echoed by Lord Robbins in his Report on Higher Education. He recommended that there should be 50 per cent more students by 1967 and 250 per cent more by 1980. Eleven new 'plate glass' universities were opened by the end of the decade: Sussex, East Anglia, Warwick, Lancaster, Essex, Kent, York, Strathclyde, Sterling, Heriot-Watt and Dundee. Young people with a technical bent could opt to study at one of 32 new polytechnics. But despite state-of-the-art laboratories and the buzz created by Labour around the 'white heat of technology', science remained far less popular with British youth than the humanities and the arts.

If science was not cool, art schools were. Britain had more art schools per head of population than anywhere else in the world. Establishments such as St Martins, Chelsea College of Art, Hornsey and Glasgow produced many of the movers and shakers of the 1960s. Mary Quant, a fashion student at Goldsmith's College before opening her uber-trendy boutique, Bazaar,

'Adult appearance was very unattractive ... I saw no reason why childhood could not last for ever.'

FASHION DESIGNER MARY QUANT, SPEAKING IN 1965

CHILLING OUT
A hippy-dressed couple in the crowd at a free concert in Hyde Park in 1971. The most celebrated of the free Hyde Park gatherings was a concert given by the Rolling Stones in July 1969, shortly after the accidental death of the group's ex-guitarist Brian Jones.

in the King's Road in 1955, would later write: 'The art schools were a great forcing house of talent, not just clothes but music, design, food, lifestyle, everything.' John Lennon of the Beatles, Keith Richards of the Rolling Stones, Ray Davies of the Kinks and Pete Townsend of the Who were all products of the art schools.

Soundtrack for a new generation

Music was at the heart of youth culture. Making it in the pop world was a way out of a boring, routine job and young would-be musicians in every city in Britain wanted to be part of it. Liverpool was the undisputed capital of this new culture, giving the world the Beatles, but Newcastle spawned the Animals, in Manchester it was Herman's Hermits and the Hollies, the Moody Blues and the Move came from Birmingham, while London produced the Rolling Stones, the Kinks, the Who, the Small Faces and the Pretty Things. At one time Bristol alone could boast 300 home-grown bands.

Young people who didn't make it onto the road to stardom after leaving school, but went straight into a job in an office, shop or factory, could still buy into the teen dream. They could not vote or marry (without parent's consent) until 21 (reduced to 18 in 1968), but teenagers still had more spending power than would have seemed possible a decade before: between 1951 and 1974 average wages increased six-fold. And there was so much more to spend money on.

Few teenagers could afford King's Road prices, but there were plenty of other choices. A run-down lane behind Regent Street called Carnaby Street fizzed into life with boutiques selling fashionable 'gear' in the wake of a young Glasgow tailor, John Stephen, who had arrived there in 1953 and was soon opening branches all over Britain. Barbara Hulanicki, who had first come to notice when the *Daily Express* offered 'something cool and shifty' in pink gingham with a matching headscarf for 25 shillings, opened Biba in a former chemist's shop in Kensington in 1964. County girls tended to prefer the romantic 'milkmaid' style cotton dresses of Laura Ashley. Boutiques with zany names sprang up all over the country selling mini skirts, coloured tights, skinny rib jumpers and knee high boots to girls, flared hipster trousers, flowery shirts and Cuban heeled boots to young men. Clothes, which had previously been modelled by elegant, languid-looking women, were now photographed on young, stick-thin girls of whom Neasden-born Lesley Hornby – known as Twiggy for reasons everyone could recognise – and Jean Shrimpton were the most famous. Behind the camera lens were working-class young men from London's East End – David Bailey, Terence Donovan, Brian Duffy.

Looking back on the style-setters of the Sixties, journalist Francis Wyndham would write: 'Possibly no other society so small in number has tattooed its image so indelibly across the face of a whole generation … often talented and malignantly ambitious, they were the butterflies born to be broken on the wheel of fashion.'

ENGLAND, MY ENGLAND
Above: A Who fan dozes on a deckchair on Brighton beach in April 1980, using his parka, emblazoned with the Union Jack, as a blanket. The British flag had long been something of a symbol for fans of the group, who had first risen to prominence as a Mod band in the 1960s.
Below: One of the many different posters used by successive governments in the course of campaigns to persuade the young of the dangers of taking drugs – usually with only limited success.

Mods and Rockers

While some girls had back-combed 'beehive' hair-dos, others went to their local salon clutching a magazine picture of a glossy, geometric, Vidal Sassoon cut. Teenagers spent Saturday afternoons in the listening booths of record shops with the latest record on the turntable. They might have heard it on *Ready Steady Go*, presented by Cathy McGowan on Friday evenings with the slogan 'the weekend starts here'. For Mods, *Ready Steady Go* became a prelude to a night out – in London at the Marquee, the Lyceum or the Goldhawk in Shepherd's Bush.

Originally, Mods were teenagers who liked modern jazz; they tended to be middle-class and influenced by Continental films and fashions. They looked like the Beatles in the early days, wearing collarless jackets, winklepicker shoes and pudding-basin haircuts. Their 'chicks' were equally sharp in short skirts, pointed-toe stilettos and seamless nylons. By the mid 1960s this urban tribe had broadened – although it maintained its keen sense of fashion – to include a wider social spectrum. Their transport of choice was a Vespa, an Italian scooter.

The polar opposite of the Mods were the Rockers, motorcycle descendents of the 'Ton-Up Boys' of the 1950s. They swaggered around with long (often greasy) hair, wearing studded leather jackets and blue denim jeans *à la* James Dean or Marlon Brando in *The Wild One*. They hung out in roadside cafés, like the Ace Cafe on London's North Circular Road, listening to rock'n'roll. From different social backgrounds and with totally different tastes, Mods and Rockers were destined to clash, which they usually did at the seaside – Clacton, Margate, Brighton, Bournemouth, Hastings – on cold, wet Bank Holidays. Magistrates and the press were outraged and parents were perplexed. Teenagers seemed to have it all, so what had gone wrong? What more did they want?

Life is for living
Live it
Don't be stuck on
'DRUGS'

Know the facts.
Ask your local Health
Department for
leaflets on drugs

LIVING ON THE LAND

'England is the country, and the country is England', the Prime Minister Stanley Baldwin told the Royal Society of St George in 1924. 'The tinkle of the hammer on the anvil in the country smithy, the corncrake on a dewy morning, the sound of the scythe … and the sight of the plough team coming over the brow of the hill, the sight that has been England since England was a land …'

HIRED HAND
A farmer (on the right) hires a farm hand at the biannual Hiring Fair at Carlisle in 1945, handing over the sum of half a crown (two shillings and sixpence) to seal the bargain. Agricultural labourers from all over the country gathered to seek employment at such fairs.

PREVIOUS PAGE
Coal miners in Waldridge, a village in County Durham, gather with pit ponies, their eyes shielded for work underground, in 1963.

The pastoral idyll lies at the very heart of Englishness. When the poet Laurie Lee's memoir of growing up in a Gloucestershire village before the First World War was published in 1959 it became an instant, best-selling classic. *Cider with Rosie* recalled a time when 'the tarred road wound away up the valley, innocent as yet of motorcars … [and] nothing happened at all except summer…'. But for those who laboured in the countryside, it was often less of an idyll and more of an unceasing battle with the elements to wrest a living from the land – a battle that grew harder in the mid years of the 20th century.

There are parts of Britain that seem little changed today – Thomas Hardy would feel at home in large swathes of Wessex, as would A.E. Housman in parts of Shropshire and Burns on the Solway coast. Maybe even Wordsworth would find a corner of the Lake District that he could still call his own. But housing, industry and their infrastructure have encroached on most of Britain. First canals, then railways, then new roads – by the 1960s, motorways – cut through the countryside. Pylons started to bestride hills and valleys, sprawling, in the words of journalist S.P.B. Mais in 1935, 'wantonly across our noblest landscape like a lunatic's slashings across the face of an old master'. Such innovations as the massive electricity-generating cooling towers that came to dominate parts of Oxfordshire and Yorkshire not only changed the landscape – despoiled it in the eyes of many – but also the lives of rural workers.

Fallow land and low pay

In 1900 Britain was still primarily an agricultural country, although it was becoming increasingly hard to make a living from the land. In the 19th century the countryside had been intensively farmed by an abundant cheap labour force, but by the first decade of the 20th, the effects of the agricultural depression and cheap imports – grain from the prairies of Canada, wool, mutton and lamb from New Zealand, beef from Argentina – posed stiff competition to homegrown food. By 1939 the price of wheat had dropped by 50 per cent since the 1870s while arable land under cultivation had decreased by almost 40 per cent, down from 14.7 to 8.9 million acres; in many counties, land lay neglected and

MANUAL HARVEST
Agricultural workers gathering in flax to make linen at Killinchy in County Down, Northern Ireland, in July 1948.

overgrown. In Dorset, where half a million sheep had dotted the hillsides at the turn of the century, there were less than 50,000 by 1946. During the First World War, when German U-boats threatened imports, the government guaranteed the price of grain and fallow land was once more ploughed up, but the prosperity was short-lived. By the 1930s international competition again hit British farming. Rural poverty and unemployment paralleled that in the hardest-hit industrial areas: between 1921 and 1939 the number of agricultural workers fell by a quarter; in 1932 alone, 600 farmers in England and Wales went bankrupt.

Farm workers' wages were low – around half of what a skilled manual worker could earn, and considerably less even than labourers on building sites took home. Increasingly the 'new industries' attracted men from the land. In Oxfordshire, for example, 48 per cent of agricultural workers left the land between 1921 and 1938, with the Morris car plant at Cowley proving a particular attraction.

The first marketing boards for hops, potatoes, bacon and milk were set up in 1934. Milk was one commodity that remained profitable. Aided by the expansion of railway lines deep into rural areas and untouched by imports from overseas, great churns of fresh, warm milk would be manhandled onto trains, many of which ran through the night from the West Country to London and the Midlands. Growing urbanisation made it worthwhile for farmers to expand their dairy herds of Friesian, Jersey and Guernsey cows, while others turned to market gardening, providing vegetables and fruit for the ever-expanding towns and cities.

The electricity grid extended across the country in the 1930s – although many remote farms were not connected to mains electricity until well into the

'... the summer was all we heard;
cuckoos crossed distances on chains of cries,
flies buzzed and choked in the ears, and the
saw-toothed chatter of the mowing-machines
drifted on waves of air from the fields.'

LAURIE LEE, FROM *CIDER WITH ROSIE*

CASTING CLOUTS

The busy sheep shearing season at a remote farm at Bannisdale in the Lake District in June 1939. The sheep are long-wooled rough 'gimmer hogs' – Northern slang for ewe (female) lambs between weaning and their first shearing.

1950s or even later – and the coming of electricity transformed farming methods. Windmills and watermills were increasingly redundant as electricity drove machinery for grinding corn; milking could be done by electric pumps rather than the age-old practice of hand milking. As traditional thatched or tiled brick barns fell into disrepair and could no longer be used to house animals or store grain, farmers turned to cheaper options, replacing them with corrugated iron structures. In turn, these unsightly additions to the landscape had a propensity to rust, so by the mid 1930s most new barns were constructed with asbestos–cement sheeting.

Rejuvenated by war

Again, in 1939, war threw a lifeline to the countryside. Before the Second World War, Britain imported more than 70 per cent of its food for human consumption and animal feed. As an island nation Britain would come under siege, its essential imports threatened by German U-boats, while shipping space was required to transport war supplies and troops. It was vital that the nation become as self-sufficient as possible in food production. The slogan 'Dig for Victory' not only applied to householders digging up their herbaceous borders to grow cabbages, it also required a radical shift in farm production. Farmers were given a generous government subsidy to plant crops, and would sometimes plough through the night to qualify for their remittance. In the Fenlands of East Anglia, the Ministry

NAIL AND ANVIL
The men of the Nelson family of Leyland, Lancashire, traditionally worked as blacksmiths. Three of them are seen here in their smithy, shoeing a farmer's horse in January 1938.

RIVER HARVEST
An old fisherman photographed in January 1932 as he works on conical willow 'putcher' baskets used for catching salmon and eels. Such baskets were mainly produced in the Somerset wetlands.

of Agriculture recut drains and dykes, rebuilt banks, installed pumping machines and brought thousands of water-logged acres back into cultivation.

Many younger farm labourers sought to join the war effort, but most were 'reserved' by government regulation – that is, required to stay on the land. Farmers were assisted in their vital work by the Women's Land Army, and also by some 40,000 prisoners-of-war wearing distinctive orange bull's eyes on the backs of their uniforms to make them easily identifiable should they attempt to escape. Generally, farmers did well in the war, and farm labourers' wages rose too. Indeed, most of those who made their living from the land had a better war altogether, with fewer air raids, more chance to supplement their rations with home-grown vegetables, eggs, rabbits and game, and a more generous allocation of petrol.

The march of mechanisation

In the name of efficiency, farming gradually became more mechanised. In 1939 there were ten times more horses than tractors on British farms, ploughing and pulling carts. Usually only farmers with 300 acres or more

Above: A farming family from Manor Farm, Shipton, in the Gloucestershire Cotswolds break for tea during the bean harvest in August 1943. Below: Prisoners-of-war – some of about 2,000 men captured in the North Africa campaign – at work in an English hay field. Most farmers welcomed the contribution that these and other later arrivals made in helping to plug the shortage of agricultural labour in wartime Britain.

could afford to own one of the 40,000 tractors then in use, but even they were unlikely to own a combine harvester. Roland Thomas remembered the communal effort at harvest time on the farm he grew up on in Wales: 'At harvest time everyone joined in. When the horse-drawn reaper had cut the corn, the children joined the adults in tying and stacking the sheaves ready to be loaded onto a wagon and made into a stack. It was fun for the children, helping to pitchfork the corn higher and higher onto the stack.'

The government intended that the wartime policy of self-sufficiency in food would continue into the peace, so farmers were supported with subsidies and loans to prevent agriculture falling back into the parlous state of the 1930s. But this intention, embedded in the 1947 Agricultural Act, was to have momentous consequences, turning much farming into large-scale business ventures and making many workers redundant. As agriculture grew more productive, with increasingly efficient mechanisation and use of chemical fertilisers and pesticides to increase the yield of the land, the evidence of change was soon apparent: in 1950, there were still some 300,000 working horses on farms, but by the start of the 1960s they had all but disappeared. That in turn meant farmers no longer needed to devote acres to grazing pasture and growing oats to feed their equine workers.

COTTAGE INDUSTRY
The manufacturer of 'Granny's Home Brewed Nettle Drink' awaits customers outside her Lancashire shop in 1954.

Tractors, combine harvesters and other large-scale agricultural machinery needed wide-open spaces – a prairie model of the countryside rather than a series of pocket-handkerchief-sized fields. Large acreage growing a single crop was a more cost-effective proposition, and with fewer cattle to restrain, hedges could be bulldozed or grubbed up so the newly mechanised farmer could range far and fast without hindrance. What had been a patchwork of small fields was increasingly turned into large slabs of highly cultivated arable land. It was almost as if the medieval enclosures had never happened. Vistas of gently waving golden corn were increasingly replaced by startlingly bright yellow rapeseed crops by the 1970s.

The agribusiness approach extended to animal husbandry, too. It would once have taken around 15 hours' labour to milk a hundred cows. Now, using electric milking machines, one person could oversee the milking of several times that

(continued on page 65)

HOPPING HOLIDAYS

WORKING HOLIDAY

Above: A truck-load of hop-pickers arriving at a hop farm near Maidstone in 1950.

Left: Veteran hop-picker Mrs Selby Ayres photographed at work on a farm in Petersfield, Hampshire, in 1954.

Top centre: Workers tipping the hops into sacks to be weighed on a farm at Paddock Wood, Kent, owned by Whitbread's brewery.

Summer holidays for many of London's East Enders, at least up until the 1950s, meant just one thing: hop picking in the Kent countryside. The main workforce consisted of women who took their children with them, and as the harvest lasted for about four weeks from the end of August, that meant many children missed several weeks of school each September. The menfolk would come down to join the family at weekends, or if they were unemployed or working as casual labourers, they might come for the whole working holiday in the fresh air.

'It is, generally speaking, the poorest and roughest households which provide the largest contingent of hop pickers', concluded a survey, and many families went year after year. Clutching bundles they would catch a train, 'the 'Hopper's Special', from

London Bridge, their children hidden under the seats to avoid the ticket inspector. At their destination the 'oppers' would make their way to one of the tin or brick huts provided by the farmer, covering the floor and making 'mattresses' and pillows out of the straw provided. Upturned apple crates served for tables and chairs, and they would dig a pit for a cooking fire.

Once settled in, it was time to get to work stripping the bines. It was rough, hard work, the hours were long and the pay meagre – six bushels a shilling was the going rate in 1931. When George Orwell took an 'oppin 'oliday, he only managed to earn 9 shillings in an entire week, but then he was inexperienced. Meals would be eaten outside if possible and the day would end with a singsong round the fire, or someone telling ghost stories.

SUPPORT SYSTEMS
Top: Lunch being prepared at an outdoor 'kitchen' on Whitbread's farm at Paddock Wood.
Above: A creche run by the Salvation Army for the pickers' younger children on a farm in 1936.
Right: Experienced, skilled workers on stilts repair broken wires in a field at Wateringbury, Kent, in April 1933, ready for the next crop of hops.

number. Once hens had scratched and pecked in the farm yard and laid their eggs inconveniently in barns, while pigs had rolled in mud and slept in straw in sties. That too, though, was changing. 'Battery hens' – intensively reared rows of poultry in controlled-climate sheds – first made an appearance in 1933. Although the practice of cramming chickens into wooden compartments so they could hardly move was not new even then, it grew over the following decades, making what had been the special treat of 'a chicken dinner' cheap standard fare. Pigs were likewise contained and regimented, their snorting, rollicking days in the orchard over.

Diversify or die

The result of the new cult of efficiency was a rapid exodus of farm workers from the land. Imports of cheap lamb from New Zealand made keeping sheep less profitable, and soon gangs of shearers with machines began to arrive, moving from farm to farm – although with the introduction of synthetic textiles from the 1930s on, wool had anyhow become a less-valued commodity. Shepherds with their scattered flocks proved less easy to mechanise than other stockmen, but the decline in demand for mutton after the Second World War meant that fewer hillsides were dotted with sheep. By the early 1970s, despite the fact that well over 85 per cent of the British Isles was still countryside, only 2.5 per cent of the workforce was employed in agriculture. To survive, farmers were having to diversify, perhaps taking in paying guests for 'farm holidays', or opening farm shops to sell homemade produce. Some let out fields to campers and caravanners, or even staged pop festivals on their land. The first Glastonbury Festival, organised by Michael Eavis at Worthy Farm near Pilton in Somerset in 1970, was attended by 1,500 people – with Tyrannosaurus Rex (later known as T-Rex) heading the bill. By the 1980s the festival had become an annual event, its celebrated 'pyramid stage' serving as a hay barn and cow shed over the winter.

If farms were changing, so were the rural industries that supported them. Turning hay and straw into rope had almost entirely died out by the 1930s, but most villages of any size had a blacksmith as late as the 1950s, although probably not a wheelwright or a saddler. Smiths who no longer had sufficient horses to shoe might turn their skills on the anvil to fashioning agricultural equipment, wrought iron gates, pokers or candle sticks. Recognising the fact that bikes and cars had taken over from the horse as the principal modes of rural transport, many smiths diversified into bicycle and motor repairs or opened petrol stations on rural roads.

Wood still needed to be chopped for stakes, beams, fences and crates for fruit, and the arrival of the chainsaw in the late 1950s made that work quicker and less labour-intensive. The few coopers who remained were able to build on their barrel-making skills to produce tubs for plants and garden furniture. Wheelwrights adept at coach-building might follow the blacksmiths' example, taking up motor-related tasks like panel-beating or painting vehicles. Cottage roofs still required thatching, and this was a skill often passed down from father to son – although when times were hard householders might replace their thick, insulating, mice-harbouring thatch with tiles or even corrugated iron sheets.

The appreciation of craftsmanship shown by those far removed from its production, encouraged by rural industry associations, served to revivify some country crafts such as wicker fence making and dry stone walling. All this was on a relatively small scale – and the producers were as likely to be 'incomers' with a yen for the pastoral as displaced rural workers – but it was a potent link with the rural past and an opportunity to rethink how rural production might be in the future.

SNOWY SCENE
A postman on his delivery round near Windermere in the Lake District at Christmas 1938. The bicycling 'posties' performed a social function in remote areas, helping to bind the nation together.

HOW WE WORKED THEN

When the journalist and playwright J.B. Priestley took his *English Journey* in the autumn of 1933, he found not one but three Englands. One was new, but two were 'old' – rural England with its historic towns and cities, 'the country of cathedrals and minsters and manor houses and inns', and 19th-century industrial England, the land 'of coal, iron, steel, cotton, wool, railways …'

SERVING STEEL
A poster produced by the North Eastern Region of British Railways, promoting their service to the steel industry. The artwork for the poster was by the appropriately named Kenneth Steel.

SPARKS FLYING
Right: Men at work in a steelworks in the north of England in November 1939. Steel-making suffered badly in the Depression of the 1930s. The industry was nationalised in 1951 by Clement Attlee's Labour government, who lost the election later that year, and it was then denationalised by the incoming Conservative government. In 1967 Harold Wilson's Labour government renationalised it once more as the British Steel Corporation.

This latter England, Priestley reported, 'makes up a large part of the Midlands and the North … but it is not being added to and has no new life poured into it.' Had he extended his journey into Wales and Scotland, he would have found much the same picture: the industries that the previous century had made Britain the 'workshop of the world', exporting coal, iron, steel and textiles and building the ships to transport them, were now dying. In 1931 almost 80 per cent of the population could be categorised as working-class: some 30 million people were employed to do some sort of manual work, skilled, semi-skilled or unskilled. Many were in those traditional 'staple industries' that were no longer competitive in the world and in which Britain had reluctantly ceded industrial hegemony to Germany and the United States. And this percentage would not change substantially until the 1960s.

It was manual workers who suffered most in the Depression of the 1930s: they accounted for almost 92 per cent of the unemployed, whose numbers in 1933, at the depth of the Depression, rose to almost 3 million. More than a third of miners were out of work, and even as late as 1939 unemployment among miners was still running at 12 per cent. It was equally dire among the Lancashire cotton workers. In 1930 competition from imports and from new synthetic fabrics had caused 45 per cent of workers to lose their jobs. Women often worked alongside their husbands in the mills – the low level of wages meant that both partners needed to bring in a wage packet to support the household. Unusually, women were paid almost on a par with men in the weaving mills and many women also belonged to a trade union, like their menfolk. But when unemployment and short-time working arrived, women were among the first to be laid off.

The plight of the shipyard workers

Hardest hit of all was shipbuilding. In the first couple of years after the First World War, the yards were kept busy with orders for replacement warships, but before long a combination of factors plunged the industry into deep trouble and shipyard owners began laying men off. There was a sharp decline in world trade – and in Britain's share of the trade that was left. There had been years of underinvestment in the yards, which struggled to cope with new technologies, especially the switch from steam to diesel power in ships. Industrial relations were fractious, and there had been an exodus of skilled workers to Canada. In 1930 Cunard placed an order for a new liner with the John Brown shipyard on Clydeside: it seemed to offer the hope of salvation, and men worked round the

A row of workmen balancing on suspended planks scrape the sides of the starboard bow of the Cunard White Star liner *Queen Mary* in preparation for a coat of paint. The ship was being fitted at the King George V graving dock, Southampton, in September 1936.

clock on 'Job No. 534'. But in December 1931, with 80 per cent of the hull completed, Cunard decided that the project was no longer economically viable and 3,000 labourers who had been working on the ship were promptly sacked. Another 10,000 men and women employed on subsidiary contracts for the liner were either thrown out of work too or put on half-time shifts – and half pay. Work was halted for almost three years, only resuming when the government agreed to contribute £3 million towards the project. A swirl of bagpipes greeted the first 300 men to return to work on the vessel. The new workforce finally finished building the 81,000-tonne *Queen Mary* later that summer.

They were the lucky ones. The overall picture was bleak: by 1937, 28 shipyards had gone out of business. It was the closure of the Palmers yard in Jarrow in 1933 that led to the Jarrow March of 1936, when men from the town walked to London to bring the plight of the shipyard workers to the attention of the country. Even by 1939, when rearmament had begun to bring back orders, a fifth of Jarrow's working men remained unemployed. Mrs Pallas, the wife of an unemployed shipbuilder in Sunderland, told a journalist that when she married her husband he had been earning £8 to £10 a week – 'he's a left-handed ship's riveter, a craft which should be earning him a lot. There aren't many left-handed riveters.' But with the decline of the industry, Mr Pallas had been unemployed for 13 years. Once his wife had paid 'for the allotment rent, the burial clubs, for the children's clothes, for chapel collection' and for her husband's cigarettes, she had 'about ten shillings a week left for groceries, two shillings for milk and three shillings for anything else' that was needed to support a family of five children.

Another group of workers dependent on world trade were the dockers. Although the docks were one of the first industries to be unionised, falling exports and imports and increasing mechanisation hit them hard: in 1931 there were some 120,000 dock labourers in Britain; by 1951 the number had fallen to 81,000. The work was casual, handed out on a daily basis, and many a man hung around the dock gate in the hope of work only to be turned away as the spiral continued downwards.

Changes in transport also caused changes in work patterns. As horse-drawn vehicles gave way to mechanised replacements, men who were used to stabling, harnessing, grooming and controlling horses learned to drive vans, lorries or buses instead. The change produced almost a zero-sum equation: in 1911 there had been more than 400,000 drivers of horse-drawn vehicles, which by 1951 had fallen to 15,000; conversely, in 1911 there had only been 50,000 drivers of motor vehicles, but by 1951 that total had risen to 547,000.

The dreaded Means Test

Older, unskilled men had the hardest time finding work as the staple heavy industries inexorably declined. And the longer they were out of work, the harder it became to find a job, since employers with a large pool to chose from were apt to think that the long-term unemployed had grown rusty, if not work shy, and would no longer be able to pick up new skills or learn a new trade. It was such men and their families who suffered most from the Means Test, introduced in 1931. When their National Insurance benefits ran out, the men would have to apply to the Public Assistance Committee (often staffed by those who had administered the Poor Law until its abolition in 1929) if they were to continue to draw benefits.

In order to assess a family's entitlement, the hated 'Means Test Man' would call on them at home. He would poke around to see if they had savings or any assets that could be sold to raise a few pounds, and in making his calculations would take into account the earnings of all members of the family living at home. As a result, sons and daughters could find themselves having to support an unemployed father – a situation they more than likely resented and which the 'head of the household' invariably found mortifying. Likewise, a father might have to support an unemployed son or daughter, bringing accusations of being a 'parasite' as weeks

ON THE JOB
Cigarette clenched between his teeth, a shipyard worker peers through a porthole while at work assembling a prefabricated tug in April 1944.

LUXURY TRAVEL
A 1935 poster for the London & North Eastern Railway (LNER) promoting three new ships – the *Amsterdam*, *Prague* and *Vienna* – on their nightly service from Harwich to the Hook of Holland. They were the largest vessels in regular service to the Continent.

(continued on page 72)

DIGGING FOR BLACK GOLD – COAL MINING

Coal extracted from deep underground fuelled the industrial revolution, and for much of the 20th century it still provided Britain's main source of energy for industry, commerce and the home. But mining has always been hard, hazardous work and, since the 19th century, it has also been a highly politicised activity, both because of its turbulent industrial relations and its impact on the environment. Yet until the First World War, Britain was the world's leading coal exporter.

Miners hewed the precious 'black diamonds' from deep pits and open-cast mines in Lancashire, Yorkshire, South Wales, Scotland, Nottingham, Somerset, Cumbria, Northumberland and Kent. It was, quite literally, back-breaking work and after years down the pit many miners also suffered crippling respiratory diseases. But in deep pits their lives were always at risk – from explosions as a result of the build-up of gases, from the collapse of pit props, or from falls of rock and coal.

The General Strike of May 1926 was in support of the miners, who were trying to stop the pit owners reducing their wages. Other unions returned to work after nine days, but the miners held out until November,

when they were forced back to work having made no gains at all. In the Second World War so many colliers left the pits that in 1943 the Minister of Labour, Ernest Bevin, introduced a scheme by which 10 per cent of those eligible for call-up were directed into the coal mines, rather than the armed forces. Known as 'Bevin Boys', these conscripted miners helped to dig the coal essential for the war effort.

After the war the industry was nationalised under the National Coal Board. In the 1980s Margaret Thatcher's government introduced a programme of pit closures, which the long and bitter miner's strike of 1984–5 failed to reverse. Since that time, most of the deep pits in Britain have closed.

Of the many tragic disasters to strike mining communities, one of the worst happened at Gresford pit near Wrexham in North Wales in 1934. An explosion in the deepest part of the mine started a fire which rescue workers could not extinguish; the miners' death toll was 265. But the worst and most shocking tragedy did not happen underground. In October 1966 a slag heap slid down on the mining village of Aberfan in South wales, burying the village school and wiping out almost an entire generation of children.

COLLIERY LIFE
Top left: Coal mining was hard, physical work, often in cramped conditions. These two miners are hewing coal at the pit face in Ellington Colliery, Northumberland, in March 1951.
Bottom left: Women employed to sort and grade coal on a conveyor belt in 1942.
Below left: Two miners lighting up a cigarette after finishing their shift at Tonypandy in the Rhondda Valley, South Wales, in 1955.
Below right: Tommy Shotton enjoys a smoke by the fire at home in 1939, while waiting for the kettle to boil water for his afterwork wash.
Bottom right: In 1951 a young miner at Ellington Colliery checks his wages on pay day.
Top right: A group of 'Bevin Boys' about to descend in the cage to start their shift at Markham Colliery, Yorkshire, in 1943.

THE PRIDE OF STEAM

Above: A team of workmen preparing the King Edward VIII locomotive ready for service on the Great Western Railway.

Below: A British Railways (BR) poster of 1955 showing trains powered by steam arriving at and departing from the ICI chemical works at Billingham, Stockton-on-Tees. Every year, ICI relied on BR to deliver nearly 2 million tons of coal and 150,000 tons of other commodities to Billingham. BR also transported 750,000 tons of fertilisers, cement, bulk liquids and other products despatched from the works.

dragged into months. 'In our house I became a passenger', said Donald Kear, an unemployed machinist whose benefit was slashed when his father, a miner in the Forest of Dean, earned some overtime one month. A particular hardship for unemployed miners and their families was that they lost their coal allowance from the pit. Don Clarke, who was brought up in the mining valleys of South Wales, recalled how 'in the winter we children would watch out for "copper" Roberly, while the men would steal coal from the coal train, hide it in the woods and then collect it when the coast was clear'.

Demand for skills

There were more opportunities for skilled or semi-skilled men, particularly if they were able and prepared to travel. (A semi-skilled worker was defined in 1952 as 'basically [a] machine operator usually trained for a few weeks or months in factory schools or training departments or, more often, while working. In this semi-skilled work dexterity, care, alertness and interest in the work are the greatest assets. Neither skill in the strict sense of the word nor physical strength are needed, but first of all the ability to stand the monotony of repetitive operations.')

As heavy engineering declined in northern England, in Scotland and in Wales, so-called 'light industries' – car and aircraft manufacture, the production of synthetic textiles, electrical and household goods – in clean, electrically powered factories were burgeoning in the Midlands and the south. By the 1930s, the north

had lost its 19th-century industrial dominance. But elsewhere, skilled workers such as fitters, millwrights and mechanics could find work and even pick and chose between jobs to maximise their pay and conditions. According to the 1931 census, there were 12,000 machine-tool setters then in Britain; by 1951 the number had shot up to 112,000. But the reduced number of apprenticeships that were available in the 1930s affected later industrial development, causing a serious skills shortage both during and after the Second World War.

Workplaces were gradually becoming less hazardous. In 1919-21 more than 16,000 people had been killed in industrial accidents each year, and though there was a blip in the war years, by 1949 the figure had fallen to 9,750. This was due partly to new technologies – to electric lighting replacing gas, to steam-driven machines ceding to electric ones, although these, too, had their dangers – and partly to a general improvement in workers' health, diet and housing. In addition, legislation was passed controlling working hours (down to about 45 hours a week by 1951) and regulating working conditions and practices, such as the use of carcinogenic lubricating oils and the presence of airborne fibres – a common cause of pneumonicosis, one of the worst occupational diseases. The first legislation to limit the effects of asbestos dust was introduced in 1931, although health and safety regulations were often permissive and could be circumvented by employers.

While work might be getting safer, more regulated and productive, it was not necessarily more enjoyable. Many workers felt deskilled by mechanisation.

MILL GIRLS
Teenage girls photographed in April 1957, as they walk home after working a shift at the Lily cotton mill in Shaw, Lancashire.

A Lancashire weaver regretted that 'work inside the factory is much harder than it used to be owing to the great speeding up of machines. The toil is now almost ceaseless; the machinery demands constant attention. Thirty years ago [at the end of the 19th century] … the machinery ran much slower and the operatives had a little leisure during working hours, but all this has been abolished … Whether spinner or weaver, the textile operatives are on their feet from the first turn of the wheel in the morning till the last turn in the evening.' The change was not lost on the left-wing Unity theatre movement, who came up with this ditty:

'Move your hands and bend your body.
Without end and not so shoddy.
Faster, faster, shake it up,
No one idles in this shop'.

Charlie Chaplin's *Modern Times*, released in 1936, shows a struggling assembly-line worker as, literally, a cog in the ever faster and more impersonal industrial machine.

Domestic decline

Until the Second World War domestic service was the most significant source of employment for working-class women, particularly country girls. They might start work in a big house at 14 as a live-in kitchen maid or chambermaid, allowed just one afternoon off a week. Some compensation might be had from the camaraderie of the servants' hall, sheltered below stairs behind green baize doors. This was the domain of a posse of servants all with clearly designated functions, from bootblack to butler and from under-parlour maid to lady's maid. 'You mostly married domestics, they were the only people you ever met', declared one Leicestershire butler. 'Butlers married a house maid or a kitchen maid, or a ladies' maid sometimes.'

The number of men in service had declined sharply since the 19th century. In the years after the First World War, such work began to pall for girls too. 'My mother had two maids the whole of her life', recalled Viscountess Hambledon. 'They always stayed with her till they retired or died.' But after experiencing the comparative freedom of life in the munitions factories, many young women had no wish to don the 'badge of servitude', as the maid's white cap and apron now came to be called, then spend years in a low-paid, menial position in the hope of becoming a lady's maid or cook, or even a housekeeper. A Ministry of Labour

FACTORY WORK
An operator guiding wool from spools onto an industrial loom at the Blackwood, Morton and Sons textile factory in Kilmarnock in 1955. The factory employed around half of the town's 3,500-strong workforce.

IN SERVICE
Mrs Evans, a cook, and her daughter Margaret, a parlour-maid, in September 1937. Working in service was becoming increasingly unpopular during the interwar years, particularly among younger women.

CONSTRUCTION WORK – Ups and downs in the building trade

It is hard to be precise about the number of construction workers employed at any one time since they tended to be mobile, traversing the country from building site to building site. What is certain, though, is that the housing boom of the 1930s provided many men with work, doubling the number of unskilled workers carrying hods of bricks, building walls and laying tarmac. There was more work too for specialists such as glaziers, tilers, electricians, plumbers and carpenters. The increase in building was largely a result of government or municipal slum clearance and rehousing programmes, and an increase in the number of first time owner-occupiers buying 'semis' in the new suburbs that radiated out from London and other major cities.

Despite the emergence of large construction companies such as Wimpey, John Laing, Berg Brothers and Crouch, most houses in the interwar years were built by small firms whose methods had changed little from Victorian times. In 1934, no less than 84 per cent of building firms employed fewer than 10 workers, and at the height of the boom in 1935 there were more than 75,000 separate contractors registered in Britain, most operating on narrow profit margins. This usually meant low pay and insecurity for the workers they employed, as many of these small, undercapitalised firms survived only by selling a sufficient number of low-cost 'spec' (speculatively built rather than commissioned) houses at one end of a street to raise the money to finish building those at the other.

'There is no doubt about the deadening, debilitating effect of unemployment upon everybody ... The best intellects will not stand up against it.'

GEORGE ORWELL, *FROM THE ROAD TO WIGAN PIER*, 1937

HERRING LASSIES
Three Scottish fisherwomen carry tubs of freshly caught herring to the cleaning sheds at Great Yarmouth during the autumn herring season in 1937.

THE WORST FATE
Left: Men signing on at Wigan Labour Exchange in 1939. Throughout the decade workers in the industrial North suffered persistent high unemployment.

survey revealed that in an unnamed textile town in the north-east, only four out of 380 single women under the age of 40 on the unemployment register were prepared to consider such an option, while in Preston, just 11 women were prepared to train for domestic service out of 1,248 interviewed.

In any case, positions were being pruned back in elegant town houses and on country estates as even wealthy upper-class families felt the pinch: an increasing number of domestic situations advertised in *The Lady* and *The Times* in the 1930s were for that most put-upon of posts – that of 'cook general' in a middle-class villa with no other servants. And yet, however much they may have disliked the prospect, the Depression years gave many girls, particularly from areas of high unemployment, little choice but to go into service. By the end of the 1930s around 1.5 million women had taken up that option, most of them in private homes, while the number of men went from 61,000 in 1921 to almost 78,500 a decade later, half of them employed in hotels, clubs and other establishments.

When the domestic decline came after the Second World War, it was swift. In 1931 almost 5 per cent of households in England and Wales had resident domestic help; by 1951 that had fallen to just over 1 per cent; by 1960 it was 0.6 per cent. Even before the war young women had been taking jobs as unskilled or semi-skilled 'operatives' in the new industries of car manufacturing and light engineering in preference to domestic service. After it, there was no going back.

WORK IN WARTIME

In 1946 the novelist E.M. Forster wrote of the Second World War: 'This was total war. Everyone was in it.' Starting with conscription for men, the coalition wartime government would eventually call on all able-bodied citizens to do their bit wherever it was needed.

It was with great reluctance, and in the face of considerable opposition, that in April 1939 Prime Minister Neville Chamberlain introduced a Military Training Bill. War with Germany was becoming a real and imminent threat, but simply not enough men were coming forward to join the army. All men were to be liable for call up in their twentieth year. They would be trained and serve for six months, then would be called on for part-time service in the Territorial Army (TA) for a further three and a half years. On the outbreak of war, conscription was extended to men aged between 18 and 41 (this upper age limit was raised to 51 in December 1941), and the TA was in effect merged with the regular army into a single fighting force. The conscripts knew they were in it 'for the duration'. The Forces had to turn these 'sloppy civilians into regular fighting men ... and it wasn't done by kindness either', recalled Len Waller. 'Everyday we were marched and yelled at up and down the barrack square. We were cursed, humiliated and degraded and worked until we were fit to drop.'

Reserved occupations

However much the forces needed men – and by September 1939 the army was only 897,000 strong – the government was determined not to make the same mistake as in the First World War, when so many had rushed to enlist that war production at home had been depleted by loss of skills and manpower. Chamberlain announced that a 'schedule had been prepared of all occupations which are so essential to the war effort that persons engaged in them should not bind themselves to undertake any other form of full-time service.'

The reserved (or scheduled) occupation scheme covered 5 million men in a vast range of occupations, from poultry farmers to teachers and doctors, all of whom were exempt from military service – sometimes over a given age. For example, a lighthouse keeper was 'reserved' at 18, whereas a trade union official could be called up if he was under 30, but not once he was older than that. As a government booklet, published in 1944, explained, 'the Minister of Labour has been given the power [by Regulation 58A of the Emergency Powers (Defence) Act, passed as France fell to German troops in May 1940] to order most of us about on a grand scale. If ... he decided that it was in the national interest that five thousand people in Kensington should go to Perthshire to fell trees, then they would have had to go and do it.' Yet although Britain might be fighting 'total war', it was not a totalitarian country – 'we were fighting as a

Left: Civil Defence workers at the scene of a V-2 rocket attack on Smithfield Market in London in March 1945. Over 100 people were killed in the blast, including housewives queuing for a freshly delivered consignment of rabbits. The nurse has the letters CS, for Casualty Services, painted on her tin hat. The ambulance driver beside her was Jean Grover, whose day job was secretary to the Governor of the Bank of England.

MAKING BOMBS

A worker making a bomb in November 1941, in a munitions factory 'somewhere in England' – precise locations of armaments factories were never specified.

democracy … to destroy Nazism, not imitate it'. Therefore there were assurances that 'the elaborate checks and balances of our pre-war system would not be swept away for ever, that the rights of the individual would not be completely forgotten …'

There were exceptions and appeal procedures. Pacifists and those who for religious, moral or political reasons did not wish to bear arms could request to be put on a register of conscientious objectors. They would be called to a tribunal to try to ascertain whether their convictions were sincere and deeply held, or just opportunistic. Conscientious objectors who were allowed not to do military service might still be directed into civil defence or other war work; a few who refused to do anything connected with war, or to take a job that would permit someone else to go to war, were allowed total exemption.

A command economy

By 1941 the demands of the war had ratcheted up and it was clear that calling for volunteers for the war effort was no longer sufficient. A committee chaired by William Beveridge found that there was a serious shortage of skilled workers in the North and Midlands and in the Royal Ordnance factories, which were often sited in isolated places to escape air raids. Meanwhile, the army, navy and RAF between them needed an additional 1.7 million men and 84,000 women. The only solution was to withdraw around half a million men from reserved occupations and the munitions industry. But it was no use having a full complement of fighting men if they lacked arms to fight with, so another 1.5 million workers were needed to join the 3.5 million already employed in munitions. One part of the answer was a 'comb out' of industry to make sure that men were only working in places where they could make the maximum contribution to the war effort. The other, for the first time in Britain's history, was that women too were to be conscripted and directed.

A total of 1.5 million women were eventually drawn into the war effort. Single women and childless widows between the ages of 20 (lowered to 19 in 1943) and 30 were liable for military service. They could, theoretically, elect to join any of the auxiliary services: the ATS (Auxiliary Territorial Service), the WRNS (Women's Royal Naval Service) or the WAAF (Women's Auxiliary Air Force), but as in the case of the army, it was the ATS that had the greatest need. Alternatively, they could be directed to perform some necessary work in war production. By 1943 there were nearly half a million women occupying a huge

LAND GIRLS
Members of the Women's Land Army pile sugar beet into a clamp for storage in October 1940. Vita Sackville-West paid a grateful tribute to such women: 'Her working hours never seem definitely to end, for on the land there may always be a sudden urgent call … she gets up when most people are still warmly asleep … she goes to bed with aching muscles knowing that the next morning the horrible alarm will shrill through her sleep, calling her back to damp boots … and numbing cold. All this she … is doing so that we can eat.'

KEEPING CALM AND CARRYING ON
Using a bombed building in London as a temporary barber's shop, a soldier gives a member of the Pioneer Corps a short back and sides in 1941. The Corps were active in clearing bomb debris during the war years. Below: A poster solicits recruits for the ARP – short for Air Raid Precautions – and the AFS (Auxiliary Fire Service).

variety of non-combat roles in the armed forces, including working in anti-aircraft gun sites, delivering planes, plotting aircraft and working as signallers.

But just as many men volunteered before they were conscripted, so did some women. From the early days of the war, women provided vital services as nurses, porters and milk deliverers, while older women came out of retirement and into the classroom to replace male teachers who had been called up. Even though they sometimes met with prejudice in industries such as shipbuilding, women came to play an essential role in manufacturing, notably making bombs and aircraft parts. As a Ministry of Labour wartime leaflet put it: 'The average woman takes to welding as readily as she takes to knitting once she has overcome any initial nervousness due to sparks.' By the time fighting broke out, 17,000 women had already volunteered for the Women's Land Army. Any doubts that 'a slip of a girl' would be capable of doing heavy farm work were quickly laid to rest, and by 1943 some 84,000 Land Girls were ploughing, harvesting, milking, tending cattle and doing all the other jobs needed to ensure that the wartime population of Britain did not go hungry. Meanwhile, others volunteered for the Timber Corps. These 'Lumber Jills' (or 'Pole Cats') felled trees to provide anti-invasion barriers, pit props for the mines and all the other essential wartime requirements for wood.

In 1941 John Marchbank, General Secretary of the National Union of Railwaymen, wrote: 'It is our war because the working people have flung their energies into equipping the fighting forces, have surrendered for the time being vital safeguards of normal industrial life in order that the war trades shall be kept in continuous production and ensure swift and ample supplies of everyone's weapon.' It was, indeed, a 'People's War'.

CIVIL DEFENCE VOLUNTEERS

There were numerous ways that civilians could get involved in the war effort. During the so-called 'phoney war', from the declaration of war in September 1939 through to May 1940, Air Raid Precaution (ARP) wardens – mostly part-time volunteers – organised the distribution of gas masks, checked shelter provision and enforced black-out regulations. Once the Blitz started in September 1940 their role became central. Setting out from ARP control posts wearing tin hats to patrol the local streets during a raid, they would look in on public shelters, assess the situation when a bomb fell, pass on messages and direct rescue operations, summoning the fire services, the Heavy Rescue Squad, First Aid Parties (known as Stretcher Parties in London), ambulances, demolition workers and mortuary vans as needed.

The Auxiliary Fire Service (AFS), set up to expand the numerous peacetime fire brigades, had some 200,000 recruits by September 1939. Once the bombs started falling, the AFS volunteers – their trailer pumps often pulled by lorries or cars – proved invaluable in helping to fight conflagrations caused by incendiary and high explosive devices. The police force was similarly augmented by wartime volunteers.

The motto of the Women's Voluntary Service (WVS) was 'The WVS never says no'. This million-strong body helped with the evacuation of urban children to the countryside, ran mobile canteens, assisted those bombed out of their homes, acted as 'information points' at bomb incidents and undertook myriad other wartime tasks.

Firewatching for incendiary bombs was made compulsory after a raid on London on 29 December, 1940, wreaked terrible devastation. Spotters stood on rooftops watching for planes so that people could carry on working until the bombers were almost overhead. Even children did their bit, collecting salvage and performing a multitude of other tasks that could be counted as civil defence – the term that gave its name to the Civil Defence Service of which ARP eventually became a part.

DEFENDING BRITAIN

Top left: A mobile canteen run by the WVS delivers a much-needed cup of tea to a rescue squad after a bombing raid in January 1943.

Bottom left: A group of Civil Defence workers man a listening device in London tracking incoming bombers on 31 August, 1940.

Bottom centre: Home guardsmen waiting to be called into fire-fighting action during a fire in Cheapside, London, in 1940.

Above: A member of the LDV – the Local Defence Volunteers, forerunner of the Home Guard – gets in some rifle practice on 22 June, 1940.

Right: An ARP warden taking a tea-break outside a sand-bagged shelter.

Bottom right: Fire guards armed with buckets of sand keep watch on the roof of the Houses of Parliament in Westminster on the night of 14 November, 1942.

NEW BRITAIN

The face of Britain was transformed, sometimes literally, by the post-war construction boom and 'new industries' manufacturing consumer goods. As modern high-rise flats took the place of old back-to-back terraces, cranes became a visual symbol of this changing Britain, towering over cities up and down the land.

In 1931 less than a third of houses in Britain had electricity – most were lit and heated by oil lamps, gas and solid fuel. But by 1935 the spread of the National Grid had led to the gradual electrification of the country, and almost half of all homes had electricity; by 1938, only a third were without. One result was a boost for the manufacture of household appliances – cookers, water heaters (replacing old solid-fuel boilers), vacuum cleaners and electric irons rather than flat irons that had to be heated on the kitchen range. Some housewives even began to yearn for a refrigerator to keep food for longer than the traditional north-facing larder could: by 1968 half the households in Britain owned a fridge, around the same number that by then had a washing machine.

The dramatic decline in the availability of domestic servants after the Second World War made middle-class housewives – who now had to rely on the 'daily' or even twice-weekly 'char lady' – eye such labour-saving devices with envy. The boom in domestic appliances also had the effect of making it easier for young working-class women, who previously would have gone into service, to find factory work producing the very goods that liberated (or replaced) them.

The consumer boom was also evident elsewhere. People traded in their old wirelesses (which had accumulator batteries that needed to be recharged at a garage) with mains radios, and aspired to have a telephone or even own a car. In 1924 only 238,000 private homes in Britain were on the phone; by 1939 heavy black Bakelite phones stood in the halls of more than 660,000 residences. In 1924 only 15.4 families out of every thousand had a radio; by the end of the Thirties, the figure had increased to 68.3 per thousand. And whereas there had been 579,000 cars on the road in 1924, by 1939 there were 2 million.

The impact of the car

At this time Britain was the second largest producer of motor vehicles after the USA, but for most people cars remained a luxury item. A medium-size Morris still cost around a quarter of a working man's annual wages (on average just under £3 a week), and even with the hire-purchase packages on offer, the price of repayment was still too high. Widespread car ownership would not come until the 1960s, when a million vehicles a year rolled off the production lines in British factories. By then, much of the British car industry had been consolidated into just one firm, British Leyland, which produced 40 per cent of the cars for the home market and 35 per cent of the trucks and buses.

If the symbol of the nation's old industrial might had been the pithead shafts, 'New Britain' was located in the modern factories in Essex, around Birmingham and Coventry, and strung out along arterial roads such as the Great West Road and the A40 from London to Oxford. Car manufacture was more a question of assembling parts than building 'horseless carriages', as in the early days. Thousands of suppliers provided components, from tiny widgets to light bulbs to rubber tyres, offering new employment opportunities for semi-skilled and unskilled workers. By the mid 1970s the car industry employed about half a million people, taking home

'Let us be frank about it – most of our people have never had it so good.'

CONSERVATIVE PRIME MINISTER HAROLD MACMILLAN, SPEAKING IN 1957

upwards of £60 a week (over £3,000 a year) – more than many white-collar professionals such as school teachers or bank clerks. At full capacity Britain's car factories could have produced 2 million cars a year, but in practice they rarely attained this. By 1974 more than 30 per cent of cars bought in Britain were foreign imports, largely from Germany, France, Sweden and Japan. Far fewer British cars were exported.

Women and the marriage bar

At the beginning of the 20th century, only 29 per cent of the workforce were women and just 10 per cent of married women worked outside the home – although working-class women often took in washing, sewed clothes or assembled toys or other small items, all for derisory pay. The First World War bought an enormous change when 1.3 million women entered the workforce, mainly to replace the men who had gone to war. Yet few remained after 1921, partly because they had only ever thought of their work as a temporary wartime expedient, but also because of hostility within the trade unions to 'women taking men's work'.

Although the employment of women in the 'new industries' doubled from just under 2 million in 1923 to almost 4 million by 1938, many were less than enthusiastic about their jobs, despite the camaraderie of the workplace. Many regarded their wages as 'pocket money' (which they essentially were, since most single women handed over their wages to their mother for bed and board) and the work as 'stupefyingly boring' (which it often was, since women were employed to do the most repetitive and monotonous tasks).

The chances of promotion for women were negligible and discipline was often draconian: at Peek Frean's biscuit factory, for example, girls were not allowed to talk while working, although the management did allow *Music While You Work* to be played through loudspeakers. At J. Lyons, the food and catering company, an explosive situation developed when the women thought the rate of the conveyor belt had been set too fast in an underhand effort to improve their productivity.

Until the 1950s a 'marriage bar' covering teachers, nurses and most office workers operated in the BBC, the Civil Service and local government offices. Single women were dismissed on marriage, while married women were not employed. In industry there was often no need for a formal rule, since most working-class women accepted the cultural convention that working a 48-hour week was not compatible with running a home. Apart from other considerations, it was seen as emasculating for their menfolk and also risked raising the ire of unmarried women co-workers. But sometimes, especially if the pay was good, as

ALL LIT UP
Unperturbed by the lack of safety equipment, workmen fix lamps on Blackpool's famous Tower, ready for the big switch-on on 18 September, 1933. Stretching for five miles, Blackpool's celebrated Illuminations required nearly 300 tonnes of electrical fittings worth £500,000, as well as 30 miles of wiring and 300,000 lightbulbs. The civic authorities of the Lancashire resort promoted the festival as a way of extending the tourist season.

'GRACE, SPACE, PACE'

Above: Jaguar cars on the assembly line in 1957. The firm initially made motorcycle sidecars before moving into the luxury car market, first employing the name 'Jaguar' in 1935.

Below: At the other end of the scale was the Ford Anglia, a relatively inexpensive saloon made by Ford UK. The poster shows the model made between 1953 and 1959.

it was at Peek Frean's and Courtauld's where a marriage bar was enforced, women kept quiet about their status and left their wedding ring off while at work.

By 1943 some 7.75 million women were working or were in the armed services. The number fell to 6 million by 1947, despite government calls for women to go back to work to help with the post-war production drive. Married or widowed women increasingly opted to combine work and family by taking part-time jobs. The notion of short-time hours as a choice, rather than imposed in an economic downturn, was a new departure in British labour history. Gradually the custom spread to other sectors, until part-time work and 'job shares' were used by some employers to retain their female workers. By 1950 one in five married women was working outside the home; by 1961 it was one in three and ten years later almost one in two – a far higher proportion than in most countries.

Those looking after the children of working mothers had evolved, too. As the nuclear family became more dispersed after the Second World War, 'nan' was often too far away to be a regular help. Unless they had crèche facilities at work,

CHOCOLATE DELIGHT
Workers ice fancy designs onto Easter eggs at a Bedford factory. In the 19th century women's nimble fingers had been required in textile production; in 1936, when this photograph was taken, there were still plenty of uses for such skills in light industry.

mothers turned to childminders, often mothers of young children themselves, who took other pre-schoolers into their homes to help with the family income. From the 1950s the 'au pair' became a middle-class stalwart: usually female and hailing from France, Germany, Scandinavia, Spain or Italy, she would spend a year or so living with a family to learn English. The girls were expected to help with the children in return for accommodation and meals, but sometimes found themselves treated as servants, expected to clean the house as well as look after small children for hours on end.

Women move into retail
Some jobs had long been considered 'women's work' – dressmaking or millinery, for example – but it was the war that brought women into the retail trades. In 1914 just over half of those working in wholesale or retail haberdashery were women; by 1917, the figure was approaching three quarters. Grocers and provisions shops had always been male-dominated, but between 1914 and 1918 more than 100,000 women went to work in the grocery, bakery and confectionary trades. By 1931 the census showed that a quarter of those working in grocers and provisions shops were women, nearly three-quarters in fabric and clothing shops and 90 per cent in sweet shops. Butchers were an exception, with only 5 per cent female employees – and no doubt most of those were sitting in a kiosk handling the money, rather than chopping up carcasses. Shop work could be hard, even in

WHITE GOODS
Workers assemble washing machines in an aircraft production factory in Burnley, Lancashire, in January 1945. By that time the changeover from a wartime to a peacetime economy was already getting under way.

expanding chain stores such as C&A Modes, Marks & Spencers or Woolworths. On a Saturday in 1931 the assistants at Woolworths in Manchester had to be at their counters when the doors opened at 8.30am, and they did not close until 9.00pm. And even then the work went on: 'The girls had to fill their counters again ready for Monday morning. In the meantime ... the male staff had to clean the floors ... That meant it [could be] as late as midnight when you got out.'

During the Second World War several department stores were requisitioned for military purposes. Staff were trained in civil defence work including, after January 1941, compulsory fire-watching duties. Many shops started to recruit married women, who were exempt from conscription. Some of these stayed on to work part-time when the war ended, although many who had been promoted into positions as managers and buyers were forced to relinquish their more elevated roles when the men came back from war.

But many men no longer wanted to work behind a counter, seeking instead jobs in commerce, transport or industry. By the time of the 1951 census, just over two-thirds of shop assistants were women, with a quarter of them aged under 20. A decade later, three quarters of shop assistants were women and more than half were married. Despite the dominance in numbers, few women rose to the position of manager. Many assistants changed jobs frequently, and there were grumblings about their 'take it or leave it' attitude. They in turn had their own gripes about customers. One irritated Selfridges shop assistant vented her feelings in the

LIMITING AMBITION – From typing pool to PA

In the late 1950s, The Bodley Head published a series of books on careers for girls. They included such titles as *Air Hostess Ann*; *Jill Kennedy, Telephonist*; *Sheila Burton, Dental Nurse* and – probably the most realistic – *Pam Stevens, Secretary*. Clerical work, once the preserve of the male clerk, had since the First World War been considered suitable work for women. 'I will not be dictated to', claimed the 'new woman' stenographer – then found herself in the 'typing pool', a large room containing up to dozens of women sitting in front of typewriters, their in-trays brimming with hand-written letters and reports to be typed with impeccable accuracy and speed, as an eagle-eyed supervisor patrolled the rows of clattering keys.

A 'pool girl' could aspire to become a private secretary – providing her shorthand was sufficiently fast and accurate, her manner pleasant, her dress neat. Her star would then be tied to that of her boss as she sat in a cubby-hole office adjacent to his, answering the telephone, making his appointments – and his coffee – and picking up her shorthand pad and pencil when summoned with 'Take a letter please, Miss Smith'. Soon it would be time to pick up her handbag, take out a luncheon voucher – one of the 'perks' of an office job, first introduced in 1955 – and go out for lunch in a nearby café. By the 1960s the secretary had evolved into the 'PA', or personal assistant, the right-hand woman organising the life of her (still usually male) boss.

following little ditty in 1957: 'Modom may be outrageous, Modom may be quite tight, Modom may be demented, but Modom is always right'. Discipline remained strict: most assistants in department stores wore uniforms and were not allowed to sit down while on duty. Many younger workers lived in company hostels – particularly in London and large cities where pay was low and rents high.

Customers serve themselves

Self-service changed the face of British food retailing. No longer required to stay behind the counter, assistants either stocked shelves or worked on a till at the check-out. There had been experiments with self-service before, but the first established stores opened in the 1940s, in part to help with staff shortages. By 1960 there were 6,000 of them and by 1966 more than 20,000. Customers who were initially nervous of the idea generally came to appreciate the convenience, although many missed the sociability and personal service of small shops. So did many of those working in the new multi-aisled supermarkets, which grew ever larger as the century progressed. Staff turnover was higher than in traditional retail. Joanna Slytheman, writing of work in a supermarket, gave a clue why: 'Snatched five-minute breaks with fellow workers at break times were treats, as was the banter with more amiable customers, but it wasn't enough to compensate for the tedious monotony of the checkout.'

OFFICE PRODUCTION LINE
Women at work in the typing pool of Unilever, a company formed by the merger in 1930 of Lever Brothers, the soap manufacturers, and a Dutch margarine maker. 'Bosses' would bring in hand-written drafts to the typists, who would then return neatly typed letters ready for signature.

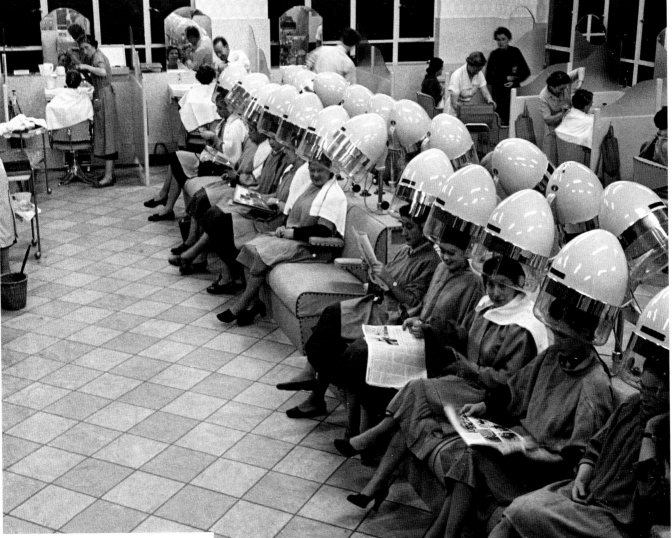

The long line of hair driers in this ladies hairdressing salon could handle more than 300 clients a day when this photograph was taken in December 1955. For many women, their 'shampoo and set' at the hairdressers became a regular part of their lives.

Equal work but unequal pay

Women were certainly becoming more ubiquitous in the workplace as the decades passed, but their pay failed to match that of men. In 1951 a survey found that most were paid less than two-thirds of what men were getting for the same work. Although the Civil Service and the state education system started to introduce equal pay for equal work at around this time, few private employers followed suit. The perception seemed to linger that women were either filling in time before marriage or working for 'pin money'. Survey after survey revealed that women were in general employed to do less skilled tasks with less chance of promotion than men – and the range of jobs they might consider was limited.

By 1975 the signs looked more hopeful for women at work: the Sex Discrimination Act passed that year made it illegal to refuse a job to a woman on the grounds of gender. In December the same year the Equal Pay Act came into force, banning discrimination between men and women in pay and conditions. In practice, though, the Act proved complicated to enforce. Disputes arose over what constituted 'equal work' and variables such as pension rights, holidays and bonuses. So its effect was diluted and the battle continued – and continues still.

In her book *Out of the Doll's House* Angela Holdsworth cites four generations of a Barrow-in-Furness family to show the changing nature of women's work in the 20th century. The great-grandmother was in service, the grandmother a shop assistant, the mother a secretary, but the daughter went out in her overalls every morning to serve as an apprentice engineer in a shipyard.

SERVICE WITH A SMILE

Air hostesses, hotel porters, chefs, cinema usherettes, stately home guides, insurance brokers, bankers, shop assistants, taxi and lorry drivers – the 'service industries' cover a wide spectrum that has grown as manufacturing industries declined. By the 1970s, the service industries employed more than half of Britain's total workforce compared to 39 per cent in 1901; by the 21st century, the proportion had risen to three quarters.

Some decried the change, arguing that the economy needed a solid manufacturing base. James Callaghan's Labour government

SERVICE WITH STYLE IN THE 1950s
Top left: A steward serves the meal and the stewardess pours champagne for passengers on board a BOAC Britannia in 1956.
Bottom left: A woman serves tea to shoppers queuing outside Barker's department store in Kensington while they wait for the sale to begin on 29 June, 1953.

introduced a tax on employment in the service sector, which the Conservatives derided as 'ludicrously old fashioned', arguing that industry itself relied on efficient banking, insurance and distribution systems. Just as agriculture had ceded to industrialisation, so manufacturing would be increasingly outsourced to other parts of the world where raw materials were available and labour was cheap. Britain would no longer be the 'workshop of the world'.

More and more people were finding white collar jobs in the public sector and in jobs that advertised, distributed and sold goods rather than making them. Growing affluence allowed people to purchase things they might formerly have made, or employ others to decorate or garden instead of doing it themselves. As more women worked outside the

home, they relied on the services of child-minders, cleaners and shops selling convenience products. Eating out at restaurants was becoming more than a once a year treat; more people were travelling and enjoying weekend breaks rather than just an annual holiday. Tourism within Britain was a growth industry, earning much needed foreign currency, while finance came to permeate our lives with mortgages, business loans and investments.

SNAPSHOTS OF SERVICE IN 1939
Top right: A bemedalled commissionaire at the London Palladium.
Right: Snacks and drinks offered for sale on a platform at King's Cross station.
Below: The celebrated photographer Bill Brandt took this picture of 'Nippies', or waitresses, at a Lyon's Corner House, on the cafe's opening day.
Bottom centre: A shoeshine man attends to a customer on a London street.

PART OF THE UNION

The failure of the General Strike of 1926 dealt a heavy blow to the trade union movement, but the economic troubles of the Depression years revived its fortunes. With the outbreak of war in 1939, the class divide was largely put aside, as workers joined forces with government to defeat a common enemy.

By 1939 more than 6 million people – almost a third of the working population – belonged to a trade union. In the 1930s membership doubled in some previously little-unionised industries, such as food and drink and clothing, while road transport saw membership rise from less than half to two-thirds. For those in jobs, wages rose slowly over the course of the decade while working hours fell slightly, and a number of unions managed to negotiate paid holidays for their members. By 1937 some 5 million people on less than £250 a year already qualified, and that figure doubled after the Holiday with Pay Act was passed in 1938. Yet the gradual strengthening of the unions did not bring more labour unrest: there were no national walk-outs for almost 30 years after 1926, until the rail strike of 1955, and fewer days were lost through industrial action between 1933 and 1939 than at any time since records began. That said, industrial relations remained tense in some industries, particularly in coal mining, where four in every five men were union members.

WORKLESS, NOT WORTHLESS
Unemployed men on a hunger march in 1935 pass through a British town on their way to London to draw attention to their plight. The march was organised by the National Unemployed Workers Movement.

Cooperation in war

With the threat of war, the cooperation of the trade unions became crucial. Without their support, wrote Winston Churchill to Anthony Eden in October 1937, 'our munitions programme cannot be properly executed'. When he became Prime Minister in May 1940, one of his first appointments was that of Ernest Bevin, General Secretary of the Transport and General Workers' Union (TGWU), as Minister of Labour. It was a good partnership: Bevin put the government's case to the workers, demanding long hours and other concessions, but he never forgot that his job was to secure the best deal for them in the circumstances.

There were strikes (although these were technically illegal in wartime), particularly in the coal mines, and trade unionists expressed concerns, as they had during the First World War, about women taking men's jobs and rises in the cost of living. But it was during the war years that 'collective bargaining' became widespread, enabling trade union leaders to have access to ministers and top civil servants in order to reach agreements on matters of industrial importance.

Consolidation and growth

Just as firms started to merge and rationalise after the war, so did trade unions: from 781 in 1945 – including some very small ones such as the Felt Hat Trimmers and Wool Formers (875 members) and the Basket, Cane, Wicker and Fibre Furniture Makers (52 members) – the total number dropped to 221 by the end of the 1990s.

From the 1950s on, much of the growth in union membership was in professional and clerical groups such as NALGO (the National Association of Local Government Officers), NUPE (the National Union of Public Employees) and ASTMS (the Association of Scientific, Technical and Managerial Staffs), the fastest-growing body within the TUC (Trades Union Congress). The increase paralleled the rising number of jobs that could be defined as 'white collar' – from under a third of Britain's workforce in 1951 to half by 1979. Those who now rose to speak at TUC conferences 'were paler and quieter men, more articulate in their talk, but usually flatter in their speeches', thought the journalist Anthony Sampson, describing the delegates from public sector unions.

From around 4.8 million in 1935, union membership rose to 7.7 million by the end of the war and 9.5 million by 1955, reaching an all-time high of more than 12.6 million in 1979. Thereafter, it fell: by the end of the century there were fewer people unionised than in 1955. The TGWU helped set a trend by amalgamating with nine other bodies in 1970, increasing its membership by 60 per cent. In the 1970s ASTMS similarly expanded into banking, insurance and other areas.

Female exclusion

By that time an increasing number of women, particularly older, married women, were going out to work. In 1951 there had been 7.1 million women in the labour force; by the end of the century the figure was nearer 23 million. But trade unions could be patriarchal organisations: in 1953 the Union of Post Office Workers even passed a motion at its annual conference calling for a return of the marriage bar. Female union participation continued to be low: in 1945 just two out of ten union members were women, by 1979 this had crept up to three. There was a higher proportion of women in unions such as NUPE and USDAW (the Union of Shop, Distribution and Allied Workers), both of which had 65 per cent female membership, but there were few women leaders.

'I ... can never forget the support and encouragement which the trade unions ... gave during the darkest days of 1940 and are giving with all their hearts today.'

WINSTON CHURCHILL, SEPTEMBER 1941

MARCHING FOR MORE
Two thousand members of the Electrical Trade Union on a march in London on 13 February, 1954, organised to press for better pay.

ALL-OUT STRIKE
Pickets demonstrate outside the Grunwick photo-processing laboratory in Willesden, North London, in June 1977, bearing posters of individuals they accused of strike-breaking. The strike, over union recognition, lasted for almost two years and attracted support from Labour Party politicians as well as trade unionists. It was led by Jayaben Desai, a woman from an Asian background, like most of the largely female workforce. The strike was called off in July 1978, without the strikers' demands being met.

By that time unions were being widely blamed as over-ready to strike. When the power of the trade unions was raised for discussion on *Any Questions* in 1956, Lady Isobel Barnett commented wryly, 'Call the House of Commons out and I don't think we'd notice for quite a long time.' British cinema audiences were regularly entertained with manifestations of the so-called 'British disease' in films such as *I'm All Right Jack* (1959), with Peter Sellers as militant trade union leader Mr Kite, or *The Angry Silence* (1960) in which Richard Attenborough played a young trade unionist victimised for opposition to a wildcat strike. In *The Rag Trade*, a TV sitcom starring Sheila Hancock and Barbara Windsor in the early 1960s, Miriam Karlin played the shop steward who called 'Everyone Out' at least once an episode. In fact, in the real Britain the number of working days lost to strikes in the 1960s was a tiny proportion of the total — far more were lost to sickness.

Strikes seem to come in waves. From the mid 1950s on, there were large national strikes by railway workers, bus men, dockers and printers, all for better pay and working conditions. Between 1957 and 1962, unofficial 'wildcat' strikes flared up, usually over the rising cost of living or redundancies. Steeply rising prices, pegged wages and the devaluation of the pound in 1967 led to another round. In 1970 there were 3,906 disputes, and even though some were short-lived, they added up to 11 million working days lost, a figure that rose in 1972 to almost 24 million. In an attempt to improve the situation, the Advisory, Conciliation and Arbitration Service (ACAS) was set up in 1975, following talks between the CBI and the unions, to provide a forum for solving industrial disputes by negotiation.

The 'winter of discontent'

But strife continued. A wave of strikes by low-paid public sector workers, road haulage and others in the winter of 1978-9 contributed to Margaret Thatcher's election victory in May 1979. Mrs Thatcher made no secret of her desire to 'curb the unions' by making closed shops and secondary picketing illegal and requiring a secret ballot of members before a strike could be called. The Prime Minister had the NUM in mind when she spoke of 'the enemy within', but most people accepted that she thought much the same of all unions. The result was a period of confrontation, marked by bitter disputes in the steel and coal industries. It was not until the late 1990s that a national minimum wage and employee consultation were introduced — the latter as a result of a directive from the European Union.

THE END OF THE DAY
Right: Several generations relax beneath a National Union of Mineworkers' banner nearing the end of the Durham Miners' Gala in 1969.

THE PROFESSIONALS

'Education, education, education' was as much a middle-class mantra in the interwar years as it was in the final decade of the century. Study was the road to qualifications and a professional career, but the path to social mobility remained an uneven one.

By 1940 almost three times as many working-class children were in secondary education as had been at the turn of the century, but a middle-class boy was still more than four times more likely to go to grammar school. The bottleneck to university was even narrower. By 1940, around 8.5 per cent of middle-class boys went to university and 1.4 per cent of working-class boys. For girls the figures were tiny: just 2.2 per cent from the middle-class and 0.2 per cent of working-class girls managed to squeeze through the college portals.

The route into the professions was increasingly through educational qualifications rather than on-the-job training. As a 1954 survey of social mobility pointed out, 'the scholarship boy had overtaken the self-made man' – largely. Although society was increasingly meritocratic, the old school tie and what one's father did still counted for a great deal. Just as skilled manual workers – welders, printers, compositors and the like – tended to expect their sons to follow them into the same firm, or at least the same industry, so it was among lawyers, doctors and clergymen, and more than a third of those sons did so. The Civil Service had been open to competitive examination since 1871, and more working-class and lower-middle-class boys were slowly climbing that particular tree.

Something in the City

The City remained a place with its own rules and conventions. Only Rothschilds were ever made partners at Rothschild's merchant bank, while at James Capel's only one partner out of the ten appointed in the interwar years hailed from humble stock. Hierarchies persisted: at the Lombard Street offices of the Guaranty Trust Co. of New York, partners used a separate entrance, separate dining room and separate lavatories from other employees. While hoi polloi were allowed to nip out to a nearby ABC café or Lyons Corner House for a cup of tea and a bun, they were forbidden to enter Fuller's in Gracechurch Street, which was for management only.

After Hitler came to power in January 1933, many Jews fleeing from

INSURANCE MATTERS
A bowler-hatted broker discusses business with an underwriter in the central hall of Lloyd's in the City of London in April 1939. The underwriter would either accept the risk involved (or part of it) and initial the slip, or else decline the trade.

'SELL NOW'

'Are stockbrokers parasites or valuable servants?', *Picture Post* asked, and in the service of 'greater transparency' the Manchester Stock Exchange opened its doors to the public in May 1954. Bert Hardy – celebrated for his pictures of all aspects of British life – went to photograph the stockbrokers at work. The impression was one of 'Bedlam let loose – in 3D sound', at a time when 'every deal is chalked up on a blackboard running the length of the House'.

Nazi persecution made a successful career in the City, both in banks and on the stock exchange. Some, like Siegmund Warburg, made a point of trying to help other Jewish refugees to establish themselves in Britain's financial industries. But not all city outsiders were emigrés. Harley Drayton, the son of a gardener, started his working life in 1915 as an office boy in an investment bank: by the 1930s he was the managing director and a country gentleman. Gilbert Garnsey, son of a long line of Somerset butchers, rose to be second in command at Price Waterhouse, dying in 1937 before he could seize the reins of power.

At that time the life of a clerk in a City firm was still Dickensian. As an office boy, Dougie Phin had to operate a hydraulic lift and collect buckets of coal from the basement for the fires, but his 'first duty ... was to fill up the ink wells' for the clerks who sat on high stools at 'old-fashioned sloping desks with a big brass rail round the centre'. It was not until after the Second World War that some City firms abandoned both the stools and the laborious task of adding up columns of figures and entering them in ledgers by hand. Adding machines, addressographs and other forms of mechanisation were stoutly resisted.

'If I had come to work with a soft collar and a coloured shirt, people would have asked if I was still in my pyjamas.'

A MERCHANT BANKER ON THE CITY'S DRESS CODE IN THE 1950s

By then employers were bringing in more women to work in the City, operating telephone switchboards, typing letters and operating adding machines, but there were limits to what they were allowed to do. The Stock Exchange – a private body – refused to admit them at all. As late as May 1968,

when student and workers' protests were erupting all over Europe, its members voted 1,366 to 663 to continue the men-only policy, turning down a female applicant, Miss Muriel Bailey, who had worked in the Square Mile since 1925. Miss Bailey had not even sought admission to the trading floor of the Exchange, understanding that 'the presence of women on the "floor" would be an embarrassment to Members'. But she proved to be tenacious and persisted: women were finally accepted in March 1973 (by which time Miss Bailey had become Mrs Wood).

By 1971 some 390,000 people worked in the City, most of them commuting by train to Cannon Street or Liverpool Street stations. 'City gents' still wore bowlers and stiff collars. Firms were small, directors wore black silk top hats and messenger boys in livery scurried around the Square Mile delivering bills and cheques. Most jobs were offered on the basis of a personal recommendation.

But gradually the City was changing and expanding. New, plate-glass buildings were erected on old bombsites. Some firms even relocated to the suburbs – as far as Croydon in the case of the insurance company, Price Forbes. Mechanisation in the form of punch card accounting systems, photocopiers, telex machines and answerphones had, by the mid 1970s, begun to ease out the duty legers and messenger boys. Bowler hats started to disappear, as did the City-wear of black jackets and striped trousers, (although rolled umbrellas persisted for longer). And rather than being addressed as 'Clerk', that generic species started to be addressed as 'Mr'.

A changing job market
The structure of the 'professions' was changing. At the start of the 20th century, 'higher professionals' were not part of the industrial economy: they worked in law, the church, medicine or the armed forces. The only possible exceptions were engineers, including architects and surveyors. By the 1950s that situation had changed: the number of clergymen had declined, while that of engineers and those engaged in the sciences and commerce had increased hugely.

In the 'lower professions' it was much the same: by 1951 there were 69,000 laboratory technicians (a category not recognised in the 1911 census) while the number of draughtsmen increased from 59,000 in 1931 to 134,000 in 1951. By 1948 more boys from grammar schools were taking up engineering apprentices on leaving school than any other work. The 'managerial' class was growing as industrial and commercial concerns amalgamated. Smaller businesses were gradually eliminated from the

STUDIES IN CONCENTRATION
Above: Law students at the Middle Temple Inn in London prepare for the traditional rites of being called to the Bar in 1951.
Below: The architect Sir Misha Black working on designs for that year's Festival of Britain.

marketplace and people such as architects, lawyers, publishers and designers were increasingly likely to be found working for large firms rather than being self-employed. The public sector grew apace after the Second World War, with local authority planning and social services, housing, transport and leisure departments all expanding their reach. At the same time the nationalisation of railways and the gas, electricity, coal, iron and (briefly) steel industries meant employees were now working for the state rather than in private industry – and this had an important impact on the role of managers. In 1951 some 8 per cent of workers had jobs in the public sector; by 1971, it was 27 per cent.

This expansion did not necessarily help professional women: while the number of schoolteachers almost doubled between 1921 and 1951, the number of women teachers fell. In professions such as medicine and law, women tended to be nurses or GPs rather than consultants, solicitors rather than barristers, and although there were some significant women in radio and television, most programme-makers were men until the 1980s. In 1939 there were no women in the Civil Service *corps d'élite*: the Foreign Office excluded women altogether, and it was not until 1955 that Evelyn Sharp (later Dame Evelyn) was appointed as the first Permanent Secretary in Whitehall. In the fast-growing fields of science and technology, women were hardly represented at all until much later in the century. Women constituted just 1 per cent of engineers in 1951 – exactly the same percentage as in 1911.

In politics, the days of Trollope's Duke of Omnium were on the wane. On the Conservative benches in the House of Commons, 55 per cent of MPs in 1951 were professional men (there were not many women), often lawyers, compared to 40 per cent who were businessmen and farmers (some of them substantial landowners). In Labour ranks, 49 per cent of MPs in 1979 were from the professions (many working in the trade union movement); only 35 per cent were (or had been) manual workers.

Careers in law – solicitors and barristers

Solicitors fought shy of regulation for much of the early 20th century. They were, after all, men of standing in the community, and if sometimes a solicitor's accounts inexplicably got mixed up with those of their clients, that was just a matter, as one historian of the law put it, of 'the marginal fringe' who kept their accounts in a muddled way. In 1941, though, lobbying by the Law Society resulted in the Solicitor's Act, which required solicitors to arrange to have their accounts audited

'EXCELLENT SERMON, VICAR'
A farmer and his family shake hands with their local rector in the village of Parracombe in Devon after a Sunday morning service in July 1954. Church attendance, falling throughout the 20th century, was becoming a cause for concern after the Second World War. 'Are we a pagan country?' asked journalist James Hodson in 1946. 'The church each week has 5 million attendances, the cinemas have 40 million.'

Women were not allowed to take the examinations to qualify as a barrister or a solicitor until 1922.

annually when they applied for their certificate to practice, and a fund, to which all solicitors were required to contribute, was set up to compensate clients for misappropriation. Much of the problem had arisen from solicitors who practised alone, and increasingly, as in other professions, smaller practices amalgamated to cover a wider range of expertise. Meanwhile, legal departments of civic authorities, companies, banks and city institutions grew to deal with the increasing complexity of commercial, tax and planning law.

Numbers of solicitors grew steadily: in 1945 there were just under 13,000 in practice; by 1960 the figure had risen to more than 18,000, with 700 more were entering the profession each year. In 1965, of the 22,000 solicitors practicing in Britain, almost a third were located in Greater London – 1,600 of them in the City alone. Metropolitan firms might give their time to newer forms of commercial activity such as oil, but in the suburbs, as in the rest of the nation, the bulk of a day's business might well be taken up with conveyancing (much of it probably done by managing clerks) and probate, with some litigation in magistrate's courts to vary the load.

The other 'arm' of British law is made up of barristers, who are required to be members of one of the Inns of Court that educate and regulate them – Gray's Inn, Lincoln's Inn, Middle Temple and Inner Temple. By the mid 1960s there were over 2,100 qualified barristers, 1,600 of whom worked in London. Some chambers specialised – in tax, for example, or maritime, libel, divorce, criminal or other branches of law – while others were more generalist.

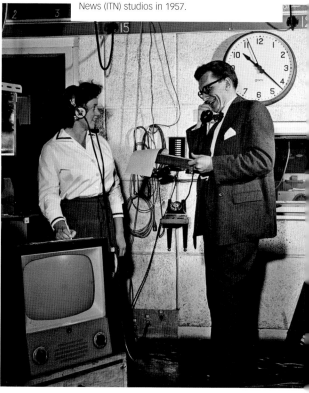

MODEL CITY
Sir Herbert Manzoni, Birmingham city's surveyor and engineer (on the left), and Mr Shepherd-Fidler, the city architect, photographed in 1954 with a scale model of the new ring-road scheme and development they were planning for the city.

Introducing legal aid

Probably the most significant development for solicitors in the 20th century was the introduction of the Legal Aid scheme for those unable to pay for the services of a lawyer. There had been less ambitious schemes dating back to at least the 16th century, but it took the Second World War to effect radical change, as it became clear that urgent matters like insurance, property claims and divorce could lower the morale of men and women serving away from home if they could not afford the services of a lawyer.

A committee was set up to look into the whole question, and the Legal Aid and Advice Act was subsequently passed in 1949. It was not achieved without difficulty, as Harley Shawcross, Attorney General at the time, recalled: 'The Legal Aid and Advice Act was an obvious much-needed reform, but it involved considerable negotiations with the legal profession whose earnings were likely to be affected.' Under the Act, legal advice and representation in the courts became free of charge to those with limited income and savings, although if the litigation is successful, claimants could be expected to repay their legal costs. The scheme is funded by the government but administered by the legal profession itself, and solicitors and barristers taking legal aid cases are paid fees.

The coming of the NHS

'The money worried them ... They put off bothering the doctor with a night call until in desperation – about midnight – they'd send. Well, if they couldn't pay we never charged them. Of course we didn't.' So one doctor told Jonathan Gathorne-Hardy, recalling the life of a GP in the 1930s. He went on: 'When I came here a farm worker in Lincolnshire was paid 28 bob [shillings] a week. That was their wages. You couldn't charge people on that. In many cases they had Friendly Societies, and they paid a penny a week and the doctor got a retainer. So much a quarter. You had to have a whole lot [of patients] to make anything at all ... But the whole thing has changed. It had to because it's been realised that the health of the community is not the business of an individual, it's the charge of the State. It must be. That's not socialism, it's common sense. It must be, and that's how the National Health was started.'

In the 1930s Britain's medical services were in an increasingly chaotic state, with care split between separate providers. In 1929 the Poor Law infirmaries had been transferred to the control of city and county councils, becoming local

EYES FRONT – OFFICERS IN TRAINING
Princess Margaret inspects a line-up of cadets at the Sovereign's Parade at Sandhurst Military Academy in July 1970. The aim of Sandhurst is to be 'the national centre of excellence for leadership' for officers in the British army, which included many of the Princess's relations.

authority hospitals paid for out of public funds and staffed by full-time doctors and nurses. Local authorities were also setting up nurseries and antenatal and child-health clinics at this time. Then there were the voluntary hospitals, which remained outside local authority control, and the insurance-based panel doctors in private practice, known as the '6d doctors', who enjoyed autonomy in the services they provided. Eileen Whiteing, a middle-class child in Surrey in the 1930s, recalled, 'There was no question of rushing out to find a chemist who could supply the doctor's prescription, as his own errand boy would cycle up with the medicine bottles after the evening surgery ... doctors made up most of their own remedies on their premises, often in view of the patient.' But increasingly, some doctors were losing out as patients who could not afford their fees turned to the out-patient departments of local authority hospitals.

Then came the war, and an urgent need for an integrated health service to cope with the casualties expected from air-raids. But there was no consensus how to bring it about. Should insurance be extended and the autonomy of the doctor (and the voluntary hospital) be left intact? Or should doctors become state employees? The post-war Labour government took its lead from the Beveridge Report and the National Health Service (NHS) Act was introduced in 1946. To get around fierce opposition from doctors, the Minister of Health Aneurin Bevan 'stuffed the doctors' mouths with gold' and they largely retained the privileged position they had

A teacher helps a pupil with his work in a classroom at Walsgrave Colliery School (now Eburne School) near Coventry. Teaching was one of the few professions open to women, but even here the number of women teachers fell from the 1920s onwards. By the time this photograph was taken in 1952, that situation was just beginning to change.

traditionally held. For the state, funding hospital consultants and their equipment generally predominated over the requirements of GPs. The 1959 Mental Health Act gave doctors the power to section (detain) patients indefinitely, and the 1967 Abortion Act put the responsibility for decisions concerning the termination of pregnancies on the shoulders of the medical profession. An inquiry in 1975 concluded that this last should be self-regulating, since 'the most effective safeguard of the public is the self-respect of the profession'.

GPs start to grumble

In the 1960s, Paul Ferris wrote of the the typical GP – or 'family doctor', as he probably preferred to be called – that 'What he can do best (it's suggested) is to act as family counsellor, look for undetected ill health (diabetes, anaemia, cervical cancer) and become a kind of social worker, especially with chronic invalids and old people. Since many of his patients will have "emotional problems" at the root of their illness, he can try to use simple psychiatry with them.' For such multiple services Britain's 24,000 GPs were earning on average £2,765 for their NHS work, plus about £1,500 in expenses and maybe some small additional income from private patients or examining candidates for life insurance. Doctors considered themselves overworked and underpaid, and in 1963 their frustration boiled over, leading to a series of confrontations with the government.

GPs who felt they had somehow become the dogsbodies of the health service could contrast their lot with the happy situation of consultants. Exemplified by Sir Lancelot Spratt in Richard Gordon's novel *Doctor in the House*, filmed in 1954

with James Robertson Justice in the surgeon's role, the consultant was the most exalted figure in medicine. In 1965 a typical consultant at a London teaching hospital worked for the NHS for up to nine half-day sessions a month, spending the rest of his time seeing private patients in Harley Street. Depending on seniority and reputation, he or she could expect to earn a handsome salary.

The nursing profession

If the consultant was a formidable figure for junior doctors, Matron played that role for nurses. Nurses had fought a '30 years' war' to have their professional status recognised, ever since the days when nursing had been seen essentially as domestic work. The first 4,005 State Registered Nurses (SRNs) were admitted by examination in 1925. By 1933 there were over 26,000 nursing staff in Britain's hospitals; six years later the total was over 33,000 – the vast majority female. Nurses' training was strict, with trainees required to live in hostels attached to the hospital where they worked – there was no place for married women until acute shortages of hospital nurses forced a change in policy in the 1950s.

A committee was set up in January 1946 to sort out how nurses would fit into the pending NHS, asking such questions as 'What is the proper task of a nurse? What training is required to fit her for that task?' The committee's main preoccupation was the wastage of young nurses during training, and its solution was to recruit more 'nursing orderlies' to perform routine tasks. Would-be nurses were in future to be treated as students rather than junior employees; part-time

MEDICAL PRACTICE
Above: A GP (General Practitioner) discusses symptoms with a patient in his surgery in 1950, four years after the National Health Service (NHS) Act decreed that medical treatment would be free at the point of delivery.
Below: A nursing sister photographed in 1944 at her station outside the Infant Ward of the Children's Hospital in Birmingham – the first hospital in the UK to isolate sick children in individual rooms.

nurses – often married women – and male nurses were recruited to make good the shortages.

But student nurses continued to be unhappy with their conditions, and in August 1948 they staged a public protest in Hyde Park. Such action shocked the *British Journal of Nursing* to its core: 'Twenty years ago young women of sound principle ... would [never] have presumed to have assessed their talents in the same category as those of our incomparable Miss Nightingale even in private, much less from a coal cart to a public audience in Hyde Park!' Nevertheless, the students got almost all they were asking for in the way of a training allowance from the Whitley Council – one of a number set up from 1919 on to improve industrial relations in many areas of work. Predictably, claims from other parts of the profession followed.

HARD WORK
Student nurses studying in the School of Nursing at St Bartholomew's Hospital (Barts), London, in 1968.

Hospital routine

Nurses spent hours in the sluice, cleaning and disinfecting bed pans and sterilising syringes – at least until the first pre-packed sterile needles started to be delivered. When they went into the dining room they had to take off their aprons; if they changed wards they had to change into a fresh uniform. The apparent obsession with cleanliness and order was, in fact, vital in the days before antibiotics, when cross-infection was the greatest fear.

Hospital life remained regimented. Matrons could be dragons, and all had high standards. Ward rounds were terrifying occasions as nurses were expected to be able to tell Matron the exact nature of each patient's illness and treatment. And Matron's eagle eye missed nothing: the 'hospital corners' of a patient's bed, pillows in line with the tucked ends pointing away from the ward entrance, top sheets turned down precisely the length between elbow and fingertip. She would check whether a nurse's starched white cap was askew or if she had a ladder in her regulation black stockings, and that no patient had the temerity to cross her or his legs under the bed clothes (to avoid the danger of thrombosis). Ward sisters could be formidable too. Even though nurses were expected to respond instantly to every request, the admonition 'Don't run nurse!' regularly echoed down the ward.

Yet nurses' patience with petty regulations and low pay was running thin. In 1962 the Royal College of Nursing held an all-night vigil for better pay. Four years later the Salmon Report recommended changes to the senior nursing structure and introduction of a hierarchy of 'nursing officers' – in effect, the end of 'Matron'. In 1972 a million letters sent to the Minister of Health, Richard Crossman, demanded more pay for nurses. In 1974 the unthinkable happened: 'ministering angels' went on strike, marching on Downing Street. The Halsbury Committee, set up to look into the matter, recommended a 30 per cent pay rise.

TOWN OR COUNTRY

The 20th century saw a revolution in British housing. Before the First World War nine out of ten families lived in rented homes, many of them in poor condition. By the end of the century millions of new homes had been built, millions more rejuvenated and more than two thirds were owner-occupied. Government, local councils, developers and the public all played a part in shaping this changing social landscape.

'So there it is, our own contemporary vernacular spread thinly but ubiquitously over English hill and dale – or what was hill and dale before the speculative builder or the municipal councillor so aptly interpreted people's instincts and carpeted them with this intricate jungle of red peaked gables and evergreen hedges, multi-coloured chimneys and winding, tree-shaded avenues.' So wrote the editor of the *Architectural Review*, J.M. Richards, in 1946.

There had been an acute housing shortage after the First World War and since the 'Geddes Axe' fell on government spending in 1922, breaking the promise of 'homes for heroes' for returning soldiers, the shortfall of houses in Britain built up to nearly a million by 1930. With rents pegged at pre-war levels, there was little incentive for landlords to acquire or improve property for rent. In 1914 only one per cent of the population lived in local authority housing, 10 per cent were owner-occupiers and the rest lived in privately rented accommodation or dwellings provided by philanthropic bodies such as the Peabody Trust. The story of the middle years of the 20th century is how this situation changed, how so many were rehoused – 12 million Britons, almost a third of the population, either became council tenants or owner-occupier families between 1919 and 1937 – and how this transformation affected the landscape of Britain and the way we lived.

The spread of suburbia

Although it was reluctantly recognised that private enterprise on its own would not be able to supply housing of the quantity and quality now required, progress remained slow. The 1930 Housing Act allocated funds specifically for slum clearance and though this did not take effect until 1933, the legislation – together with cheap land, a pool of available labour and ready money for mortgages – did bring about action at last. By the time war broke out in 1939, the problem of the slums – dark, insanitary houses unfit for human habitation – was half solved. Some 245,000 slum houses had been demolished or boarded up and 255,000 replacement homes had been built, plus 24,000 specifically to house those in grossly overcrowded accommodation. (Nearly half a million slums remained, but in many cities and towns the Luftwaffe would soon help with demolition.)

What had been built to replace these dank, malodorous dwellings? Almost 90 per cent of the total 4 million houses that were built between the wars were on suburban estates of remarkably homogenous character. As Richards noted, 'from Becontree to Wythenshawe, from Port Sunlight to Angmering-on-Sea, the

NEAT SUBURBAN SPRAWL
A typical street in Ilford, east of London, in 1936. 'Always the same long, long rows of semi-detached houses,' wrote George Orwell of the Thirties' penchant for suburban development. Out-of-town estates required new standards in roads to accommodate the demands of cars as well as commuters.

MOVING IN
A poster from the mid 1930s promotes the household removal services of the railways, which included free estimates, packing and unpacking and door to door transit by rail and road.

startling consistency of suburban character – despite its notorious vagiaries in detail – indicates its origins in the living present. It could be no other age but ours.' Local authorities built houses for rent, while private 'spec' (speculative) builders constructed for sale, but both largely opted to build out-of-town estates.

Local authorities built to standards laid down by the Tudor Walters Report of 1918. This recommended that houses should be built of such quality that they would last 'for at least 60 years', with 'a minimum of three rooms on the ground floor (living-room, parlour and scullery) and three on the floor above – two of these being capable of containing two beds'. The report also specified a larder and a bathroom as 'essential'. Influenced by the 'garden city' movement from the turn of the century, the suggested density of houses was low: a maximum of 12 to the acre in towns, eight in the country, with a preference for estates arranged in cul de sacs and crescents with houses clustered, village-like, round green spaces.

By 1935 the Wythenshawe estate, built on 2,500 acres of farmland 12 miles from Manchester, housed 35,000 people in a series of 'cottages' served by a four-lane 'parkway', the first in Britain. Becontree, near Dagenham in Essex, covered some four square miles and provided housing for 112,000 people when completed in 1935, making this single estate larger than Norwich, Bath or Preston at the time. The houses varied in size to provide for different families' needs. All had gas, but few had electricity, even for lighting, since the overwhelmingly working-class tenants argued that they could not afford electricity. In contrast, the St Helier estate near Carshalton in Surrey had no gas when it was built, just electricity for lighting, heating and cooking. A feature of these newly built estates was the battle between the utility companies to supply the tenants. 'If you decided to have gas instead of electricity, your cooker came almost free', remembered Hetty Gates.

Yet although these new estates were often the size of small towns, many lacked amenities. Becontree had no street market – the lack of which was much regretted – and only one shop for every 240 people, compared to one for every 40 or 50 in traditional towns. On the Downham estate in Kent, there was only one pub – albeit the largest in Britain – for 35,000 residents. The residents of Becontree had five pubs, whereas in London's East End, where most of them came from, they would have walked past a pub every 60 seconds or so. They also had few doctors (one to 8,000 people), but there were 30 schools, 27 churches and two cinemas – the Princess, opened in 1932, was described as 'palatial'. Only 11 garages were provided for rent, since it was assumed that if a family could afford a car they would want to move from a council estate.

'Hearts are light, eyes are bright In Metroland, Metroland'

FROM THE LYRICS OF A POPULAR SONG

A 'home of your own'

One million of the 4 million houses built between the wars were the work of local authorities; private builders were responsible for the rest – 3 million homes, most of them for sale. Some 275,000 houses were built in 1937 alone, at the peak of the building boom. By 1938 around 3.25 million people owned their own home (or were buying it on a mortgage). Most of these new home-owners lived in the more prosperous south of England and parts of the Midlands. In the 1930s more than twice as many people were buying their own homes in the south than in the north – in areas of high employment, families were unable to contemplate such a move. Merthyr Tydfil in Wales historically had a high level of home ownership, but only 20 new houses were built for sale there in the whole of the 1930s.

A 'home of your own' had become the realisable dream of increasing numbers of lower middle-class white collar workers – clerks, foremen, inspectors, supervisors, all anxious to distance themselves from the respectable poverty in which most had grown up. A new house in the leafy suburbs, away from the grime of city centres, held out the promise of a new life. A regular wage of £200 a year could secure a mortgage; with repayments as little as 9 shillings a week (around £1 to £1.50 was more usual), plus council rates, this was also within the means of skilled manual workers. In London *The Evening News* was able to sustain a weekly 'Homeseeker's Guide', with pages of new houses for sale in the suburbs. Building material prices had fallen, labour costs were depressed, mortgages were easy to obtain with repayments spread over 25 or even 30 years. In some parts of the country £250 would buy a modest bungalow, although in Greater London new-build houses generally fetched from £400 to £1,200.

Transport – private and public

Transport was a vital factor in the development of the suburbs. Numerous houses were built along the arterial roads that radiated out from London and other large cities – residences that the cartoonist Osbert Lancaster sneeringly described as 'by-pass variegated'. But the point of such roads had been to ease the flow of traffic in and out of

PRIDE AND JOY
Helped by his children, a suburban householder polishes the family's Standard 8 outside their home in 1953.

urban centres. When the increase in traffic started to clog these vital arteries – and anxieties grew about the straggle of houses 'blotting out' the countryside – legislation was passed in 1935 to halt the urban sprawl, or rather to redirect it.

In fact, the development of the suburbs around most cities owed more to trolley buses, trams and coaches than to cars. Around the capital the suburbs depended above all on the extension of train services and the London Underground, which enabled people to commute each day from 20 miles and more outside the city, travelling back and forth to homes deep in what had been countryside. The charms of this 'Metroland' in leafy Buckinghamshire and other Home Counties, beloved of the poet John Betjeman, were the subject of widespread advertising by London Transport. By 1934 the 'tube' was carrying 410 million passengers a year and exciting modern stations, many designed by Charles Holden, marked their routes.

Suburban happiness

The rural aspirations of the suburbs were reflected in the design of the houses and in the layout and naming of the streets – not that they were called streets, as that would have sounded too inner-city. Roads in suburban estates were named 'Close', 'Crescent', 'Walk' or 'Avenue', while modest semi-detached houses would have a name-plate on the front wall or gate proclaiming 'The Laurels', 'The Firs', 'The Spinney', or perhaps a name that evoked a honeymoon or holiday, such as 'Coniston', 'Lynton' or 'Charmouth'.

Houses on private estates were generally more ornamented than on council ones – not always to their advantage. They might have elaborate chimneys and gables, a small porch, a bay window and most likely red, scalloped tiles above the pebble-dashed external walls; some faux 'beams' (strips of dark stained wood) were often nailed onto the frontage recalling some historic era. Most of these 'Tudorbethan' dwellings were semi-detached, each identical to its neighbour but not necessarily to other houses in the road since variety was prized. The Farm Estate in Catford, South London, offered would-be home-owners a choice of 'Queen Anne, Jacobean, Georgian or Tudor' styles, with the option of bottle glass or leaded panes in the windows. What all the houses had was a garden back and front, with an individual front gate. The garden might be handkerchief-sized in the cheaper houses, but it still offered privacy between its clipped privet hedges.

> *'We were all so proud of our houses, and each occupier named his house . . . Ours was called "Arcadia" which means "simple happiness". That's what we had . . .'*
>
> GRACE FOULKES, RESIDENT OF A NEW ESTATE IN HORNCHURCH, ESSEX, IN THE 1930s

ISLAND IDYLL
Two young boys make their way home along a grassy track on Lewis and Harris in the Outer Hebrides in 1955. Connected by a narrow isthmus into one landmass, Lewis and Harris jointly constitute the largest island in the Western Isles. The islanders mainly lived by crofting and fishing, although the traditional hand-woven Harris tweed was, and still is, exported all over the world.

Country and village life

If the town was encroaching on the countryside, there was also concern that the countryside itself was continuing to empty out. Unable to find work, young people were moving to the cities, leaving 'townies' with disposable incomes free to buy up the 'quaint' cottages that the locals could no longer afford. They did not live in them full-time, but instead used them as 'weekend' cottages. Reports had been written about the phenomenon even before the First World War, but there seemed no way to staunch the drift as the 20th century progressed.

Rural depopulation would become a self-fulfilling prophecy: as Britain's agriculture became less competitive, and as traditional cottage industries became absorbed into urban mass production, more people left the land. There were then fewer people requiring and using public transport. In his 1963 cost-cutting

SELLING UP
Curious villagers and visitors inspect the wares up for auction in a house clearance sale from a thatched, picture-postcard cottage in Chipping Campden, Gloucestershire, in 1954.

PARISH PUMP
A woman in 1950 fills her bucket from a tap on the green at Wark, a modest Northumbrian village on the North Tyne river that was once the capital of Tynedale. Its name derives from the Anglo-Saxon word for an earthwork. Many villages depended on pumps and natural springs long after towns had mains water supply.

exercise Dr Richard Beeching, the chairman of British Railways, recommended axing 6,000 miles of railway lines. In 1950 Britain had 21,000 miles of railway track and some 6,000 stations: by 1975 this network had shrunk to 12,000 miles of track and just 2,000 stations, cutting hundreds of villages off from easy access to towns – and cutting people off from work.

The 'big house' once occupied by the lord of the manor was also under threat as land prices fell and the cost of maintaining such stately piles became prohibitive. Some were knocked down in the decades after the Second World War; others, with much of their land sold off, became country clubs, hotels or conference centres. Village schools and chapels were sold and turned into 'des-res' homes. Churches remained, usually with falling congregation numbers and soon to be locked against vandals unless a service was underway. Many villages became unable to sustain a pub and as post offices, once the hub of the community, were closed, village shops went too. While retirees and urban escapees brought in some new life, the trend of villages turning into 'ghettos of the elderly, the housebound and the wealthy' seemed unstoppable.

Villages within commuting distance of an urban conurbation suffered a different fate, being transformed into dormitory towns. Some light industries were set up in villages with good road links. Silver End and Bataville, both in Essex, were built as model villages for employees, continuing the 19th-century tradition of Lever Brothers at Port Sunlight, Titus Salt at Saltaire and Cadbury's at Bournville. At Silver End the homes were for the workers of Crittalls, a company that made the metal window frames so particular to 1930s architecture. At Bataville, developed by a Czech entrepreneur to house workers for the Bata shoe

CONSTRUCTION-KIT HOMES
A mother sees her small daughter off to school from their prefab in Bromley-by-Bow in 1946. The area had been badly damaged in heavy bombing during the Blitz. Prefabs were intended as emergency housing to last for ten years, but most stood for much longer. Though most have now gone, argument still rages over the Excalibur Estate in Catford, built by Italian and German POWs in 1945-6, as conservationists and some of the residents try to fight off council proposals for demolition and redevelopment.

factory, there were all the facilities of a thriving village, with a dental surgery, community hall, bank, telephone exchange, school, playing fields and cinema.

New Ash Green in Kent, originally planned as a joint venture between the Greater London Council and private developers and built from 1967 on, proved a success, serving as a precursor to Poundbury near Dorchester, built from 1988 to realise the deeply traditional architectural vision of the Prince of Wales. Aided by new technologies as the century progressed, the 'home-working' movement, by which people set up offices at home, gave a new lease of life to some villages. In scenic areas pretty villages managed to retain their charms as tourist destinations, while traditional craftsmen often found that 'incomers' were more likely to maintain an 'authentic' thatched roof or a dry stone wall – though they often paid less regard to tradition when adding an extension or conservatory.

Going up fast

The devastation caused by bombing in the Second World War greatly exacerbated the housing problem. Nearly half a million houses were destroyed or uninhabitable, and a great many more were damaged. Given that 2 million couples married during the war and the birth rate had risen, the need for homes was acute. At war's end there were 94,000 people on the housing waiting list in Glasgow alone; of those more than 40,000 were actually homeless. As an emergency measure, more than 150,000 two-bedroom, prefabricated bungalows were erected between 1945 and 1949. Although 'prefabs' were small and basic – critics called them 'chicken coops' and 'rabbit hutches' – to most of those re-housed in them, they were a considerable improvement on pre-war accommodation, not least in having bathrooms and fitted kitchens. A few of these 'short-term expedients' would last into the 21st century.

One of the attractions of prefabs was that each one stood in its own little garden. Since before the First World War, it had been recognised that the British, unlike their Continental neighbours, were just not 'flat minded'. Apart from the modernist experiment of Quarry Hill in Leeds – a huge block of local authority flats that admirers thought looked like 'Beachy Head at sunset', but detractors saw as 'soul-less … something of a grey elephant' – only a few three- and four-storey blocks of flats were built in the 1930s.

'There is no doubt that this country must save space by building upwards and that many people will have to live in flats ...'

DAILY MIRROR, FEBRUARY 1943

Yet planners argued that flats were essential if the countryside was not to be carpeted over completely with suburbs, leaving inner cities as wastelands. The County of London Plan of 1943 recommended that almost two thirds of the city's residents seeking to be rehoused in their familiar districts should be accommodated in blocks eight or ten storeys high. Increasingly in the post-war years, the municipal housing problem was 'solved' by the construction of high-rise estates. The Alton Estate in Roehampton (built 1958-9) was among the earliest to mix tower blocks and low-rise houses. But it was soon apparent that although planners and architects might relish vertical buildings, they did not suit many of the people who had to live there, particularly those with children. At Crawley, a new town in Sussex, the percentage of flats was scaled down from 14 to 2 per cent. The end of tower block development was hastened by the structural failure of the 22-storey Ronan Point in London in May 1968.

A political issue

Housing dominated the Conservative party conference held in Blackpool in October 1950. Nudged by Harold Macmillan, soon to become Minister of Housing, the Tories adopted the ambitious target of building 300,000 new houses a year – 100,000 more than the ruling Labour administration, which had prioritised local authority building over homes for private ownership. The Conservatives won the 1951 general election and by 1954 had exceeded their house-building target, largely as a result of stimulating the private sector by making it simpler and quicker to acquire building licenses and also making it easier for potential buyers to obtain mortgages on houses or grants to renovate older properties.

By the 1960s, an increasingly wide variety of housing options was available to those who could afford them. There were new-build estates in the 'commuter belts' growing up around major cities – the electrification of some main railway lines made commuting feasible over longer distances – and there was a growing appreciation that the inner cities had something to offer, with the 'gentrification' of areas formerly characterised by run-down, multi-occupant Georgian and Victorian houses. Solid Edwardian mansion blocks were refurbished and large, uneconomic old houses were turned into flats. The reclaiming of the inner city coincided with the relocation of industries, eventually allowing former industrial and commercial properties to be redeveloped as 'work/live' spaces, while many city warehouses – particularly around ports or major rivers – lent themselves to the Manhattan concept of 'loft living', as 'rooms' became 'spaces' and gardens migrated upwards to roof terraces and balconies.

VOTES FOR HOMES
An election poster trumpets the Conservative government's record in house-building since coming to power in 1951, a factor which helped them to win again in 1955. Housing was the key post-war domestic concern.

POST-WAR DEVELOPMENT
Built on the site of the Woolwich Arsenal, Thamesmead was planned by the Greater London Council (GLC) as a large social housing project for up to 100,000 people. The area was liable to flooding – hence the raised pedestrian walkways and first-floor accommodation. The first tenants moved in in 1968; this photograph was taken in 1972.

STREET GAMES

The list of outdoor games from childhoods past is rich and various. Playing hopscotch on a grid chalked on the pavement. Group skipping with a long rope, held at either end by two friends, chanting: 'All in together, girls/Never mind the weather, girls ...' or 'Matthew, Mark, Luke and John/Went to bed with their trousers on'. Boys rolling marbles, girls tossing five stones or jacks, small children spinning a top or whipping a hoop. Riding a bike as if it were a bucking bronco, roller-skating, skateboarding, skidding along on a homemade go-cart fashioned by attaching old pram wheels to an orange crate. Playing cricket with a piece of wood, an up-turned box for a wicket. Playing football with the goal chalked on a wall, or marked out by discarded jumpers. Chasing games of 'tag', 'he' or 'it', playing 'Grandmother's Footsteps', or 'What's the Time, Mr Wolf?'

In days long gone the street was a playground. There were so few cars it was possible to claim the road for

whatever children's activity was the craze of the moment. No one could be territorial and say 'You can't come into my garden', because no one had a garden and the street 'belonged' to all those whose house doors opened onto it.

Most mothers would be glad to get the children 'out from under my feet' and at the end of the day might take a break, arms folded, resting in the doorway, watching the children play, laughing at their chants and songs, which they would have once sung themselves. Some songs would be traditional, others might once have been topical. 'Kaiser Bill went up the hill/To conquer all the nations …' was still being sung in Wiltshire as late as 1952, according to Iona and Peter Opie, experts in children's lore and literature.

Then there were the games that were played only when mothers were not around: swinging from a lamppost, knocking on doors and running away, posting stones through letterboxes, letting down car tyres.

URBAN PLAY
Top left: Boys of various sizes playing High Jimmy Knacker against a wall in 1950.
Bottom left: A game of street cricket in Millwall near the Thames in 1938, with the funnels of a ship dominating the background skyline.
Bottom centre: Snow always makes a welcome change. These children are enjoying sliding around on an icy road on the Isle of Wight in 1940.
Below: A young brave shoots from a coal-hole in a game of 'cowboys and indians' played in a London street in 1954. In an article for *Picture Post* Noel Streatfeild, the author of *Ballet Shoes*, wrote that this was 'no place for a healthy youngster'. Streatfeild backed the paper's campaign to 'get children off the streets and into the parks'.
Bottom right: The youngest child and her doll are the centre of attention outside a house on Bath's Royal Crescent in 1955.
Top right: Children playing hopscotch at a community centre run by the Make Children Happy charity near St Katherine's Dock, East London, in 1972.

MAKING A HOME

A house did not become a home until people put their stamp on it with their own possessions. British homes grew steadily more comfortable as the century progressed and individuals had more choice over decor and furnishings. But the tastes of designers and style-setters did not always chime with the tastes of the majority.

When tenants moved into their house on one of the new London County Council estates in the 1930s, they would find the exteriors painted white, usually with Brunswick green for the front door and woodwork. Tenants had a limited choice of colours for the interior: either 'ochre' (which some optimistically referred to as 'buttercup yellow') or pale green for the walls, the woodwork 'a sort of beige, pastry colour'. The bedrooms were distempered with a mixture of whitewash and size, the ceilings painted white with a dash of blue to make them look even whiter.

At first the authorities had been wary about papering the walls since in the slums, from which many of the tenants had moved, wallpaper meant bugs. But gradually they relaxed and, as one tenant recalled, they were allowed to choose 'from a book [that the decorators had] with half a dozen patterns ... But if you wanted to go out and buy your own paper you could, and the council would still

TEATIME IN WALES
The Jones family gather for tea in their South Wales kitchen in July 1943, with clothes airing overhead on a pulley-operated rack. This homely scene was not quite as spontaneous as it appears. The Crown Film Unit was recording the family, contrasting the peaceful domestic life in Wales with the horrors inflicted by the Gestapo on the Czech village of Lidice, and speculating how life might have been under the Nazis.

put it up for you. Most people waited for the council decorators, though, because they really couldn't afford to pay for paper and paint.'

Most people's dream on moving into a new house was to leave their old, heavy furniture behind and start afresh. When Mr and Mrs Baldwin in R.C. Sheriff's 1936 novel, *Greengates*, decided to sell their gloomy Victorian house off the Edgware Road and move to a new estate in the Home Counties, they sold off all their old furniture and 'wandered miles through a labyrinth of sideboards and bedroom suites; they glutted themselves upon weathered oak and well-nigh suffocated themselves in mattresses and quilts.'

A new suburban semi might have wood panelling in the hall, or if that was too expensive the walls would probably be covered with anaglypta paper up to dado-level, brush-grained and varnished to match the woodwork, which was likely to be brown-painted 'oak'. Alongside a hat stand, the telephone, if there was one, would be sited in the hall to discourage lengthy conversations. By 1930 there were more than a million telephone subscribers in Britain and phones were an index of prosperity. In Epsom, Surrey, almost one in three households was on the phone, compared to one telephone per 47 households in Merthyr Tydfil, South Wales.

MODERN LIVING
A housewife prepares dinner in her fully-fitted 'galley' kitchen in 1968. The room is light and bright, with a stainless steel sink unit and easy-to-wipe cupboards and surfaces. Personal finishing touches include a pepper mill – still quite rare in Sixties homes – a step-stool and vibrantly coloured tea-towels and accessories.

Floors, fires and furniture

Downstairs, parquet floors were popular with those who could afford them, parquet-patterned linoleum for those who could not. In the dining room and the living room there would be rugs, often Turkish, with a small crescent-shaped wool rug in front of the coal fire in a mottled tiled grate, which – joy of joys – did not need weekly blackleading, just a quick dusting. Upstairs, the bedrooms would probably have a square of carpet, with a dark painted or varnished border round the edge, or again linoleum. The bedroom suite would perhaps be light oak, walnut or maple, comprising a wardrobe, dressing table and chest of drawers, and perhaps twin beds, which were becoming fashionable, each with its own peach or pink satin-covered eiderdown.

Since few homes had central heating, there would be a coke-burning boiler in the kitchen to heat water, coal fires in the living rooms and perhaps a two-bar electric fire in the bedrooms for the lucky ones. The kitchen and the bathroom would be the most modern rooms in the house. The bathroom, usually with a separate – very small – lavatory, would be tiled with a boxed-in bath, shiny chrome towel rail and fittings, and an aquarium motif or two. Eau de Nil and duck-egg

WASHING DAY

A woman strings her washing line across a street in Halifax, West Yorkshire, in about 1964. Getting the family clothes washed and dried was an onerous weekly task in pre-automatic washing machine days. One of the most popular detergents was Daz, whose makers cottoned on to the power of blue to make whites look whiter. This poster is from October 1953.

blue were popular colours for the kitchen, which would have a sink and draining board, a stand-alone gas cooker, a hatch so plates could be passed through to the dining room, and probably a small table where the family would eat breakfast. Covered with a blanket, the table would double as an ironing board, with the iron often plugged into the light fitting above, since many homes only had a circuit for lighting. Few people had a refrigerator; food was kept in a pantry built on the north wall of the kitchen. With no washing machine, washing was done in a deep sink in the scullery, using a mangle to wring out the water.

'Autumnal tints' were popular colours, the downstairs walls often papered in oatmeal with a border of leaves or swags of fruit in browns, muted oranges and greens. The living room would have a three-piece suite in uncut moquette, although boxy-shaped rexine chairs and sofas were becoming very *à la mode*. In the corner would stand a large wood or Bakelite wireless round which the family would sit to 'listen in'. The dining room would have another suite – dining table (with extending leaves for when 'company' came), chairs and matching sideboard, above which might be seen a set of three ducks flying upwards, getting smaller towards the picture rail, from which a reproduction print of Constable's Haywain or some sunset or battle scene might hang over the fireplace.

Not everyone could buy new, but there was always the temptation of furnishing a house on the 'never-never'. The Board of Trade estimated that almost three quarters of the furniture sold to the working classes was bought this way. But until the law was changed in 1938 it was not a system designed in the interest of consumers, who often incurred high rates of interest and could find their furniture repossessed if they fell behind with a couple of payments.

The war invades the home

The furniture and décor of the 1930s were destined to last well into the 1950s. During the Second World War materials were scarce since most factories were turned over to war production, and paper and wood were needed for more martial purposes. Windows were covered over with a gummed paper lattice to prevent shards of glass injuring the occupants of houses damaged by bombs; broken windows were replaced with opaque material. Roofs with tiles missing could be covered for months in tarpaulin or roofing felt to keep the rain out, until replacement tiles – and a roofer – could be found. Rooms were made dark by heavy blackout curtains and the fact that the electricity voltage had been lowered.

Little furniture was made in the early days of the war, since timber imports had been drastically cut and home-grown wood was needed for military uses. Plywood was withdrawn in 1942 as it was required in aircraft production. Furniture manufacture came to a standstill as firms used up their pre-war supplies of timber. The Blitz and subsequent bombing attacks intensified the problem – as houses were destroyed, furniture became firewood. Carpenters were also in short supply. Only men or women aged over 40 were allowed to work in the furniture industry: younger men and women were called up or drafted into war work.

Since rationing was not considered appropriate – some people needed no furniture, while others required an entire houseful – an allocation system was introduced: people could buy furniture only if they could prove that they needed it. It was important that no more labour or materials went into making furniture than was necessary, but on the other hand manufacturers had to be discouraged from producing cheap, shoddy goods to sell at inflated prices to people desperate for essential items. The answer was to control both price and quality through a 'utility furniture' scheme. A standard design would be specified, using minimum materials and labour, while ensuring that the furniture was well-made.

Plain and simple – 'utility furniture'

The Board of Trade produced a booklet of designs influenced by the Arts and Crafts movement and Scandinavian designs. To modern eyes utility furniture looks pleasingly simple, but to a public accustomed to neo-Jacobean styles with barley-twist legs and elaborate carving, the designs seemed drab – many was the handy husband who got out his tool box to chisel a design into a plain cupboard door or bed-head. The 'utility furniture' was only available to 'priority classes' with a permit issued to bombed-out families or to newly-weds setting up home. Prices were regulated, but to buy an item also required a certain number of units – a wardrobe took eight units, a kitchen chair one. The only exempt items were cots, playpens and high chairs. To the fury of housewives, curtains, towels, sheets, pillow-cases and mattresses required clothing coupons.

In 1946 an exhibition called 'Britain Can Make It' (a spin on the wartime mantra 'Britain Can Take It') was held at the Victoria & Albert Museum displaying new pieces intended to carry the best of war-time furniture design into the

MOTHER'S LITTLE HELPERS
As the middle classes learnt to live without servants, mechanical and electrical aids were increasingly welcomed. Here a woman vacuums her curtains in 1937.

'Our front room was never used. It was kept pristine [for] formal occasions … It seems crazy now. The house was so small we all sat crammed in the kitchen. But that was the way then.'

A WOMAN REMEMBERING THE 1950S

peace. The exhibition commentary was by John Betjeman and one-and-a-half-million visitors came to gaze on exhibits he titled the 'Working-Class Utility Kitchen', the 'Middle-Class Kitchen with Dining Recess' and the 'Suburban Living Room for a Hard-up Curate (whose wife clearly had a weakness for pottery)'. It was not to everyone's taste. 'I don't like that steel furniture. I wouldn't buy it. It's not at all snug or cosy,' commented one woman of utility furniture in 1946. And in any case visitors were soon amending the exhibition's title to 'Britain Can't Have It', since almost all of the nation's slowly recovering production had to go for export to repay the massive post-war debts – mostly to the USA. The utility scheme was finally wound up in 1952.

Moving with the times

By that time, though, there was a growing determination to 'spring-clean the nation'. The Festival of Britain in 1951 showcased new materials and designs for the home. The lure of the modern permeated everything – textiles, wallpaper, carpets and furniture. Synthetic fabrics such as nylon and terylene were easy to care for and came in bright, cheerful colours that did not fade. Many carried designs based on crystal structures – nature, as in designs of the 1930s, but now seen through a powerful microscope. Wallpapers were printed with patterns called 'Insulin' and 'Boric Acid'; a carpet had a design based on the structure of nylon.

Other new materials such as fibreglass inspired futuristic-looking furniture – Eero Saarinen's tulip chair designed for Knoll, or Robin Day's stacking chairs. Wire basket-seats and tubular-steel legs on tables and chairs made pre-war wooden furniture seem dark and bulky. 'Labour-saving' and 'easy-wipe' were the buzz words

GRACIOUS LIVING
Lord and Lady Sackville at home at Knole, their family estate near Sevenoaks, Kent, in 1949. Built in the mid 15th century, the house is one of the great houses of England, reputed to have 365 rooms and 52 staircases. The Sackville family, including the writer Vita Sackville-West, had been its owners and occupants since 1603. But many stately homes faced an uncertain future after the Second World War, forcing their owners to move with the times. The Sackvilles handed Knole to the National Trust in 1946, with an endowment towards the upkeep of the house, retaining the park, some of the contents and a 200-year lease on certain apartments.

of the decade. Most middle-class women, whose mothers might have had a maid or at least a cook-general, would be lucky if they had a 'charlady' who 'did' for them once a week. Home appliances were falling in price and many housewives aspired to an electric washing machine, perhaps a twin tub, or at least a spin drier to lighten the load on washdays. Vacuum cleaners, designed to glide across swirly-patterned fitted carpets, were shaped like rockets and sputniks in homage to the new fascination with space. Formica, invented in the 1940s, was now seized on by women tired of endless scrubbing. 'Lucky the mother whose table is Formica-topped', declared the advertisements, showing a housewife with her feet up, enjoying the gleaming surfaces in her fitted kitchen.

In the 1950s spending on household items more than doubled, but since money was often tight, do-it-yourself (DIY) became a way of life. Many couples spent their weekends emulsioning walls and glossing woodwork, laying vinyl floor tiles, ripping out old fireplaces, nailing hardboard over panelled doors to make them look modern, or crazy-paving a patio. New magazines such as *Practical Householder* and Barry Bucknell's television make-over series catered for DIY-ers, and firms like Black & Decker began to manufacture domestic-scale power drills and workbenches. Meanwhile, women's magazines pumped out the message that all a woman needed to make her husband successful and herself happy was a labour-saving, gadget-filled home.

COMPACT LIVING

Above: London designer Richard Hamilton in his flat equipped with a 'bachelor's column' incorporating a cocktail cabinet, lighting control panel, radio, television screen, bookshelves and a home office. The column went on show at the 1958 Ideal Home Exhibition.
Below: The Leyton family of Halton near Lancaster anticipated the Sixties vogue for space-saving bunk beds when they converted a bus into a family home in 1948.

The return of homely clutter

In reaction to all these 'gay' (a very Fifties word) homes, trend-setters of the late 1960s and 70s re-embraced the dark and exotic. Victoriana came out of the attic. Palm-filled cache-pots stood again on spindly-legged bamboo side tables, fringed curtains in moody plum or rich brown were draped across windows. Homes were also influenced by Continental or Eastern styles as the DIY trend gathered pace. Rooms were 'knocked through', floorboards sanded, 'Nordic' shag pile or Spanish 'Casa Pupo' rugs covered floors, folk-weave fabrics hung at windows, three-piece suites ceded to less comfortable 'G plan', and sideboards were discarded in favour of 'room dividers' housing ornaments and books. Stripped pine was the wood of choice for tables, set with teak bowls and coloured Scandinavian glass, while rustic brown Denby or Dansk pottery was preferred to floral bone china. Those of a more hippyish persuasion went in for mirror-encrusted Indian fabrics, peacock feathers, joss sticks in brass vases – and a great deal of lounging about on cushions on the floor rather than in chairs.

Of course, such trends were not universal. While people might admire contemporary styles on display in exhibitions, when it came to parting with their hard-earned cash, most reverted to the traditional. Nevertheless, the burgeoning consumer society of the day seemed distant from Ernest Bevin's claim that 'Half the trouble in England is that we suffer from a poverty of desire'.

STAYING IN

In the first half of the 20th century, radio cast its spell over the nation, bringing music, entertainment and news into almost every home. In the second half, it was the turn of television. But unlike the effect of radio, the pull of the 'magic box' was so powerful, it ended up displacing hobbies, family games – even conversation – from our leisure hours.

On the outbreak of the Second World War, almost every home in Britain had a wireless receiving its signal from an aerial usually strung from the roof to a pole at the end of the garden. Mass production had brought the price of sets down: in 1931 a three-valve, all-mains set cost around £15; by 1934 the price of a model such as the Ecko 'superhet' (containing a device that improved reception) with four valves and a speaker had dropped to £8.8s, while Philco's so-called 'People's Set' cost only £5.5s.

The first Director General of the BBC, the austere and formidable Scot, Sir John Reith, had a clear idea of the organisation's function. It was to 'contribute consistently and cumulatively to the intellectual and moral happiness of the community', and a glance through the pages of the *Radio Times*, the weekly listings magazine first published in 1923, shows how that ambition was realised. Most programmes were live, offering a mixture of music, comedy, talks, news and weather forecasts. *Children's Hour* was broadcast at teatime, or while mother was cooking supper.

LISTENING IN
The Cooper family gather round their wireless to listen to Prime Minister Winston Churchill speaking on 19 May, 1945 – after VE Day but before VJ Day. During the war the radio was an all but indispensable medium for information and entertainment

Early broadcasting rules
No news could be heard before 6.00pm because the newspapers considered this unfair competition and the BBC acquiesced. Nor, for the same reason, were the results of sporting events given, though the events themselves were broadcast and the roar of the crowds was often heard. Newsreaders wore evening dress, even though they could not be seen, and were criticised by the *Daily Mail*, among others, for their 'over-refained' Oxford accents. Sundays were a radio wasteland. Reith was 'more anxious about the general religious policy of the BBC' than anything else, so there were no broadcasts on Sunday mornings or early evenings for fear of discouraging church-going.

It was not until the Second World War that Reith's 'lowest common denominator' programming mix of light music, quizzes and comedy was finally permitted on the Sabbath. In the 1930s a survey of radio listeners overwhelmingly selected variety shows as the nation's favourite listening fare. *Bandwagon*, broadcast on Wednesdays at 8.15pm from 1938 to 1940, was so popular that cinema managers noted that their takings fell that evening, and organisations such as the Women's Institute found it prudent to hold their meeting on another night. Starring Richard Murdoch and Arthur Askey, it was supposed to be set on the flat roof of Broadcasting House, where the pair kept a menagerie of animals. They had a charwoman, Mrs Bagwash, whose daughter's name was Nausea, and Askey's catch phrase 'Ay thank you' was soon on everyone's lips.

On the outbreak of war, regional radio stations were closed down and most programmes pulled, so that all an anxious public could hear were uninformative news bulletins and an endless repertoire of Sandy MacPherson playing the BBC Theatre organ. But within days the government realised that the radio was essential to morale. Soon the schedule filled up again with talks, plays and comedies, the most popular of which was *ITMA* (It's That Man Again) staring Tommy Handley. *ITMA*'s catchphrases and whacky characters – Colonel Chinstrap, Funf the Spy, Mona Lott and others – were the social glue of wartime Britain.

THE BOX IN THE CORNER
The white light from the television screen illuminates the mesmerised faces of children intently watching a programme in 1956. Not everyone was as satisfied as this audience appears to be. One viewer from the 1950s recalled: 'On Sundays there was a programme called *All Your Own* with Huw Weldon, and children who had made cathedrals out of matchsticks would come on and show us how clever they were … it was most annoying.'

United by the BBC

Many people had formed the habit in the 1930s, when Reith's edicts restricted light music and jazz, of listening to English-language stations broadcasting from Europe, such as Radio Normandie and Radio Luxembourg. Although these shut down on the outbreak of war, the ingrained habit meant that in the early days of the war many people tuned in to such stations as Radio Hamburg to hear the German propaganda broadcasts of 'Lord Haw Haw' (William Joyce). In response, the BBC introduced the Forces Programme in January 1940. It was soon broadcasting 12 hours a day to listeners in homes all over the country, not just the Forces. Its output was mainly light entertainment – 'drip listening' that could be dipped into. But *The Brains Trust*, first transmitted in January 1941 with a panel of five individuals discussing philosophy, art and science, regularly drew an audience of 10 million to hear the team debating such thorny issues as 'Why can you tickle other people, but not yourself?' and 'Is Vera Lynn bad for morale?'

DAN DARE
Nine-year-old Philip Hunter test-reads an American *Marvel* comic to compare it with the *Eagle*, a British children's favourite. The brainchild of Reverend Marcus Morris, *Eagle* was launched in 1950 and was instantly successful, with the first issue selling 900,000 copies

HEARTH AND HOME
The Wallaces spend a companionable evening in their living-room in 1946, she knitting, he reading the newspaper. A sewing machine sits under its cover on the cupboard beside Mrs Wallace; the ubiquitous wireless is on the cupboard beside her husband.

With the blackout, petrol rationing and air raids, the radio became of great importance during wartime, both for information and morale. The restriction on the timing of news broadcasts was dropped in the nation's hour of need and the nine o'clock evening news bulletin became a fixed point in most people's lives, as they gathered round the Bakelite or wood-encased set in the living room. Since it was harder to get out to concerts, the BBC became a rich source of music, and the Corporation continued its policy of commissioning new works from British composers, needed all the more since most of Wagner's music and quite a lot of Richard Strauss (and even Sibelius's *Finlandia* after Finland capitulated) were no longer played. Since the 1930s the BBC had sponsored the Promenade Concerts – staged at the Albert Hall after the Queen's Hall was demolished by an air raid in 1940 – and the wartime 'Proms' included new works by Vaughan Williams and Benjamin Britten.

But it was not just classical music that people tuned in to hear. With the advent of the 'talkies' in 1929, the BBC became a lifeline for musicians who suddenly found themselves redundant from cinemas, having previously made a living accompanying silent films. Popular classics and dance music played by such bandleaders as Jack Payne and Henry Hall filled the airwaves, while jazz and 'swing' from America would also occasionally blare out of radio receivers whose reception was improving all the time. So too would the songs of 'crooners', the most popular of whom in the 1930s was Al Bowlly. The BBC shunted dance music to after 10.30 at night (Reith again), when in many homes the rug would be rolled up so couples could practice dance steps from diagrams in the *Radio Times* or dance magazines, ready for Friday night at the local Palais.

New kids on the block

The radio had speeded the decline of sheet music, since fewer evenings were spent playing music than listening to it, either on the radio or on a record-player. Brittle shellac records that revolved at 78rpm on a wind-up gramophone were gradually replaced after the Second World War by vinyl substitutes, either 45rpm 'Extended Play' (EPs) or 33⅓rpm 'Long Play' (LPs). Vinyl records were less fragile, but they scratched easily and could bend if left somewhere warm. The plain brown-paper envelopes, with a circle cut out to reveal the disc's title, were replaced with laminated sleeves printed with photographs and information on the artist and music. LP covers soon developed into an art form.

By the early 1960s most teenagers longed for a hi-fi record player, advertised by Curry's as a 'magic box' on which to 'spin their platters'. A Dansette could be bought for around 11 guineas (£11.11s). It was the size of a small suitcase, ideal for a teenager to take up to his or her bedroom, where they could play pop singles with a lightweight stylus. An extra two guineas would buy a model with an auto-change spindle, allowing several records to be loaded at once – as one finished, the arm automatically lifted off to allow the next record to drop down.

Drinking Tizer and eating crisps, the nation's youth began to groove in their bedrooms, not just to hi-fi sounds but also to pirate radio stations accessed via 'trannies' (transistor radios). The best-known of these was Radio Caroline, started in 1964 and moored offshore to avoid restrictive broadcasting regulations. To counteract the appeal of the pirates, the BBC reorganised its radio transmissions in 1967, dividing the Light Programme into two, with the new Radio One, playing the latest pop hits, appealing primarily to the young.

Something for the grown-ups

Downstairs, parents might be listening to Radio Two, the other half of the old Light Programme, now home to middle-of-the-road music compered by the likes of Jimmy Young and Terry Wogan. Or to Radio Three (formerly the Third Programme), home to classical music and serious talks and plays, or Radio Four, the re-branded Home Service. Or they might be playing their Frank Sinatra records on a more substantial piece of furniture, the radiogram; as the hybrid name suggests, this combined a record player and a valve radio, and came in shiny wood with plastic or gilt trim to suit any décor. By the 1970s

SPINNING THE PLATTERS
Teenage girls play 78rpm records on a portable record player, a much-desired object for all young people in the 1950s.

'The TV when it arrived was a Bush 12 inch. Dad bought us a Dansette record player and three records: Edmundo Ros, David Whitfield and 'Itsy Bitsy Teeny Weeny Yellow Poker Dot Bikini'.

MAUREEN LIPMAN REMEMBERING THE 1950s

'GO TO JAIL!'
A 19-year-old drama student, Veronica Hurst (second from left), playing Monopoly at home in Tooting with her mother and sisters in 1951. The UK version of the US boardgame, substituting London streets for the Atlantic City originals, first came out in 1935.

stereo radiograms had arrived, with enveloping sound issuing from two symmetrical loud speakers. They in turn gave way to transistor radios that could be carried around the house, some equipped with cassette tape players that could also play back music.

Entertaining each other

Television posed no competition for other home entertainment until well into the 1950s. An evening at home might mean playing a game. Mahjong was popular in the 1930s, as were pick-a-stick, beetle, hangman, charades, consequences and various word games, while most newspapers had begun to print a daily crossword. Jigsaws got ever larger and more complicated, and there were jigsaw lending libraries since no one wanted to do the same one twice. Alternatively, the family might sit down together to play a boardgame such as Tiddlywinks, Ludo, Snakes and Ladders, or in later years Monopoly, Cluedo, Diplomacy, or, later still, Trivial Pursuit. Draughts and chess were perennial favourites.

There was also time for hobbies, such as embroidery, sketching or painting. Men and boys tended more towards making model airplanes, squeezing ships into bottles, fiddling with home-made radio equipment, or collecting stamps and coins. Many people had a Box Brownie camera. Columns in newspapers and magazines catered for most such interests, but this active world would dwindle in the face of the newcomer to the sitting-room.

New show in town

On 26 August, 1936, almost 7,000 people crammed into the Radiolympia Exhibition at Earl's Court in London to see the first television pictures with sound, transmitted from Alexandra Palace some 10 miles away. Sets with tiny screens were available, but only those in close proximity to the Alexandra Palace transmitter could pick up the flickering black-and-white images without a booster,

FIFTIES FAVOURITES – The Goons and other radio fun

Favourite radio programmes of the 1950s and 60s included the music programmes *Housewives' Choice*, along the lines of *Music While You Work*, and *Two-Way Family Favourites* linking British troops serving in occupied Germany with their families and friends back home. A roll-call of the nation's favourite programmes included such long-running shows as: *Top of the Form*, a quiz for school children; *The Billy Cotton Band Show*, with Cotton's signature 'Wakey, Wakey!' call, which later transferred to TV; *In Town Tonight*, an early example of a chat show with celebrities; *Desert Island Discs*, launched in 1942, and *Woman's Hour*, 1946, which are both still popular today.

Comedy was always an important part of the BBC's output, attracting large audiences. Fifties favourites included *Educating Archie* with ventriloquist Peter Brough; *Hancock's Half Hour*, another show that successfully transferred to TV; *Take it From Here*, starring Jimmy Edwards as Mr Glum and June Whitfield as Eth, the long-suffering fiancée of Ron Glum; *Round the Horne* with Kenneth Horne; and last, but not least, *The Goons*, a surreal weekly event starring Spike Milligan, Harry Secombe and Peter Sellers that creased up the nation, spawning a horde of imitators of its zany voices, including the heir to the throne.

A NATION OF HOBBYISTS

Above: A Manchester man painstakingly crafts a model of a Spanish galleon on his dining-room table in 1936.

Below: Women attend a class in flower-arranging at the Corn Exchange, Dorchester, in March 1952 in preparation for a forthcoming Flower Arrangement Show.

while the sets themselves cost a fortune – between £50 and £125 at a time when the average wage was around £3 a week. The spread of television was slow to begin. *The Spectator* declared it 'a mere toy or hobby for the well-to-do, [that] will make little change to our social life'. In any case war terminated the experiment for the time being: the plug was pulled on television in September 1939 during the transmission of a Mickey Mouse cartoon and it remained off-air until June 1946, when it resumed with the same cartoon.

Even then it was still radio that exercised the greatest pull on the British public. At its peak *Dick Barton – Special Agent* drew 15 million listeners daily, Richard Dimbleby's *Any Questions* and *Down Your Way* were both popular, as was *Variety Bandbox* starring Frankie Howerd and Benny Hill, who made his radio debut in 1947. *Mrs Dale's Diary*, the story of a GP's wife, started in 1948 and ran until April 1969. Another weekday serial, *The Archers*, conceived in conjunction with the Ministry of Agriculture as 'an everyday story of country folk' to inform and encourage farmers and smallholders, first aired in January 1951. It is still running today, the longest-enduring drama serial anywhere in the world.

Radio had the advantage that the listeners could do other things at the same time – many a pair of socks, baby's matinee jacket or child's school jumper has been knitted in that way. The situation was different with television – 'of course, knitting remains undone', noted Judy Haines, after her family got to the

TUPPERWARE PARTY
Plastic food containers first developed in the 1930s, and the Tupperware brand was launched in 1946. Pursuing an innovative marketing strategy, the resealable boxes were sold at 'parties' in people's homes, where friends and neighbours gathered to experience the products, as seen here in 1963.

top of the waiting list for a Pye set in Chingford in 1947. At the time there were just 300,000 television sets in use in Britain, and even five years later there were fewer than 2 million, partly because signals could only be received around London and major cities. But in 1953 the coronation transformed television's fortune. As many as 20 million watched the ceremony in Britain, most of them on someone else's TV, but afterwards everyone wanted a set of their own with an 'H' shaped aerial on the roof.

The first TV 'soap' to challenge *Mrs Dale* and *The Archers* was *The Grove Family*, the story of a lower-middle-class family that took its name from the Lime Grove studios. Programmes such as *Come Dancing* (1950), *What's My Line?* (1951), which made a star of the irascible Gilbert Harding, 'the rudest man in Britain', *The Black and White Minstrel Show* (1958) and *The Quatermass Experiment* (1953) were brand-new for TV. And whereas BBC radio had generally been circumspect about news and current affairs, television proved willing to court controversy with programmes such as *Panorama* (1953), another Dimbleby fiefdom, and later, on ITV, *World in Action* (1963). The *Wednesday Play*, broadcast from 1964 to 1970, gained a reputation for gritty social realism vividly delivered in Jeremy Sandford's *Cathy Come Home*, a harrowing drama about homelessness watched in 1966 by an estimated 12 million people – almost a quarter of the population – coinciding with the creation of the homeless charity Shelter.

The ITV challenge

In 1955 everything changed again. 'Auntie', as the nannyish BBC had been nicknamed, was challenged by a brash newcomer that promoted itself as 'giving viewers what they want' instead of what the BBC 'deems is best for them'. On 22 September that year, the night of ITV's launch, BBC radio ran a 'spoiler' in which Grace Archer died in a fire. ITV came in the form of regional franchises – Granada, Thames, ATV, Harlech, Grampian – and at first only 190,000 homes could pick them up, but by the end of the 1950s it had attracted an audience share of 70 per cent to pacey serials such as *Emergency Ward Ten*, the all-singing, all-dancing *Sunday Night at the London Palladium* (hosted from 1958 by Bruce Forsyth), game shows with cash prizes such as *Double Your Money* and *Take Your Pick* and the talent competition *Opportunity Knocks*. For a while presenter Hughie Green seemed to be everywhere. ITV was commercial not just in its programming,

He who prides himself on giving what he thinks the public wants is often creating a fictitious demand for low standards which he will then satisfy.

SIR JOHN REITH, DIRECTOR-GENERAL OF THE BBC, 1924

but in being funded by advertising. Viewers were soon humming snatches of jingles – 'Murray Mints, the too good to hurry mints' and 'Mash means Smash' – and using the ad breaks as time to put the kettle on for a cup of tea.

In the 1960s and 70s, television jumped on a nostalgia bandwagon with series like *Dad's Army*, *The Forsyte Saga*, *Dr Finlay's Casebook* and *Upstairs Downstairs*. Exotic places, wildlife and ancient civilisations came to seem almost commonplace thanks to series in the mould of Armand and Michaela Denis's *On Safari* and David Attenborough's *Life on Earth*. Highbrow offerings such as Sir Kenneth Clark's *Civilisation* (1969) and its scientific equivalent Jacob Bronowski's *The Ascent of Man* (1973) contrasted with hugely popular US imports like *Bonanza* and *Peyton Place*. 'Soaps' came into their own, in particular with *Coronation Street*, although *Crossroads* rivalled its popularity for a time. Comedy more than held its own with *The Likely Lads*, *Fawlty Towers*, *The Morecambe and Wise Show*, *The Good Life*, *The Liver Birds*, *Steptoe and Son*, *Monty Python's Flying Circus* and the renegade *Till Death Us Do Part*. Regardless of the strictures of Mrs Mary Whitehouse and her 'Clean Up TV' campaign, first launched in 1964, edgy satire had a huge popular impact with *That Was The Week That Was*.

Colour reached Britain on BBC2 in 1967 and soon spread to the other channels. With the Apollo 11 mission two years later, when it became apparent that you could watch men on the Moon live from the comfort of your living room, viewers began to feel that there might really be no need to go out at all.

A NATION OF GARDENERS

The passion for tending gardens is a national trait that stretches right across the social classes. The soul of Britain could be said to reside in its gardens, from the sweeping grounds of stately homes to the postage-stamp sized plots tucked behind urban houses. Gardening enthusiasts get out in all weathers to tend these havens of tranquillity and beauty and to reap the benefits of fresh home-grown vegetables.

COUNTRY GARDENER
Allotments played a crucial role in keeping the nation fed in wartime, but for many gardeners, like this elderly gentleman contentedly surveying his plot in Devon in July 1954, the tradition of growing vegetables went back far beyond the war.

'Here in the spring, when the trees are burgeoning, the ground is covered for three weeks at a time with the azure snow of bluebells, and later in the summer you find the tall, over-weighted spires of wild Canterbury bells, no doubt descended from flowers escaped long ago from older enclosed gardens of the monasteries and manors.' So wrote Osbert Sitwell of his home, Renishaw in Derbyshire, where his father, Sir George Sitwell, had laid out a spectacular garden. Writing *Left Hand, Right Hand,* the first volume of his five-part autobiography, it is not surprising that his thoughts in wartime turned to the beauties of the garden of his childhood. Gardens, parks, pots on patios define the British identity: if parks are the lungs of our cities, gardens are the heart – private, individual, happily absorbing hours of their owner's time and attention.

Influential experts

The first decade of the 20th century was a heyday for the domestic garden. Gertrude Jeykll's cottage-garden-influenced herbaceous borders, full of lupins, hollyhocks and roses, were reproduced on a small scale in many British gardens for the rest of the century, although not always with the care that Jeykll gave to colour combinations or to fastidious 'underplanting', so that no bare earth showed and flowers seemed to float in drifts of delicate colour and scent.

Vita Sackville-West and her husband Harold Nicolson bought Sissinghurst in the Weald of Kent in 1930 and set out to restore its derelict garden, creating a series of linked 'rooms', each with a theme or a single colour – of which the white, with its 'white clematis, white lavender, white Agapanthus, white double primroses and white lilies …', became the most copied. Sackville-West contributed a weekly gardening column to *The Observer,* starting just after the Second World War. In it she wrote of her love of old roses, subtle, small flowers and 'gloomy hellebores', and her dislike of most floribundas, showy flowers, 'double' varieties and chrysanthemums – 'shaggy things as big as Old English sheepdog's faces'. In the view of Anne Scott-James, woman's editor of *Picture Post,* Sackville-West's articles 'change[d] the face of English gardening more than any other writing'.

While Sissinghurst was a hybrid of aristocratic great-house grounds crossed with the cottage garden, modernists such as Christopher Tunnard anticipated the decking of the late 20th century with a 'rational landscape' that exiled anything unruly, sentimental or fussy, concentrating instead on low-maintenance shrubs, uninterrupted views and smooth sweeps of paving. Tunnard was instrumental in setting up the Institute of Landscape Architects in the late 1920s. Particularly in the years after the Second World War, this institution would bring the tenets of great 18th-century garden landscapes to communal urban spaces and the banks of motorways.

CITY AND SUBURBAN GARDENERS
Above: Eighty-year-old Mr Webb in his back yard at Sansom Street in Camberwell, South London, demonstrating that no space is too small to create a garden. In March 1939 he won eight prizes for his efforts.
Below: Mrs Graves of Mitcham in Surrey, mowing the front lawn of her surburban home surrounded by herbaceous borders full of lupins.

FLORAL DISPLAY
Queen Elizabeth, the royal consort, inspecting the prize-winning garden of a prefab in Marylebone, London, in July 1950.

Many of those rehoused on council estates in the 1930s had a garden of their own for the first time. The majority of tenants knew nothing about horticulture but soon learned; observers from the Mass Observation project, surveying a number of new estates, found that less than a fifth of gardens were neglected and that most people 'treasure their garden and look after it well'. London County Council officials walked the streets peering over hedges, then awarded silver cups and medals for the gardens they judged best-kept. Most were a blaze of colour throughout the summer, 'every single inch used for growing flowers of every kind', while vegetable patches in the back garden yielded potatoes, cabbages and Brussels sprouts — some gardeners were 'even ready to give celery and cucumbers a try'.

In the 1930s most newspapers printed weekly gardening columns, while gardening part-works, encyclopedias and other gardening books sold well. Mr Middleton's weekly gardening talks were among the most popular radio programmes on the BBC. 'Gardening is today man's chief hobby', claimed the author of *All About Gardening*, with some justification, on publication in 1931.

In the suburbs, the innovation of including 'French windows' in many 1930s houses turned the garden into an 'outdoor room' — at least in summer. Eagerly collected cigarette cards from packs of 50 offered 'gardening hints' showing how a terrace could be constructed, often of 'crazy paving (concrete slabs broken up into irregular shapes), so that tea could be taken while gazing at the lily pond or watching the trim lawn being mown — probably with an Atco mower. Lawns tended to be rectangular, mowed in straight, broad stripes, with a path (crazy-paving again) down the middle and herbaceous borders on either side. There might be a shed at the bottom of the garden, usually a male domain, where the lawn mower was stored with neatly hung garden tools and shelves full of chemicals used to control slugs, snails and fungal invasions.

(continued on page 142)

TEA ON THE LAWN
The author Hammond Innes and his wife enjoy the tranquillity of their garden in Kersey, Suffolk, in the summer of 1952

DIGGING FOR VICTORY

If ploughshares had to be turned into swords in wartime, so flower gardens had to become vegetable patches. Since Britain imported up to 90 per cent of its foodstuffs, the island nation was extremely vulnerable when war was declared on 3 September, 1939.

An immediate campaign was launched to make the country as self-sufficient in food as possible. And it was not just farmers who were exhorted to plough up fields; everyone was encouraged to 'Dig For Victory'. The Ministry of Agriculture, in conjunction with the Royal Horticultural Society, distributed a series of 'Growmore Bulletins' with advice on digging up lawns for vegetable patches and replacing flowers in borders with 'good croppers' such as runner beans and turnips. Every inch of soil could be productive: the recommended 15 inches of earth shovelled on top of corrugated iron Anderson bomb shelters in back gardens could be used

to grow marrows or tomatoes. Flat dwellers could cultivate vegetables in window boxes or potatoes in a dustbin.

The Women's Institute organised lectures to encourage women to dig, plant and prune for victory. Allotments would prove a saviour: an Act passed in 1939 empowered councils to take over unoccupied land to grow vegetables – and keep chickens and maybe a pig too. Soon rows of cabbages, peas and beans flourished in public parks, recreation grounds, railway embankments, football pitches and private, gated squares. The forecourt of the British Museum sprouted onions, beans and lettuces, as did the moat around the Tower of London. After the ravages of the Blitz, allotments were dug on bomb sites. By 1945 around 1.5 million allotment holders were producing 10 per cent of

the country's food. The British had absorbed the wartime adage: 'If you don't grow it, you don't have it.'

THE GARDEN FRONT
Top left: Residents of London's East End tend allotments dug on a bomb site in the shadow of St Paul's Cathedral in 1942.
Bottom left: Two postmen inspect a good crop of cabbages on a vegetable patch outside their Post Office in July 1941.
Bottom centre: While their babies sleep or sit in their prams, women plant cabbages at Peckham Health Centre's Home Farm on Bromley Common, where these young mothers and their children were evacuated during the war.
Bottom right: Boys from Dury Falls Council School in Hornchurch, Essex, arrive for a session on their allotment. The boys ran a shop where they sold the vegetables they grew to the public.
Top right: An Anderson shelter was not complete until it was covered with a thick layer of earth to help protect it from bomb damage. Here, a woman in Clapham, South London, waters the vegetables she has planted on the shelter's roof in 1943.

BEST IN SHOW
Competitors arrive with their exhibits for a flower and vegetable show organised in 1933 by the Teddington branch of the Unemployed Allotment Holders.

Keen gardeners would aspire to a greenhouse, or at the least a cold frame, since plants would be raised from seeds bought in packets from Carters or Suttons, carefully labelled and left to germinate in pots before being planted out. Those with a large garden – and an income to match – might have a 'summer house', a wooden construction with glazed windows, a real 'outdoor room' where croquet sets, tennis racquets and similar equipment could be stored.

Rock gardens, so beloved of the Victorians, made a comeback in 1930s suburban gardens, largely because they were a useful way of using the rubble generated by the building construction and left behind in the soil. Seed manufacturers produced a range of miniature (or dwarf) rockery or alpine plants – saxifrages and campanulas were particularly popular. And then there was the fence or hedge – of laurel, yew or privet – to give the privacy so valued by suburbanites whose gardens, like their houses, were, in fact, semi-detached.

Putting on a show

If back gardens were private spaces, front gardens were the public face of suburbia, for display rather than recreation. A low wall would mark the boundary between road and private property. Paving (sometimes coloured) would be much in evidence, maybe with a concrete sun dial or bird bath centrally placed. A half-moon shaped flowerbed would often sit under the window, filled with colourful annuals and perennials 'to make a good show' for passers-by. A gnome or two might have taken up residence – perhaps sitting on a toadstool, smoking a pipe or 'fishing' in a non-existent pond. The front gate, carefully latched, would be of wood (or later fancy black-painted wrought iron), perhaps in a starburst design, most likely painted green, another Thirties homage to nature.

The Second World War transformed gardens into mini-allotments or even smallholdings, but with the restoration of peace there was a desire to replace rows of leeks, carrots and cabbages with flowers once more. If nothing much could be bought to brighten up inside the house in the years of post-war austerity, a few cheap packets of seeds could do the trick outside. And roses were a particular desideratum – standard roses marching alongside the paths in crimson red, or the best-selling Peace rose, a golden-yellow bloom with pink edges reputed to have been the last flower flown out of France before the German occupation. Harry Wheatcroft, with his luxuriant moustaches and sideburns, was the 1960s face of rose-growing, genetically breeding and grafting ever more colourful varieties which eager gardeners were prepared to join a two-year waiting list to purchase.

The Chelsea Flower Show was revived in 1947 (the grounds of the Royal Hospital had been an ack-ack gun site during the war). The National Garden Scheme (NGS), which encouraged those with lovely gardens to open them to the

DEMONSTRATING HOW IT'S DONE
Percy Thrower, one of BBC television's gardening experts, potting up geraniums in 1957. Thrower presented *Gardener's World* from 1969 to 1975.

public for charity, joined forces with the National Trust in 1948 and thousands flocked to visit. *Gardeners' Question Time* was first broadcast on BBC radio in 1947 and from 1956 Percy Thrower became the Mr Middleton of television on *Gardening Club*. As package holidays introduced more people to the influence of the Continent, terraces became patios furnished with barbecues and large terracotta pots planted up with geraniums.

The biggest transformation came as plant nurseries were usurped by garden centres that sold everything a potential gardener could desire – from plants for all seasons and all places to labour-saving equipment such as 'hovver' mowers and lawn sprinklers. But gardeners still relished talking about their trials and triumphs, so local gardening clubs flourished and flower and produce shows continued to be well attended. In the growing line of much-loved BBC gardening gurus – Fred Streeter, Dr D.G. Hessayon, Percy Thrower – the baton was passed to Geoff Hamilton, who in 1985 moved *Gardener's World* to his own garden. That same year, gardening writer Chris Baines sowed the seeds of a new trend – gardening to encourage wildlife, rather than exclude it, claiming: 'Just a few minutes of quiet relaxation amongst the trees, with bird song and bumblebees for entertainment, and even the most exhausted of city workers is ready for anything.'

'No one can make a garden by buying a few packets of seeds or doing an afternoon's weeding. You must love it and then your love will be repaid a thousandfold, as every gardener knows'

MARGERY FISH, FROM *WE MADE A GARDEN*, 1956

GREEN INITIATIVE
Marie Burns (on the right) and other young volunteers take up spades and forks to clear land in Wood Green, North London, and turn them into allotments in January 1976.

FEEDING THE FAMILY

Mealtimes became less communal as the decades passed by. Even Sunday lunch, that celebrated feature of British family life, became something of a rarity. In its place a new generation embraced the convenience of takeaway meals and ready-made TV dinners.

With unemployment rising to almost 3 million in 1933 and short-time work endemic in declining industrial regions, 'feeding the family' was a daily battle against hunger. It was a question of stretching inadequate supplies and eating cheap cuts and offal – scrag end, pig's trotters, sheep's heads – and even that not every day. Women went round markets at the end of the day to see what could be picked up for a few pence. They filled the children up on potatoes, or bread and dripping, frequently going without themselves to ensure that the rest of the family were fed – not well fed, perhaps, but fed.

The housewife was a key figure in these mid years of the 20th century when fewer women worked outside the home (although some were obliged to take in home working, for a pittance, to supplement the family income). The relative lack of domestic appliances until well after the Second World War meant that housework, washing, shopping and cooking added up to a full-time job.

BRITISH TRADITION
A Sheffield housewife prepares a filling Yorkshire pudding to go with the Sunday roast in 1947.

COMMUNAL EATING
Right: Three generations of the Maycock family, all living in the same house in Twickenham in Middlesex, sit down to Sunday dinner in 1946.

TASTY FARE
A West Indian-born father sits with his daughter at the kitchen table in their Birmingham home, as mother puts the finishing touches to dinner.

FARMHOUSE KITCHEN
A farmer's wife makes pastry in the kitchen of her 16th-century Essex farmhouse in 1949, while her husband sits by the fire enjoying his pipe and the paper, his feet resting on a home-made clippy mat (rag rug).

A middle-class menu

The Lawrence family lived in Wallington in Surrey. Henry Lawrence, a successful businessman, commuted to the City and the family enjoyed a comfortable lifestyle with seaside holidays and help in the house. As Eileen Lawrence (later Whiteing) remembered her upbringing in the 1930s, they had plenty to eat. For breakfast the family 'always had the usual bacon and eggs or tomatoes or poached eggs or kippers, or (on Sundays) cold small pork sausages with, of course, toast and marmalade to follow.' In Eileen's recollection 'breakfast cereals hadn't really been invented' – or perhaps her mother chose not to buy those that were then available, such as 'Mr Force' or Scott's Porage Oats.

After breakfast the children went off to school, until '… at one o'clock, unfailingly, we all came home from school and sat down to a hot meal … steak-and-kidney pie or pudding, lamb chops, veal cutlets, steak casserole, steak and onions, Irish stew, or plaice and Dover soles (cod and herrings and suchlike were despised by us as being "common"!).' Lunch was rounded off with a hot pudding – 'steamed sultana pudding or syrup sponge, fruit tart or rice pudding'. Eileen recalled school ending at about 4 o'clock, then 'we would return home on our bicycles, and at five would sit down to a proper afternoon tea, with

'Housekeeping is the very linch-pin of life's daily round.'

FROM AN INTERWAR EDITION OF MRS BEETON'S
BOOK OF HOUSEHOLD MANAGEMENT

white and brown bread and butter, and jam or fish paste, plus a great variety of cakes'. Not surprisingly after all that food the children had only a 'light bedtime snack of biscuits and milk or homemade lemonade (or cocoa in winter)'. But the grown-ups sat down later to have 'supper, or "late dinner" as it was often called. I had never heard of "high tea" as eaten in the North until many years later.'

On Sundays lunch in the Lawrence household 'was invariably a roast joint of some kind – beef, pork or lamb in turn, with the trimmings of horseradish sauce, apple sauce and mint sauce (all fresh) respectively … The Sunday pudding was always rather special … a trifle, or fruit jelly, or stewed prunes with blancmange. But … we always had fresh cream added, plus delicious peeled almonds.'

Replenishing supplies

Supplying such a menu required thorough and constant attention to family housekeeping. Although milk and bread would have been delivered, and Mrs Lawrence may have telephoned her weekly order for dry goods – flour, sugar, tea, coffee – to the grocer, she would still had to go shopping most weekdays, since without refrigeration food did not keep for long. She might have called first at the grocers for cheese cut from a large block – most likely cheddar or possibly a regional cheese such as Stilton, Cheshire, Wensleydale or Red Leicester. Butter would also be cut, weighed and wrapped up for her, bacon and ham sliced by a hand-operated machine that could be set to the thickness of slice required by the customer.

Tins of fruit or vegetables might be on her list at the grocers, as well as packets of biscuits. Already by the 1930s less food was being weighed and bagged up in the shop – or sold 'gross', which is what the word 'grocer' derives from – and more was coming from the wholesaler in tins and packets. Household names included Tate & Lyle sugar, Oxo cubes, Bovril, Carr's Water Biscuits, Bournville Cocoa, Typhoo Tea. By the 1930s, family grocers were in competition with chains such as Home and Colonial, Liptons and International. Then it would be off to the greengrocers, maybe the chemists, then finally to the butcher, who would chop up a carcass to provide the particular cut the housewife wanted for stewing, braising, frying or roasting.

Rationing – getting used to queuing

The Second World War changed shopping habits. Food rationing came into effect in January 1940 and coupons as well as money were required for commodities such as butter, cheese, fats, sugar, meat, preserves and soap. Housewives had to register with and go to a specific retailer. The amounts allowed of different foodstuffs varied throughout the war – in 1941, for example, the cheese ration fell to just one ounce per person per week. In December 1941 a points system was introduced. The tariff varied, but a tin of red salmon might require 32 points, while baked beans and tinned pilchards required two apiece. The choice was the housewife's.

PACKAGED PRODUCTS
Above: Rowntree had been in business for 90 years in 1953, when this advertisement for their jelly appeared.
Below: A housewife and her daughter check the groceries in her weekly shop in 1955. Many of the brands are still on sale and familiar today.

Rations were guaranteed, but some things were never rationed – vegetables and fruit, for example, offal, fish and bread (although this last was rationed after the war ended, from 1946 to 1948). But non-rationed foods were often in short supply – or disappeared altogether. A rumour would go round that a shop had got in a new supply of something and a queue would immediately form, with housewives waiting up to a couple of hours in the hope of a 'nice piece of fish', only to reach the front of the queue and find it had all been sold. Rationing allocated fair shares, on the whole, and no-one needed to go hungry, but diets were monotonous and housewives had to use all their ingenuity, often creating 'mock' dishes using substitute ingredients such as powdered eggs and parsnips. Rationing of meat, butter and cheese continued until 1954 – and queuing continued, too.

Getting the self-service habit

It was in an attempt to cut down on queues and save on labour that some of first self-service grocery shops were opened in Britain. The Co-operative Society claims to have opened the first, in London, in 1942 when labour was in short supply. A Tesco's self-service opened in St Albans in 1947 and within four years almost half of Tesco's shops had been converted. In 1952 Sainsbury's opened their first purpose-built supermarket, in Eastbourne. The trend was unstoppable. By 1966 there were more than 20,000 self-service shops and supermarkets in the country. Yet not everyone took to picking up a wire basket and serving themselves. Eileen Cook remembers going to her local corner shop in the 1950s virtually every day 'to catch up with what was happening'. When self-service took over 'shopping was

COOKING AND THE BOX – A perfect partnership

Television proved an ideal medium for showing people how to cook. One early exponent was Marguerite Patten, who had worked for the Ministry of Food during the war, devising recipes for rationing and giving cookery demonstrations around the country. But the first true television chef was Philip Harben, a plump intellectual with a goatee beard and striped butcher's apron, who turned up on the BBC

almost as soon as transmission was resumed in June 1946. *Cookery*, which he compered, ran until 1951.

Fanny Cradock – seen above with husband and 'Bon Viveur' partner Johnnie in their South Kensington home – followed in Harben's footsteps. A devotee of the French master Escoffier, she whipped up elaborate dishes employing lashings of cream. Wearing evening dress and throwing

out such phrases as 'This won't stretch your purse', Fanny became the first star of television cooking.

Delia Smith was from an altogether different mould. Starting her culinary career as a washer-up in a Paddington restaurant, she soon graduated to cooking and her no-nonsense presenting style – and the fact that her recipes worked – hit the right note with aspiring cooks everywhere.

more anonymous … No longer did shops assistants have time to chat with customers – they were too busy stacking shelves and working at the checkout.'

But supermarkets were the way of the future. In the 1960s, with more women going out to work and an increasing number of families owning a car, with a fridge in the kitchen and probably a chest deep-freezer in the garage, shopping became something done once a week in a supermarket, instead of being a time-consuming daily activity. The traditional high street suffered. When Retail Price Maintenance was abolished in 1964, small shopkeepers found the level playing field dug up overnight, since supermarkets could offer discounts they could not match. And another challenge came from a new breed of corner shop, run by Asian immigrants prepared to put in long hours, who stocked foods for their fellow immigrants that increasingly tempted the palates of the native-born British.

New tastes

The 'herring savouries' of the 1930s had morphed into cod fish fingers by 1955, while frozen peas were taking over from the processed tinned variety, but meals for many families were so predictable people knew what day it was from what they had to eat. Alison Pressley recalls: 'Food in our house was an absolute ritual. If you asked me what I had for dinner on the first Monday of 1950 and the last Friday of 1959, I'd be able to tell you.'

But eating habits were changing. By the 1960s food manufacturers and supermarkets were combining to offer convenience. One of the biggest changes was the advent of white sliced bread. It 'came like a bolt from the blue' for Christine Fagg of Manchester. 'Before you were forever hacking at a loaf with a half blunt knife, and now you could make sandwiches with real ease … and the children could help themselves.' By 1969 the British were eating 42 million sliced white loaves a week, as well as other 'instant foods' that required no preparation: Angel Delight, Vesta boil-in-the-bag curries, packet soups, Smash instant potato. Christine Fagg liked Cambell's condensed soups 'because you could put a mushroom or tomato soup over some cooked meat and get an instant sauce. It was wonderful to be able to open a tin and just dish it up – no washing up to do either.' Towards the end of the 1970s the pot noodle appeared, imported from Japan and soon beloved of students everywhere.

The British meat and two veg was under attack in another way. With families becoming less nuclear, entertaining at home involved fewer family gatherings over Sunday roast and more dinner parties on Saturday evenings. 'Continental dishes' would often be served: garlic and tinned Italian tomatoes stirred into mince to make a version of spaghetti bolognese or lasagne, often followed by Black Forest gâteau. Cheese fondue and Chicken Kiev were also popular, served from a hostess trolley that kept food warm. When Elizabeth David's *Mediterranean Food* was published in 1950, olive oil moved from the medicine cupboard to the kitchen, omelettes took over from scrambled eggs, and a pasta dish was no longer a macaroni milk pudding. Aubergines and other exotic vegetables arrived, while hard-boiled eggs were removed from salads, which now accompanied quiches rather than corned beef. And to accompany this new fare, wine might be served – a bottle of chianti, or Riesling, or perhaps Mateus Rosé.

CUBIST COOKING
Oxo cubes were first produced in Germany in 1866, although the name dates from 1899. They became an essential ingredient for most home cooks, adding flavour to stews and gravies without the trouble of boiling bones for stock.

HERE'S ONE I PREPARED EARLIER
Above right: Philip Harben, Britain's first television cook, making *Soupe a l'Oignon* in one of five fortnightly programmes devoted to European cookery and broadcast in 1953.
Right: If anyone can claim to have taught the nation to cook, it is Delia Smith. Here she is in 1973 promoting her first BBC series, *Family Fare*.

A DAY OUT SHOPPING

In the 20th century, shopping has gone from queuing for necessities to a national pastime. High streets became more uniform as expanding department stores and chains took over, displacing individual family businesses. Then came the threat from the malls and the convenience of out-of-town shopping with free parking provided. No one as yet had even dreamed of the internet and the world of online shopping.

'Doing the shopping' suggests necessity – the chore of getting in essential supplies. 'Going shopping' sounds a more pleasurable activity altogether, involving window-shopping, browsing, taking a break for coffee or tea, then coming home with a lighter purse and a satisfying clutch of glossy carrier bags, rustling enticingly with tissue paper. Both forms of shopping were essentially women's work (or pastime) and both changed fundamentally over the course of the 20th century. In the transformation of the high street one of the most significant changes is the decline of the small independent shop, from 'madam shops', selling fashion, to traditional grocers and butchers, the first affected by the march of 'chain stores' and increasing popularity of department stores, the latter by the rise of supermarkets. Between 1957 and 1966 alone, the number of independent shops in Britain fell by almost 100,000 out of a total of nearly 500,000, and the headcount of those working in them dropped by around 160,000.

TREASURE TROVE
A smartly-dressed woman inspects the wares on offer in the window of a Dundee jeweller's shop in 1955.

The rise of the department store

The figures for department stores went the other way, from an estimated 150 in 1910 to more than 500 by 1950, largely due to the spread of suburbia and improved transport, which allowed customers to travel to shop in them from across a far larger area. This trend was pronounced in the 1930s, when advances in mass production techniques meant increased choice and rising incomes (for those in work) made it possible to buy more. Many of London's most famous department stores – Dickins and Jones, Swan & Edgar, Selfridges, Liberty's, Barkers, Derry & Toms, D.H. Evans, John Lewis, Gamages, Simpsons in Piccadilly, Peter Jones in Sloane Square (voted best building of 1939 in *Architectural Review*), Harrods and Harvey Nichols in Knightsbridge – were either newly built or had recently undergone radical redesign and refurbishment, and in many cases extensions.

It was much the same in towns and cities up and down the country, from Whitakers in Bolton to Bobby's in Southport, from Fenwicks in Newcastle to Jarrold in Norwich. The whole shopping experience had changed as floor layouts were opened up, making it easier to browse, and women in particular flocked to admire the merchandise and other attractions that stores laid on to pull in customers. Imperious shop-walkers no longer interposed themselves between the customers and the merchandise, and shoppers were encouraged to handle goods before parting with their money. In the 1930s, department stores could provide a delightful day out. Many of their tea rooms laid on music. At Kennards of Croydon, customers could hear 'strains of light music from the inevitable trio or quartet, often of ladies only, hidden behind a bank of palms and plants', while the elegant Dome Restaurant in Dickins & Jones held a tea dance every weekday afternoon.

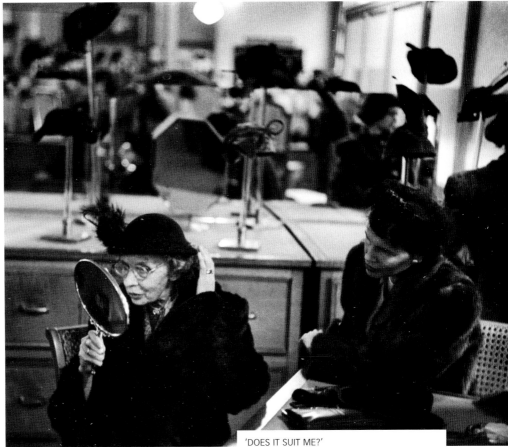

'DOES IT SUIT ME?'
Bargain hunters try on sale-priced hats in a London department store in January 1950. Both ladies are wearing fur coats – to own a fur was an aspiration for many women in the Fifties. Fake fur also started to become popular, not, as later, for ethical reasons, but because it was cheaper than the real thing.

'Why go to the West End – there's Bentall's of Kingston', advertised the suburban Surrey store, and to make sure that they delivered on their promise the store hosted baby shows, imported the floral decorations from the Royal Box at Ascot every summer and serenaded customers with a 'gypsy band' as they travelled up and down the escalators – another new attraction. They also displayed *Bluebird*, the car in which Malcolm Campbell broke the world land speed record in 1935, hired a Swedish gymnast to dive 63 feet down the atrium into a tank of water, and staged a circus on the ground floor with the lion kept in the lift overnight.

No one outdid Selfridges in stunts to get the store noticed. In 1932 they filled 6,000 square feet of floor space with the products of Sheffield steelmakers. A million pounds' worth of diamonds in burglar-proof octagonal cases were displayed in the window for a month. These were then replaced with the plane flown by aviatrix Amy Johnson. In 1933 Selfridges constructed a temporary tennis court so that Suzanne Lenglen, six times Wimbledon ladies singles champion, could give tennis lessons. Simpson's of Piccadilly, a stunningly modernist store designed by Joseph Emberton, arranged for three light aircraft to land on its roof, while Kennards hired three baby elephants to promote their 'Jumbo Sale' in Croydon.

'The customer is always and completely right!'

MARKS & SPENCER'S SLOGAN, 1953

'Gardens in the sky'

The creation of roof gardens added another dimension. The Co-op in East Ham had a roof garden open to customers that boasted 'a cafeteria, flowerbeds, crazy golf ... a lily pond, fountain, kiddies' playground, giant telescope ...'. Back at Selfridges, the landscape architect Margery Allen was commissioned to transform

RICHARD SHOPS
32 DARLEY STREET

the 'vast grey empty expanse [of roof] stretching from one end of Selfridges
Oxford Street store to the other'. Working before the store opened to the public
each day, Allen and her team carried hundreds of tons of earth, rocks and manure
up in the lift to create an English garden with 'old-fashioned flowers', a lily pond,
dovecote and gazebo, a rose garden, winter garden and fragrant garden. There were
sculptures by Jacob Epstein and Henry Moore, and shoppers could take coffee,
lunch or tea and watch mannequin parades. Yet even this was surpassed by the
magnificent one-and-a-half-acre garden atop Derry & Toms in Kensington, with a
Spanish garden based on that in the Alhambra in Granada, a Tudor-style garden,
an English woodland garden with over 30 species of trees and a flock of pink
flamingoes pecking among the plants to the delight of customers taking tea.

Standardising the high street

Already by 1933 a book complained that 'On almost every high street you will
find the same shops'. There was likely to be a Boots the Chemist, an ABC
('Aerated Bread Company'), a Lyon's tea shop, an Express and a United Dairy,
Home and Colonial, the International, a Maynards (sweet shop), a Dewhurst's
(butcher), a Mac Fisheries (started by Lord Lever in an attempt to support the
Hebridean fishing industry), a Timothy White's (hardware), a W.H. Smith (books
and stationery), a Dorothy Perkins (named after the popular climbing rose, and
selling clothes), Evans Outsize, Cresta Silks, C&A (budget clothes from Holland),

the Times Furnishing Company, Montagu Burton (men's tailoring), the shoe shop chains Freeman, Hardy & Willis, Dolcis, Bata and Lilly & Skinner – and, of course, a Marks & Spencer and F. W. Woolworths. In 1933 the thousandth branch of Boots was opened in Galashiels in Scotland, and there would be another 200 by 1939, selling pharmaceuticals and a range of what were then considered 'health foods' such as Ovaltine and Bovril.

Marks & Spencer's had started as a market stall in Leeds in 1884 selling 'nothing over a penny'. It moved indoors and upmarket, and by the 1930s had narrowed its focus to concentrate on haberdashery and clothes: its flagship Pantheon store in London's Oxford Street was described as displaying a 'forest of apparel'. By 1939 there were 234 M&S branches to be found at the 'top end' of high streets – that is, away from such places as fish'n'chip shops – all over Britain. Woolworths, which had opened its first British store in Liverpool in 1909, was even more ubiquitous. It flourished in the hard times of the 1930s, its red and gold fascia signalling the 'democratisation of desire' so potent in that decade. 'Mr Woolworth's success is due to the fact that millions of people can spend

SUPERIOR SERVICE
A commissionaire helps a customer to find a taxi outside Fortnum & Mason in Piccadilly, London, in 1953.

sixpence [the maximum price for its goods] at five different times, or threepence at ten different times, who never at any time have half a crown to spend', suggested a book published in 1934. By 1937 there were 711 Woolworth stores providing necessities and small luxuries, and somewhere for children to spend their pocket money.

The demands of war

During the Second World War, department stores and chain stores along with all other shops had to cope with rationing – clothes went 'on the coupon' from June 1941 – and with shortages, not just of goods but also of staff, since around a quarter of them enlisted or were conscripted. Harrod's fashion workrooms were put to good use making uniforms, parachutes and even aircraft parts, as they were in Howell's in Cardiff. Since shops were invariably located in the centre of towns and cities, many were wrecked by bombs. In September 1940 John Lewis in Oxford Street suffered bomb damage estimated at £2 million, but staff continued to trade from trestle tables on the pavement. Binns of Sunderland was bombed in 1941 but also managed to carry on trading, while the newly built Lewis's in Liverpool, which was requisitioned for the Civil Service before it even opened for business, was almost destroyed in May 1941. During the blackout and the Blitz, shops shut as early as 4 o'clock in winter so staff could get home before a raid started, although many stayed on to fire-watch on the premises. Large stores provided air-raid shelters for their customers – Dickins & Jones' basement was particularly sought-after.

When 'the lights went on again'

After the war, shops could again illuminate their window displays and switch on neon signs, but they did not

AN EYE FOR A BARGAIN
Above: A mother and her children examine the goods in the window of a Woolworths store in Chertsey, Surrey, in 1945.
Below: Marks & Spencer's ubiquitous underwear undergoes close scrutiny in the Oxford Street branch in 1955.

have much to sell for some years, since most manufactured goods went for export. They did what they could to respond to changing customer needs. The House of Fraser introduced a 'Junior Miss' department, and in 1947 Dickins & Jones opened a 'Young Londoner' section. But the real change was on the streets rather than in the established stores.

In 1955 Mary Quant, a young art student who had no desire to 'grow up' into a world of twinsets and pearls, opened a boutique on London's King's Road with her husband-to-be Alexander Plunket Greene. It was named Bazaar, it sold trendy (but not cheap) clothes and its impact was huge. By the 1960s boutiques were mushrooming, selling distinctive, different clothes for the young. There was Bus Stop, Miss Chelsea and Laura Ashley, which favoured the milkmaid look and was a great hit with debs and the young marrieds. The most celebrated of all was Biba, started after a mail-order gingham dress designed by Barbara Hulanicki and offered to *Daily Mirror* readers had shown there was a massive unfulfilled market for inexpensive yet cutting-edge fashion.

CLOTHES ON RATION
A small crowd eagerly surveys the goods on display in the window of Selfridges' Oxford Street store as a shop assistant pins a card on a dress indicating how many coupons were required for its purchase. Clothes rationing came into effect in June 1941.

The swinging Sixties

The first Biba shop opened in Abingdon Road in Kensington in 1964 but soon moved to Kensington High Street. Queues would form outside to get into the dark, gold-accented Art Deco interior where they could buy large hats, knee-high suede boots in moody colours such as mulberry, rust and cocoa, feather boas and skimpy dresses. Out-of-towners could buy the same desirable clothes by mail order. In 1974 Biba took over the entire seven-storey premises vacated by the defunct Derry & Toms, including the roof garden. By then Biba was selling soft furnishings, wallpaper and even food – including tins of baked beans with the Biba logo. But despite attracting a reputed million customers a week, the company had overstretched its resources and it was forced to close the following year.

The department stores, anxious to capture a slice of the new youth market, opened stores within stores: 'Way In' in Harrods in 1967, 'Miss Selfridge' in 1966 and 'Top Shop' in Peter Robinson's department store in 1964. Barker's staged a 'Youthquake' fashion show that year, with models showing off the clothes of young designers straight out of art school to a background of loud pop music. The retailing revolution even penetrated the staid world of three-piece suites and mahogany furniture represented by Maples, Catesby's, Waring & Gillow and the furniture departments in the major stores. In 1964 the designer Terence Conran, who had worked on the Festival of Britain in 1951, opened the first branch of Habitat in the Fulham Road in west London, and soon young homeowners were saving up to buy chicken bricks and earthenware pasta jars. There were Magistretti chairs from Italy, tableware from Scandinavia, pine beds and duvets, all available to buy, rather than having to order then wait for delivery.

Purchasing power was boosted by the arrival of plastic credit cards, the shopper's 'flexible friend'. Barclaycard was the first to be introduced in Britain, in 1966, and held the field until Access arrived in 1972. Allowing for instant gratification, credit cards would increasingly take over from cash, cheques and hire purchase for all except major items such as cars.

Moving on, moving out

The high street had been the traditional venue for shopping, but by the 1930s planners had increasingly begun to think that it was wrong to mix up traffic and pedestrians. The devastation of city centres caused by the Blitz and subsequent bombing raids during the war provided an opportunity for a rethink. The first pedestrian precinct – Chrisp Street in Poplar, East London – was an exhibit at

FASHION ICONS
Above: Clothes designer Mary Quant poses with a French copy of *Vogue* featuring the model Twiggy on the front cover in 1967.
Below: Shoppers enjoy the intimate atmosphere of the Biba store in Kensington Church Street, which opened in 1965.

the Festival of Britain in 1951. Coventry and Plymouth, where air raids had laid waste the city centre, were rebuilt with grand shopping boulevards, with car parks and delivery yards provided to the side, so that shoppers could wander untroubled by the presence of vehicles. New towns took up the trend: Harlow had precincts reserved for pedestrians, while traffic was barred entirely from Stevenage town centre, the first town in the country to do so.

Large shopping centres attracted more shoppers – most arriving by car. Initially the vehicles could be accommodated on reclaimed bombsites nearby, but as redevelopment continued, multistorey car parks were built adjacent to, over or under the shops. In these purpose-built centres the shopping experience was quite different from that on the high street. Gone was the mish-mash of individual premises, replaced by neat shop units arranged in straight lines, with banks and large stores that were allocated corner sites. In some, the shops were set back behind colonnades, rather in the style of the 18th-century Pantiles in Tunbridge Wells. Trees were planted and slabs of colour enlivened the view, as did the occasional clock tower or fountain. Benches were set out for weary shoppers or their bored husbands.

New shopping precincts often turned out to be windy places and as time went on became no-go areas at night when all the shops were shut. The result was that precincts were converted into malls, either by covering them over with glass roofs or, in the case of the Bull Ring in Birmingham (1964), the Elephant and Castle in London (1965) and the Arndale Centre near Leeds (1967), by enclosing the whole complex behind walls that made artificial light essential at all times, with piped music and hot or cold air blown in to give an impression of life. Such developments were often derided: the Arndale Centre in Manchester (1972-9) was said to have 'the longest lavatory wall in Europe'. Gradually voices called for more organic complexes that incorporated architectural features of existing towns, as in the Lanes in Carlisle, or at least façades, as at Banbury in Oxfordshire (1974-7).

It did seem, though, that most shoppers liked the enclosed mall – really a modern version of the traditional covered market – so more were built, most of them US-style on the edge of conurbations. Brent Cross, Bluewater, Lakeside, the MetroCentre in Gateshead and many more provided the required mix of department stores, chain stores and supermarkets, offering an enveloping, dawn-to-dusk shopping experience in one ever-larger space. As it had been for centuries, though, the largest shopping complex in Britain remained London's West End, comprising over 6 million square feet of retail space on Oxford Street, Regent's Street, Bond Street and the labyrinth of smaller streets all around.

LEFT BEHIND
Not everyone would race to partake of the new shopping experience. These two elderly ladies were photographed in London's East End in 1960, talking outside a traditional haberdashery and drapers shop.

MAKING CHRISTMAS SPECIAL

In the depth of the Great Depression of the 1930s, housewives were urged to 'remember specially in their Christmas shopping the claims of our own country and the Empire countries beyond the sea'. But for many a child of an unemployed worker, Christmas Day would be much like any other. There might be a 'silver-wrapped tangerine and a pink sugar mouse' and perhaps a tin whistle for some in their stockings, although as Eileen Lawrence noted, 'There were not so many decorations in the shops, nor for so long' as there would have been in better times before or after.

Christmas shopping was bleak in wartime, too. Sidney Chave, a London laboratory technician, noted that it was 'a bit dismal' in 1940. 'Meat is rather scarce. There is a great deal to be had, but not much choice, nuts scarce and dear. Figs and dates are absent.' Frank Edwards, a buyer for a London munitions factory, found that in the

'big stores in Kensington' there were plenty of shoppers, but 'Things are much more expensive than this time last year, and everyone seems to be purchasing practical gifts; things to wear and use are the order of the day. Most of the stores have a toy fair for the children, but I saw few children, which is doubtless accounted for by evacuation. There were not many decorations, but there was plenty of colour about, and all the departments looked bright and cheerful.' Fewer shops had a Santa Claus in a grotto, although some shops did their best to look seasonal, with strands of cotton wool draped across their scant stock to represent winter 'snow'.

Nevertheless Sydney Chave must have managed to achieve some Christmas shopping, since he found that he and his wife had to use a pillow case, rather than a stocking, for their small daughter, Jillian, since 'she had so many presents'.

THE SEASONAL SPIRIT
Top left: For children, Christmas lost none of its magic in the early war years. This little girl takes advantage of the sandbags to get a good view of Selfridges window in Oxford Street in 1939.
Bottom left: A little girl tells Santa what she wants for Christmas in 1977.
Bottom centre: Buying turkeys at auction in Smithfield Market in 1937.
Bottom right: Shoppers jostle to get to the counters in a busy Woolworths at Christmas 1955.
Below: The lights on London's Oxford Street in 1960.
Right: Shopping done, a mother in Bristol uses a wheelbarrow to get her children, presents and Christmas tree home in 1935.

ON THE MOVE

Trains had been a part of people's lives since the early decades of Queen Victoria's reign. At the turn of the century steam power was joined by the internal combustion engine and before long cars, motorcycles and buses began to displace the horse. Already enamoured of the bicycle, the public seized on the new opportunities for travel, becoming ever more mobile as the century progressed.

STREAMLINED
The 'Coronation' train pulled by the A4 class locomotive *Dominion of Canada*, on a poster advertising the LNER's streamline service to Scotland. Both the locomotive and the train – named in honour of the coronation of George VI in 1937 – were designed by Sir Nigel Gresley.

PREVIOUS PAGE
Two young women have an early evening snack on a street in Elland, West Yorkshire, on their way home to remove the curlers and get ready for a night out in 1977.

Speed was a motif of Britain in the 1930s and 'streamlined' was a word often used of design as well as processes, suggesting modernity and a sense of urgency. The figurine commissioned for Rolls-Royce cars before the First World War from the sculptor Charles Sykes – the forward-leaning silver lady, wind rippling through her hair – still epitomised this restless drive for progress. (The mascot was variously known as the 'Spirit of Ecstasy ', the 'Silver Lady' or, more irreverently, 'Ellie in her nightie' after motoring fanatic Lord Montagu's mistress who was the model for the figure.) By the 1930s even the homely Austin and Ford family cars were losing their boxy shapes in favour of curves and slimming down.

The streamlining of cars culminated in Malcolm Campbell's aerodynamic *Bluebird*, in which he set a new land speed record of 301mph on the Utah salt flats in 1935. Henry Segrave, an earlier holder of the land speed record, broke the water speed record with his arrow-like *Miss England II* on Lake Windermere in 1930 (he was killed in a subsequent attempt to beat his own record). But the nearest ordinary people came to experiencing such thrilling, streamlined speed was when they travelled by train.

Steam-powered speed

By 1938 nearly 2 million train journeys were taken every year. Southern Railway had spent £21 million in modernising – largely electrifying – its lines in the commuter belt round London, as were lines round other large cities. Long-distance trains were still powered by steam and two of the 'Big Four' railway companies now abandoned an earlier gentleman's agreement and entered into competition to provide the fastest train journey ever. The testing ground was the run from London to Scotland.

London, Midland and Scottish (LMS) trains steamed up the west coast to Glasgow, while the London & North Eastern Railway (LNER) took the east coast to Edinburgh. Both took a leisurely eight-and-a-quarter hours to cover the 400 miles from London to Glasgow or Edinburgh, yet railway advertisements showed trains pulling ahead of cars, boats and aeroplanes in the race north. To give substance to this claim, in 1935 LNER upgraded its service from King Cross to Newcastle with the 'Silver Jubilee' train, so called to mark George V's 25 years on the throne. The train was painted to look like a silver bullet, which looked thrilling, and it was pulled by a new A4 class locomotive. On 27 September, 1935, the train touched 112mph, a record for steam. The service cut the journey

TRAINSPOTTING
Schoolboys in Newcastle upon Tyne in 1950 carefully note down the numbers of the steam locomotives as they leave Newcastle Central Station. A railway modernisation programme got underway in the 1950s to convert from steam to diesel power, but diesel engines would never delight the souls of schoolboy trainspotters in the same way as smutty steam.

time to Newcastle to just four hours and was such a success it was extended to Edinburgh. Not to be outdone, LMS produced the *Coronation Scot* in anticipation of the coronation of George VI. Another streamlined, aerodynamic locomotive, *Coronation Scot* reached 114mph on 29 June, 1937. But the crown went in the end to *Mallard*, an A4 steam locomotive designed by the LNER's chief engineer, Sir Nigel Gresley, which achieved 126mph on a downhill stretch near Grantham on 3 July, 1938. It was the fastest speed achieved under steam anywhere in the world.

Back to basics

Little more than a year after *Mallard*'s triumph, the railways went to war. Trains were painted battleship grey, their streamlined cladding removed and carriage lights replaced by blue bulbs that made it impossible to read. Soon they were crammed with troops, or hauling trucks of war matériel and supplies around the country.

In 1948 Clement Attlee's Labour government nationalised the railways, taking the 'Big Four' companies into public ownership as British Railways (BR). A survey in 1951 revealed that a majority of people thought that the service was worse after nationalisation, but John Harris looked back fondly on his local train service in the early 1950s. 'We were quite dependent on the Newquay–Truro line', he

FRIENDLY SERVICE
A woman and toddler give a milkman's horse a sugar lump in the Elephant and Castle district of London in 1949. Horse-drawn deliveries were still common after the war, and some urban breweries continued to use dray horses well into the 1970s and beyond.

COUNTRY ROADS
The long-distance London to Glasgow coach, operated by the Northern Road coach company, on a bleak stretch of open road in 1952.

recalled. 'Some of the hamlets only had five or six little houses. If the water supply went down it was the train driver who delivered churns of water. It was a brilliant service. You could send a basket of eggs or a few chickens two or three stations down the line.'

But this was not a way for the railways to make money. The fact was that one of BR's aims – to provide a social service – was incompatible with the other, which was to turn a commercial profit. A long-awaited modernisation programme, converting from steam to diesel, got underway in the 1950s, but it was costly and the railways were losing money. Then in 1963 the 'Beeching axe' fell. After an intense census of railway use, BR chairman Dr Richard Beeching recommended that passenger services be cut by a third: more than 2,000 stations were closed and some 6,000 miles of track were ripped up.

Fares were going up too. Passengers had replaced freight as the main users of rail transport, and in 1964 fares were reorganised to make them pay for the privilege. Previously they had been set at a standard rate: threepence a mile for second class and fourpence-halfpenny for first (third-class carriages had been upgraded to second in 1956). In future, travellers would pay more and train travel dipped as a result, only reviving with the introduction of the long-distance InterCity 125s in the 1970s, so called because this was the speed at which they could travel – it was no faster than *Mallard* had achieved in the 1930s, but the 125s could maintain it for more of the journey. In 1994 the Conservative government, continuing the pursuit of privatisation begun under Margaret Thatcher, started to sell off the railways. Few people had welcomed nationalisation, but fewer still celebrated privatisation as trains grew more crowded, track more desperately in need of repair and ticket pricing all but impossible to comprehend.

On the roads

Well into the 1950s, coal and milk were still being delivered to the door by horse and cart, while the Steptoe-like rag-and-bone man's horse remained a familiar sight in many towns. The majority of people got about on foot or by public transport. In Coventry, a centre of the car industry, it was bikes and buses that formed 'the memorable image of town traffic in the early 1950s: dense, surging columns of

RAILS ON ROADS
Trams running along the Thames embankment
in 1932. Although it is dark and lights are ablaze,
this photograph was actually taken at midday
during one of London's infamous smogs.

pedalling workers released from factories at the end of the day; long, snailing
queues of workers, shoppers and schoolchildren waiting to board the bus home.'

Trams were on the way out by the 1950s: the last ones ceased running in
London in 1952, although they continued to operate in Glasgow for another ten
years. Many people looked back with nostalgia on the tram era. Kenneth Beck,
who travelled to and from school by tram in Dunfermline, Fife, in the Thirties
remembered the 'open-top tram cars ... I recall climbing the stairs to the top deck
and the way the tramcar used to sway.'
Trolley buses, powered by connection
to overhead electric cables, were first
introduced in 1949 and were known as
'whispering death' for the way they
glided silently along. They were
vulnerable to power cuts and were
never as popular as trams. 'The trolley
buses weren't as steady ... They were
always coming off the [electric] line,
and the driver would have to get out and use a long pole to put [the trolley
connection] back ...'. Smoking was still allowed upstairs on buses: '... it was a
bit like an opium den. No windows open and blue with smoke.'

Yet people generally found travelling to work by public transport
companionable: 'You seemed to meet the same people at the bus stop every
morning, so you'd make some comment about the weather, and if you were sitting
next to someone of the same age group, you'd end up saying, "Well, where did
you go last night?" and you'd have a chat all the way to work, and then often

*'The trams were dead reliable. Even when it
was really foggy or snowing, that didn't stop
them, and you could hear them coming as
they rattled along the tracks.'*

MARY GREENHOUGH, REMEMBERING TRAMS IN BRADFORD IN THE EARLY 1950s

TO AND FROM WORK

Above: Workers at the Bristol Aeroplane Company set off home after a shift in the factory in July 1939. The men in the long snaking queue are waiting patiently for a tram.
Below: A bus conductor stands on the rear platform of a London bus in 1951, checking that all the passengers are safely on board before ringing the bell to tell the driver to move on.

you'd meet the same people on the bus home and ask how their day had been.' But the ravages of war and long-term lack of investment meant that the 'buses were often chock-a-block in the mornings,' recalls a London woman. 'I'd line up to get on, and then it was packed, my hair might get caught in someone's coat button … Sometimes they'd be very late, and then two or three would turn up at once. It was grim when there was thick fog [the Clean Air Act was not passed until 1956]. The buses would creep along, so then you knew you were going to be late. And I'd be sitting there tense. I had to clock in at work, so I'd be thinking, I'm losing money here and I might even get the sack.'

An alternative in London and in Glasgow was to take the underground. An underground network had been tunnelled under both cities in the 19th century, but London's had been greatly extended in the 1930s with lines running out to the new suburbs. The familiar, pocket-sized, diagrammatic tube map was designed by Harry Beck in 1931.

Tube trains continued to run during the war, and despite the government's initial objections London's tube stations were used as air-raid shelters, with as many as 72,000 Londoners taking shelter nightly. Several stations were in fact hit and many were killed – 17 at Marble Arch in Sept 1940, more than 60 at Balham in October and, worst of all, a direct hit on Bank station in January 1941 that killed 117 people. The tube was taken into public ownership with the railways in 1948 and the few remaining steam trains were replaced as the electrification of lines was completed. No new lines were added until the Victoria, begun in 1968. The extension of the Piccadilly line to Heathrow airport started in 1977, followed by the Jubilee line out to Docklands which commenced in 1979.

On the road on two wheels

A hugely popular form of transport, both for leisure and to get to work, was the bicycle. By 1934 there were more than 10 million cyclists on British roads, double the number of just five years earlier, and bike design was improving. Frames were increasingly made of steel on all but the cheapest bikes and derailleurs equipped bikes with a range of gears that made going uphill easier – although such innovations were not allowed in competitive cycling for some time. A typical Raleigh or Triumph with gears cost about £5.10s, or 5 shillings a week on 'deferred terms'. Dick Cunningham remembers being given a new bicycle as a child: 'I chose a Raleigh – guaranteed for 50 years – and insisted on having a three-speed gear and a milometer and also a large saddle-bag.'

When the first families moved out from London to the new council estate in Becontree in the 1930s there was little local employment available, so many of the men cycled back the ten miles or so to their former jobs in the East End every day. For most of the year, this belted-raincoat-clad column would leave when it was still dark. For some, the trick was to catch up with a lorry then hang on to its tailgate and be towed for an easier, if not safer, ride.

Motorcycles served much the same function as bikes but at greater speed. In 1930 there were more motorcycles than cars on the roads, most of them manufactured by Triumph, BSA, Royal Enfield or Norton. Lillian Smith's father 'did not have a car – a Ford 8 – until 1939. Before that he had a motorbike and sidecar. Mum rode pillion and we three children in the sidecar. Dad was a devotee of speedcar racing and we travelled to different events. My memories are of noise and dirt.' As cars became more affordable, motorcycles lost their place as the standard form of transport. In the 1960s they came to prominence as the transport of choice for 'rockers' – as did Italian scooters, Vespas or Lambrettas, for 'mods' – but from the mid Sixties bikers increasingly went for more reliable Japanese machines and the British industry went into decline.

Triumph of the car

By the outbreak of the Second World War there were just over 2 million cars on British roads. A Hillman Minx 'family saloon' cost £159, an Austin 7 £125, a Ford 8 around the same. Cheapest of all, at £100, was the Morris Minor, first produced in 1931. Yet even this was more than a year's wages for most working-class men, so until after the war car ownership – or certainly the ownership of new cars – remained the preserve of the middle classes. Motoring was still seen as something of a luxury and leisure activity, the car to be taken out of the garage on a Sunday, washed and waxed, and then driven for 'a spin' in the country, before being put back in the garage for the rest of the week.

TWO WHEELS
The Skeel brothers of Cambridge demonstrate their willingness to repair any age or make of bicycle in about 1950.

ANIMAL TRANSPORT
A Fair Isle farmer, proud owner of one of only two motorcycles on the Island in 1955, makes use of the sidecar to transport his sheep.

Sometimes extended families, or even neighbours or workmates, might club together to buy a car. And not everyone bought a car new, of course: the secondhand market was thriving. In 1930 Barclay Hankin bought his first car – 'a 1927 Austin 7 with a "special body", a hood, side screens and a small dicky [seat]' – for the 'princely sum of £10' from a secondhand dealer in Shepherd's Bush. The car had a top speed, just, of 50mph and did a creditable 50 miles to the gallon of petrol on long journeys, but it did have one major fault – it used a pint of oil every 50 miles. Despite this, the car 'was a huge joy ... taking us everywhere, including two trips to Scotland. Two people could get to Oban (500 miles) for less than £2 [petrol was about a halfpenny a gallon], but it usually meant camping for two nights on the way. In winter it was distinctly cold, so we wrapped legs and shoulders in rugs and, if necessary, stopped at a convenient town and walked round Woolworths to get warm.'

With post-war manufacturing shortages, secondhand car dealing became a flourishing trade, with the epithet 'used car salesman' entering the language as a metaphor for a dodgy-dealing wide boy. It was the introduction of Ministry of Transport (MOT) tests in 1960 that put an end to the worst practices by instituting compulsory checks to prove the roadworthiness and safety of all vehicles more than 10 years old (reduced to three in 1967).

Choice and affordability

Growing affluence and consumer-friendly hire-purchase helped to increase car ownership to one household in four by 1956. By the Sixties, some 60 per cent of cars were bought on HP and cars on the roads more than doubled in that decade, from 5.6 million to 11.8 million. There was a wide variety of models, and each make had its own identity. There were the sexy, sleek and expensive, epitomised by the E-Type Jaguar, launched in 1961 with a top speed of 150mph (not that it could go that fast legally on the Queen's Highway after 1965). The E-Type had 'pulling power', a quality shared by other nippy sports cars such as the MGA and Austin Sprite. Ford family cars progressed from the Popular to the Anglia, then the Cortina, first produced in 1962. There was the Triumph Herald, the Standard 10, the Morris Minor or, for the better-off, the Rover 100 or perhaps a Volvo – a Swedish import.

Then there were the 'miniature' cars. The three-wheeled 'bubble car' was little more than a covered motorbike – and taxed as such – without even a reverse gear. The Messerschmitt, which looked like a cockpit on wheels, was launched in 1953; two people could just squeeze in, getting in and out by swinging the whole front of the vehicle open. But it was the Mini that became the iconic car of the 'swinging Sixties'. Designed by Alec Issigonis, with its engine placed sideways to save space, it was launched in 1959 and Britain fell in love with it. Costing just £469 new, the Mini was the perfect town car: easy to park, yet capable of carrying four people.

MAKE MINE A MORRIS
A range of cars, British-made and imported, at the 1954 Earls Court Motor Show in London, where a Ford Popular was priced at £390.

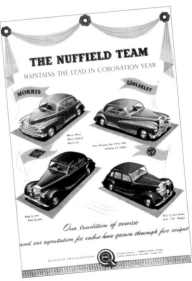

CORONATION SPECIAL
A poster for Nuffield cars – Morris, Wolseley, Riley and MG – in the coronation year of 1953.

FLYING – The aeroplane shrinks the globe

IMPERIAL AIRWAYS

The increasing affordability of air travel did more than almost anything else to broaden people's horizons in the 20th century. The Wright brothers had made the first powered flight only in 1903, yet by 1920 pioneer airlines, graduates of flying experience in the First World War, were already launching passenger travel. In the interwar years, intrepid pilots like Amy Johnson and Jim Mollison flew impressive 'firsts' – to Australia, to South Africa and back. Flying was dangerous but glamorous – only the well-to-do could afford it – but this began to change after 1945 with a new generation of planes. For the population at large, the real revolution came in the 1970s, with the proliferation of charter flights and package tours. Holiday-makers whose options had previously stopped at Dover found first the Continent and then the whole world opening up before them.

With the massive increase in car ownership, parking became a major challenge in towns and cities, and the first parking meters appeared in Mayfair in 1960, charging sixpence for two hours. Yellow lines were painted by the kerb to show motorists where they were not allowed to park. Many of the meter's early custodians, the traffic wardens, were ex-servicemen, as were those other 'knights of the road', patrolmen with the Automobile Association (AA) and Royal Automobile Club (RAC). All wore similar, peaked caps, but there was one major distinction: where AA and RAC patrolmen were welcomed by motorists, traffic wardens were vilified as yet another incursion on the motorist's freedom.

Curbing the mayhem on the roads

By the 1930s, road accidents were at epidemic proportions – in 1934 alone there were 7,343 deaths and 231,603 injuries – and dealing with the carnage placed considerable strain on Britain's services. In *The Car In British Society* Sean O'Connell comments: 'The treatment of road-accident victims caused a serious drain on the resources of many rural hospitals. Smaller cottage hospitals on popular motoring routes were most vulnerable, at times becoming "weekend casualty stations".' Half of those killed were pedestrians. The newly appointed Minister of Transport, Leslie Hore-Belisha, called it 'mass murder'.

Some measures had already been taken. Legislation in 1930 limited to one the number of pillion passengers on a motorbike, made third-party insurance for drivers compulsory, introduced the Highway Code, limited the hours that bus and lorry drivers could work, and gave local authorities the power to regulate traffic through one-way streets, roundabouts, road signs and traffic lights, originally known as 'traffic control robots'. The 1934 Road Traffic Act reintroduced the 30mph speed limit (it had been abolished in 1930 except on exceptionally dangerous stretches). It also introduced a driving test for new drivers and allowed local authorities to install pedestrian crossings: 19,000 'Belisha beacons' were duly set up in London to mark these new crossings. The moves were not as effective as Hore-Belisha had hoped, although casualties did reduce in built-up areas where the speed limit was enforced.

There was much opposition to all of the safety measures, with both press and public complaining that legislation was a constraint on freedom. It was a chorus that would resurface whenever governments tried to improve road safety. Further measures included the introduction, in 1965, of a 70mph speed limit on motorways; the fitting of safety belts in cars in 1967 (although it would not be compulsory to wear them until 1983); drink-driving laws and the breathalyser test also appeared in 1967. From 1973 motorcyclists were compelled to wear crash helmets, a move which made many older motorcyclists give up altogether. The increase in rules and regulations seemed as unstoppable as the car itself.

PICNICS AND PITSTOPS

Hard boiled eggs, tomato or fish paste sandwiches, lemonade, a thermos flask of tea with milk carried separately in a screw-top jar ... Picnics are an intrinsic part of most people's childhood memories, and the rise of the car opened up a new world of possibilities for trips out involving picnicking. On Sunday afternoons families would pile into their cars to drive out to the coast or the countryside. At some point on the journey they would pull up in a picturesque spot – or sometimes not-so-picturesque, to judge by the number of people who opted to stop in a layby on a busy road. Then it would be time to get out the folding chairs, or simply spread a rug on the ground, open the picnic basket, and take tea in the fresh air.

Eating in public hardly seems a very British thing to do – even the word 'picnic' derives from the French

term, *pique nique*. Yet the British took picnics to their hearts, turning them into celebratory occasions. Posh wicker hampers prepared for special events – for an all-day sporting occasion, perhaps, such as the Henley regatta or the Eton and Harrow cricket match at Lords; or an elegant cultural gathering such as the Glyndebourne opera or a classical concert at Kenwood – might contain exotic fare: cold lobster followed by strawberries, perhaps, with a good bottle of chilled Chablis. For a grouse shoot on the moors, more robust food would be required – a large flask of soup, a raised pork pie, or ham on the bone with hot English mustard. A picnic lunch in the hay field could be simplicity itself – fresh bread with cheese and pickled onions, perhaps, washed down by home-made ginger beer. And all quite delicious flavoured with hunger and fresh air.

MEALS IN THE GREAT OUTDOORS

Top left: Camper vans, like this de luxe four-berth Bedford dormobile, brought the freedom of the road with almost home-from-home comforts. This young family enjoy all it has to offer as they share a meal on the grass in the 1960s.

Bottom left: Undisturbed by the passing traffic, a driver enjoys an after-picnic nap by the side of the Exeter by-pass in August 1960.

Below left: An elderly gentleman perches on his shooting stick to take sustenance at a race meeting in 1939.

Below: A primus stove was useful on a day out as well as on longer camping holidays, especially if the weather was not warm. Here, one young woman boils the kettle for tea, while another offers round food to a group of hungry boys.

Bottom right: Londoners have a picnic on a Chelsea bombsite on a sunny day in June 1942.

Top right: Visitors to the Chelsea Flower Show take their tea in the rain in the 1980s.

HOLIDAYS AND DAYS OUT

The day out was a Victorian innovation, made possible by the train. But with the coming of cars and coaches, the options expanded. So did the amount of time people had for travelling, thanks to the granting of paid holidays. In the 1970s cheap air travel opened fresh horizons abroad, but Britain's celebrated resorts declined as holiday-makers bought into the sun-and-sand package tour.

The Victorians had enjoyed four bank holidays a year since the Bank Holiday Act of 1871 (plus Christmas Day and Good Friday, which were considered common-law holidays). The early closing of shops and offices on a Saturday – 'early' often meaning 2.00 or even 3.00pm – also gave most people a little more leisure time than they had previously been accustomed to. It was not until well after the First World War that the notion of an annual holiday became a matter of common expectation. Only 1.5 million people were entitled to a paid holiday in 1925 – by 1937 that figure had risen to 4 million out of a workforce of around 18.5 million.

Everyone – government, employers, trade unions, representatives from the hotel and holiday industries – all agreed that workers should have the right to

SCHOOL'S OUT!
Joyful pupils at Hugh Myddelton Primary School, in Clerkenwell, London, run across the playground at the start of their summer holidays in July 1939. By the time school started again, Britain was at war.

'regular periods of freedom from daily toil, commonly described as periods of leisure', but could the country afford it? Cautiously it was decided that it probably could – or should – and in 1938 the Holidays with Pay Act was passed (although it would not be enacted until after the war), entitling more than 11 million white- and blue-collar workers to a week's holiday with pay, plus bank holidays as usual. 'The summer holiday, so recently the privilege of a minority, has become the prerogative of the millions,' rejoiced one of Blackpool's MPs.

The 'Wakes Week' tradition

But even though workers might be entitled to a holiday, not everyone could afford one. At a time when the weekly wage was around £3, a fortnight by the sea for two adults and two children cost around £10. Even so, most families did their best to find the money. 'Wakes Week' had started in the Lancashire cotton industry towards the end of the 19th century at a time when all mills, shops, post offices and schools closed for a week and everyone took a holiday – a few days at Blackpool if they could afford it, although some 'eccentrics' opted for quieter Morecambe, or even Rhyl on the North Wales coast.

The custom spread to the Yorkshire woollen mills, the Staffordshire potteries and other Midland towns, so that from mid July to mid September one town after another would close for a week – or even a fortnight by the 1930s – and its workers descend on Blackpool or another chosen resort. For that week the place

DRAGON-SLAYER
This poster of young 'George and the Dragon', an inflatable crocodile, was one of many produced by LNER to promote the East Coast line and holidays by rail. It was designed by Tom Purvis, a founder-member of the Society of Industrial Artists.

THE GOLDEN MILE
Children enjoy a donkey ride on Blackpool beach in 1955. The resort's landmark Tower rises up behind them.

would be known as Bradford or Oldham or Rochdale or wherever on sea. William Woodruff, the son of a Lancashire cotton weaver, recalls that his family saved all year to pay for the Wakes Week break, and when they packed their suitcases it was not with bathing suits, summer dresses and shorts but with provisions for the week. 'As the price of food in Blackpool was too high, we took bread, oats, a large tin of Tate & Lyle's syrup, margarine, cans of evaporated milk, fish, pineapple chunks, tea, sugar, eggs – each one marked with our name – a jar of jam, a jar of piccalilli relish, salt and sauce.' And when the Woodruffs arrived at their Blackpool boarding house, the whole family crammed into a single bedroom, preparing their food in an adjoining room shared with other families.

'If you do not like industrial democracy, you would not like Blackpool. I know people who would have to go into a nursing home after three hours of it …'

J.B. PRIESTLEY, FROM *ENGLISH JOURNEY*, 1934

Moving up the social ladder

Slightly higher up the social scale were people like the Stevens, described by R.C. Sheriff in his poignantly evocative novel *The Fortnight in September* published

BESIDE THE SEASIDE
Seaside holidays were supposed to offer sun, as this LNER poster promoting the 'beautiful sands' of Redcar promises, but all too often in Britain the reality was paddling about in the rain, like this child and her grandmother on Blackpool's sandy beach in 1945 (below).

in 1931. Mr Stevens was a clerk, the family lived in Dulwich, a respectable south London suburb, and each year the mother, father and a grown-up son and daughter went to stay in a boarding house in Bognor. It was always the same one: 'Seaview', owned by Mrs Huggett. They bought their food at the local shops, and Molly, the maid, cooked it for them. The Stevens were charged an extra shilling for use of the cruet, on top of the £3.10 shillings a week they paid for accommodation and service.

Bognor was a popular south coast resort in the 1930s, as were Brighton, Eastbourne, Worthing and Bournemouth. Of these Eastbourne was the most 'select', banning such vulgarities as slot machines on the pier, while Bournemouth was slowly unbending, claiming 'not to despise day trippers as it once did'. This social calibration continued all round the coast: Sidmouth in Devon made strenuous efforts to keep day trippers away, while the 1932 official guide to

nearby Torquay made it clear that the resort held little attraction for 'those whose idea of a holiday is compounded of Big Wheels, paper caps, donkeys … tin whistles and generally a remorseful harlequinade.' Frinton-on-Sea in Essex, where nannies often brought their employer's children while the parents holidayed abroad, was careful to distinguish itself from the nearby and more vulgar Clacton, just as Westgate tried to avoid contamination from its near neighbour Margate and its 'Dreamland' attractions. Lytham St Anne's emphasised the social if not geographic gulf that separated it from Blackpool, and Southsea kept remote from nearby Portsmouth by stressing that it was the resort 'for those who prefer their seaside stay to be spent among surroundings that are peaceful, quiet and refined, without being dull'. Bexhill, with its elegant leisure centre, the De La Warr Pavilion, considered itself to be a cut above nearby Hastings, while Scarborough even went so far as to advertise that the town had 'natural barriers' that served to keep out hoi polloi.

Simple pleasures of the seaside

Like the fictional Stevens family, middle-class vacationers tended to take the view that a good holiday consisted of staying in a hotel, if they could afford one, or a boarding-house if not. Taking a daily stroll along the promenade, they might be snapped by a seaside photographer, or could even encounter a 'Lobby Lud' figure, loitering courtesy of one of the tabloid newspapers engaged in a 'circulation war'; if they were lucky enough to identify him, they could win a reward of £5.

For many people, and if weather allowed, days were spent dozing in a hired deckchair on the promenade or sands, wearing a hat or a knotted handkerchief to keep the sun off. They could admire the municipal floral clock, perhaps, or hire another deckchair to sit and listen to a band playing on the bandstand, or stop at a café for an ice-cream or a 'knickerbocker glory' in a tall glass. Those with children might take a trip round the bay in a small fishing boat, help make sandcastles with a tin bucket and spade, collect shells and trawl the rock pools, dad's trousers rolled up above the knee. Mother would tuck up her skirt for a stately paddle in the shallows. A few might don a bathing costume for a quick 'dip in the briny',

> 'Oh, I do like to be beside the seaside! I do like to be beside the sea!'
>
> EVERGREEN MUSIC-HALL SONG, WRITTEN BY JOHN GLOVER-KIND IN 1907

AWAY FROM IT ALL
War workers enjoy a sunny day on a beach, surrounded by rugged cliffs, on holiday in Cornwall in September 1943. The west coast of the country receives more rain than the east, a meteorological fact that this Tom Purvis poster (right) highlights to promote holidays on the east coast.

EXTRA FOR THE CRUET?
A seaside landlady serves a meal to the guests staying at her boarding house in August 1952.

changing in a beach hut if they could rent one, or with embarrassing difficulty under a towel if not. Other resorts, Brighton, Rhyl and Llandudno among them, offered all this and some less staid pleasures too: fish and chips or cockles and winkles on the prom, donkey rides on the beach, peeking at 'What the Butler Saw' and playing the slot machines on the pier. The fun was harmless but could be messy, as Ivy Green recalled of a holiday in Margate in 1931. 'On "competition evening", we cheered the brave contestants trying to eat jelly with knitting needles … and watched gleefully [the men] who tried to catch eggs thrown from the Arcade roof without dropping them – what a state they ended up in!'

But it was Blackpool that really knew how to entertain the masses. It was cheap – 'twopence in Blackpool goes as far as a shilling in London [or] five shillings in Deauville, Le Touquet, Biarritz, Monte Carlo', noted the journalist Charles Graves. It was, he concluded 'a pleasure factory', made even more so by its rejuvenation in the 1930s, when the town claimed to attract 7 million visitors every year. It boasted what was reputed to be the 'largest Woolworths in the world' – many day trippers were said to spend their entire day there, never catching a glimpse of the sea. The refurbished 520-foot tall Blackpool Tower housed a glitzy ballroom, where Reginald Dixon played a 'Wonder Wurlitzer' nightly. There was an aquarium, a covered swimming pool, clairvoyants, a circus, a zoo, a tea bar,

PUNCH & JUDY – Seaside slapstick

'My idea of utter summer bliss', wrote a reader to a Sunday newspaper in 1981, 'is a deck-chair on a sun-baked beach with a choc ice watching Punch & Judy.' Why do the British on holiday find the spectacle of Mr Punch violently attacking his wife and throwing the baby out of the window so amusing? A crocodile seizing a string of sausages and a policemen arriving with his baton merely add to the mayhem – and the merriment. In its way, Punch & Judy is a small-scale version of the Christmas pantomime, with lots of deliberate misunderstandings and

audience participation. The glove puppet show had its origins in the Italian *commedia dell-arte* and the 'Lord of Misrule' probably made his first appearance in Britain in the 17th century. Samuel Pepys noted in his diary seeing a marionette show with a 'Punchinello' figure in Covent Garden in May 1662. By the 20th century, the red and white tents were a familiar fixture on British beaches, now aimed at entertaining children rather than adults. By the 1970s Punch had largely stopped beating his wife, but little else had changed.

restaurants and a seahorse tank in the basement. A miniature railway ran along the promenade, offering access to the ice rink for skating, ice hockey and other 'extravaganzas', a casino (designed by Joseph Emberton in the shape of a corkscrew) and acres of pleasure gardens.

Then there was the promenade that stretched from the north to the south pier. Known as the 'Golden Mile' – in fact just a small part of the 'seven miles of golden sands' proclaimed by the resort's brochure – it was lined by a raucous jumble of booths selling saucy postcards, candy floss and sticks of pink Blackpool rock. Visitors could have their photographs taken, record their voices, play guess my weight, ride the 'Big Dipper' or gaze on a series of titillating exhibits of dubious taste in the 'Educational Museum of Human Anatomy'. These included a 'headless girl', a collection of ashen-faced 'starving brides' – the reasons for them going without food were not made clear – and a crop of 'hermaphrodites', one of whom had a left half described as a 'wiry, strong, muscled and crop-headed man' with the right half being a 'pink and white, powdered and bejeweled woman'. For a time, there was even the defrocked vicar of Stiffkey in a barrel (until he was fatally mauled by a lion while appearing in a similar exhibit at Skegness).

JELLIED EEL ANYONE?
Holiday crowds in Southend-on-Sea in July 1956. The Essex resort was the seaside destination of choice for many of London's Eastenders.

FUN FOR ALL
The Butlin's holiday camp at Clacton in Essex opened in 1938 and closed its doors for the final time at the end of the summer season in 1983. This poster was produced to promote both the camp and train travel to it.

Holiday camps – organised fun

But even these possible delights and bizarre oddities could not fill an entire day. Holidaymakers, turfed out of their lodgings after breakfast and not allowed back by their landlady until time for high tea, would wander disconsolately around the town with nothing much that they could afford to do – and quite often in wet and chilly weather. Billy Butlin, a showman who had graduated from running a hoop-la stall to managing seaside amusement parks, hit on the bright idea of offering holidaymakers something more – a holiday camp that would keep them entertained whatever the weather.

Butlin's was not the first holiday camp in Britain: there had long been 'pioneer camps' that appealed to a spartan love of fresh air, and a few altruistic companies provided holiday villages for their workers. But Butlin's was the first to be so commercial, large and ambitious – soon it was also the most popular. The first opened at Skegness on Easter Saturday 1936, advertising 'Holidays with Pay [a reference to the legislation going through Parliament] – Holidays with Play'. It offered 'three meals a day and free entertainment from 35 shillings a week to £3, depending on the season'. The fun on offer was pretty relentless, with 'happy campers' exhorted and organised by Redcoats (helpers wearing red blazers) from the moment they were urged to 'roll out of bed' at 7.45am until lights out at 11.45pm. Meals were eaten communally and in between there were rambles, dances, fancy dress parades, beauty contests, knobbly-knees and bonny-baby competitions, swimming and fitness classes, quizzes and church services on Sundays. Butlin opened another camp at Clacton soon after, and by 1939 the two camps between them were catering for 100,000 visitors a year.

'It's the one place where the youngsters can be allowed to go off and enjoy themselves without any worries.'

BUTLINS ADVERTISEMENT, 1954

Holiday camps particularly suited families. The 'kiddies' were entertained by 'Uncle Mac' and dads did not have to keep putting their hands in their pockets to pay for rides, as everything was included in the holiday price – the entertainment was all free. For mums, there was the relief of not having to cook. There was also a baby monitoring service so parents could enjoy the evening entertainments.

Other companies offered much the same formula – there were Bluecoats at Pontin's, Greencoats at Warner's. To broaden their appeal and attract groups of teenagers, the camps laid on entertainments such as roller skating and lessons in the latest dance crazes. At a time when most young people lived at home until they married, a week with friends in a chalet was a rare opportunity to have fun away from the family. By the 1960s, as many as 3,000 young people would be staying at Butlin's each week throughout the summer without their parents.

The Colditz appearance of holiday camps was given something of a makeover in the 1970s: chalets could be self-catering if preferred, the endless megaphone cheeriness was toned down and campers were no longer required to 'wakey wakey' en masse – indeed, by that time the campers themselves had been rebranded as 'visitors'. But the tastes of holidaymakers had changed and by the late 1980s only three Butlin's remained. This was not to be the end of the holiday camp ethos entirely, however: by the end of the decade CentreParcs were beginning to spring up, largely patronised by the middle-class families, who realised how much more enjoyable a holiday (or weekend) could be if there was endless entertainment on tap for their offspring.

BABY ALARM
Butlin's evening babysitting service alerted parents if their children needed them. This notice board was in use at Skegness in 1955.

ALL GOOD SPORTS
Competitors line up for the start of a piggy-back
race at a Butlin's holiday camp in 1939.

Touring holidays

The enforced gaiety of holiday camps did not suit everyone. Others preferred to
see the countryside, a preference greatly facilitated by car ownership. 'Excursion
trains' and coaches encouraged people to 'Make the Journey Part of your Holiday'
and in 1936-7 carried some 82 million passengers. Such holidaymakers would put
up at 'B&Bs', often farmhouses where the farmer's wife supplemented the family
income by taking in paying guests or selling cream teas – or both.

Hikers, ramblers and cyclists often chose to stay at a youth hostel, which
catered for outdoor types. The first four hostels, based on the German model,
opened at Easter 1931 and by the end of the year there were three more. The
accommodation was basic but cheap at just a shilling a night; visitors could, at
extra cost, eat food provided at the hostel, or be a 'self-cooker'. There was strict
sexual segregation in the 'dorms', and no drinking, smoking or gambling; lights
out was at 10.30. But hostels were friendly places and held great appeal for those
seeking 'a tramping holiday away from the atmosphere of the big city'. Expansion
was rapid: by 1939 there were 280 hostels, many in Britain's most remote and
beautiful places, and the Youth Hostel Association had 88,417 members.

Towing one's home

In 1934 the London Motor Show had a caravan section for the first time.
Motor homes offered another way of 'getting away from it all' that was a bit more

GREAT NEWS!
AN ALL IN HOLIDAY
in
Bonnie Scotland
FROM
£15·15·0
CHILDREN UNDER 14
£10·10·0
ASK INSIDE FOR DETAILS

TARTAN TRIP
British Railways produced this cheerful
inducement to go north on a package trip to
see 'Bonnie Scotland' in 1955.

*'I'm happy when I'm hiking
Pack upon my back.
I'm happy when I'm hiking
Off the beaten track …'*

ENGLISH HIKING SONG, AUTHOR UNKNOWN

comfortable than pitching a tent in a field. Early caravans were little more than sheds on wheels, but the romantic notion of being a 'wandering gipsy' seized the British imagination in the interwar years. The Caravan Club of Great Britain had been started as early as 1907 and by the 1930s annual rallies were held, the first one at Minehead in 1932. It was quite an exclusive organisation: new members had to be proposed by an existing member, and at rallies full evening dress was expected at dances. But caravans themselves were becoming more affordable: the Rolls-Royce of caravans was the Winchester, but in 1934 Eccles of Birmingham, the largest manufacturer, introduced the National, a mass-produced four-berth caravan costing only £130.

There were few caravan parks before the Second World War, so caravans were parked by the road or in a farmer's field for the night. Or they might pitch up on a 'plotland' development, where redundant railway carriages, old coaches and buses provided a holiday – or even year-round accommodation, for those who could not afford anything else. Because of the housing shortage after the war, caravans were pressed into service as homes:

A BREAK IN THE COUNTRY
A family relax in the shade of an awning at a Camping and Caravanning Club gathering held at Hurley Farm, Berkshire, in 1934. Christine Fagg, a caravanning enthusiast for 50 years, explained why she loved it so much: 'Caravanning gave you the freedom to take to the road and just get up and go. If you didn't like one site, you could move on to another one; if you heard that the weather was bad you could go somewhere where the sun was out; if you liked a place you could stay a few days longer.'

HIKE for HEALTH
SOUTHERN RAILWAY
Go-as-you-please cheap tickets get you to the country quickest

in 1946 some 70 per cent of caravans in Britain were lived in all year round. The growth in car ownership in the 1950s made caravanning a practical way to have a family holiday – and cheap, too, since it was self-catering. Wherever they were, caravanners could buy local produce to cook on Calor gas in their tiny galley kitchen, or over a primus stove on a folding table in the open air. By the early 1960s there were 75,000 caravans and 10,000 motor caravans on Britain's roads. Most were now made of aluminum, the 11-foot-square 'Sprite' being the most popular. Farmers who had previously let a few caravans park in the corner of a field were developing caravan parks, with a standpipe for water, chemical toilets, perhaps even showers and a shop selling basic provisions. As Ray Gosling wrote: 'Where once sheep and cows grazed, now farmers milk caravans.'

Some caravan parks, particularly the 200-odd sites registered with the Caravan Club, were small and sited in areas of natural beauty. Others were large and regimented, often on clifftops overlooking the sea – perhaps in Devon, or north Wales, or the northeast coast. Many were for static caravans that never moved and were used, or let out, as holiday homes. These could be luxuriously appointed, if always compact inside and requiring preternatural neatness from their occupants. What no British holiday could guarantee was good weather, and many a wet and windy week was spent playing cards and gazing at a cold grey sea.

Change afoot

The advent of cheap package holidays abroad in the 1970s – coupled with growing affluence and a dislike of regimentation – changed holiday patterns and sounded the death knell for the Fifties-style family holiday camps. Package holidays made it 'safe' for the British to venture to foreign parts, mainly to Spain. The camps did their best to fight back. Pontin's went 'Pontinental', opening clubs in Sardinia, Torremolinos and Majorca, while Butlin's pushed the boat, or rather plane, out as far as the Bahamas. It was a long way from the 1930s, when a holiday in the Mediterranean sun had been the prerogative of the well-off, who could board the *Train Bleu* at Victoria station bound for the Cote d'Azur and a grand hotel in Nice, Cannes or Monte Carlo, or a villa at Antibes or Cap Ferrat. St Tropez was still an unspoilt fishing village to be 'discovered'. Or they might take a cruise down the Rhine or the Nile, venture on a 'Grand Tour' of Italy, or try winter sports in the Swiss Alps or Austrian Tyrol. After the war, currency restrictions and the expense of travel kept 'abroad' the province of the better-off. Those who could afford to might 'hop' over to Le Touquet with their car in a small freight plane operating from Lydd airport in Kent, or set out with the family on a cross-Channel car ferry. The young might hitchhike through France, usually with a small Union Jack sewn on their rucksack.

THE ROAD LESS TRAVELLED
A couple on a motoring tour of Northern Ireland in 1955 take a break in County Down for photographs and to check the map.

In 1950 Horizon Holidays, run by a journalist, Vladimir Raitz, hired an old US Dakota and flew passengers to Corsica on the first 'package holiday'. The all-in price of £32.10s included travel, accommodation and food, and this at a time when a scheduled BEA return flight to Nice cost £70. It was pioneering stuff: few Continental resorts had purpose-built airports, and many of the planes were unpressurised wartime models which had to fly at low altitudes – the levels of turbulence they encountered made sick bags an essential flying accompaniment. But sun and cheap wine proved irresistible attractions, and soon established airlines were offering 'package holidays' too. The most ambitious of the 'no frills' flights were those of Freddie Laker, whose Laker Airways, founded in 1966, was soon the largest independent airline in the world. In 1977 a seat on Laker's 'Skytrain' from London to New York cost just £59.

By then holidays to Europe were commonplace. To attract foreign currency, General Franco had encouraged mass tourism to Spain, transforming tiny fishing villages on the Costa Brava into a strip of hotels. At the height of the 1959 season Benidorm was attracting more than 30,000 visitors – and the British loved it. Irene Jackson recalled her first package holiday in the 1960s: 'The Spanish girls had bare legs; at home we wouldn't have dreamed of going without stockings, suspenders and stilletoes. Not for long! Off came the stockings. We bought flip flops and shortened our skirts … Alcohol was very cheap and we'd drink Cuba libres until midnight. At home girls weren't even supposed to go into pubs.' Even Blackpool hoteliers were packing their suitcases at the end of the season and jetting off for a fortnight in Torremolinos or Alicante – sunshine guaranteed – while the seaside resorts back home puzzled over how to compete.

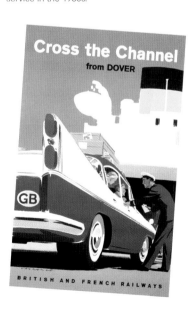

Cross the Channel
from DOVER

GB

BRITISH AND FRENCH RAILWAYS

DAY TRIPPERS

'The stately homes of England
How beautiful they stand ...' wrote
Felicia Hemans in 1827. But by the
mid 20th century many were felled by
a decline in land values and a rise in
death duties, and owners were
having to devise schemes to survive.
Longleat in Wiltshire, home of the
Marquess of Bath, is an Elizabethan
mansion set in 900 acres of parkland
landscaped by Capability Brown. In
1949 the 6th Marquess opened his
house to the public, the first 'stately
home' owner to do so. In 1966 he
added a 'safari park', said to be the
first outside Africa. Visitors drove
through the grounds – windows

ONLY HERE FOR THE DAY

Above: An RAC van stationed at Longleat in
Wiltshire gets a visit from a giraffe in May 1969.
Left: Mods ride their scooters along Hastings
seafront on August Bank Holiday Monday, 1964.
Bottom left: A sailor helps a young woman ring the
bell at a funfair on Hampstead Heath on a Bank
Holiday in 1943.
Below: A coach-load of children leaving London for
a day-trip to the Sussex coast in 1946.
Below right: Children enjoying a sunny day at the
Lido in Brockwell Park, south London, in 1947.
Far right: An open air whist drive at Broomfield Park,
Palmer's Green, Southgate, in July 1949.

shut – as big beasts padded around their cars. The Duke of Bedford followed suit, opening Woburn Abbey in 1955 and also later adding a safari park. Chatsworth, the Derbyshire seat of the Duke of Devonshire, opened in 1952 and has been consistently voted Britain's favourite 'stately home' ever since.

Other impecunious owners of great houses turned their properties over to the National Trust in lieu of death duties. Sissinghurst, renowned for its gardens, was given to the Trust in 1967 and like many NT properties added a shop and a tearoom to cater for the steady stream of visitors who arrived by coach or car. Other 'trippers' headed for Stonehenge or one of the many castles, long barrows and sites of archaeological and historical interest under the guardianship of English Heritage, as it has been known since 1983.

There were also museums, art galleries, exhibitions, fairs – and zoos. London Zoo and its outpost at Whipsnade, and others such as Belle Vue in Manchester, had been hugely popular from before the

Second World War. Madam Tussauds, with its waxwork kings and queens, historic tableaux and Chamber of Horrors, was another great draw.

Long before the popularity of 'weekend breaks', 'days out' were a treat. Lilian Olsen looks back fondly on days out in the 1930s: 'Our holidays were very few … but our outings were a planned exodus every Sunday … We piled the old bone-shakers of prams not only with kids but also with pots and pans, kettle, teapot, a bit of coal, potatoes, mince and onions.' The procession managed to board the train – 'prams in the guard's van, kids travelled free, adults a penny-halfpenny' – bound for Cramond on the Firth of Forth. From the train they walked a mile and a half to the beach: 'There was plenty of sand but a lot of boulders from which we harvested whelks and mussels.' They filled their saucepans from a public tap, made a fire from driftwood and 'cooked our mince and "tattie" dinner'. For tea they cooked

the mussels and whelks, winkling the latter from their shells with a pin. 'There was plenty of entertainment … singsongs, spoons, accordions, a penny whistle; a good gig we had while the mothers gossiped or knitted socks. We teenagers would weigh up the talent, and boldly chat them up. Dads played pitch and toss, and if we were lucky enough to be chosen as a look out [for the police as gambling was illegal], we earned ourselves a penny.' At the end of the day, 'Scruffy, happy and dirty, sand mixing with our runny noses, we retraced our steps … We were weary, sore but happy, and shouted a cheerful "Cheerio. See you next Sunday" as we parted to go our own ways.'

A work or pub outing to the seaside or the races was a festive occasion for many in lieu of a holiday. At the end of a grand day out, with a crate of beer packed on the coach, people sang 'In the Quartermaster's Store', or 'Daisy, Daisy, Give Me Your Answer, Do', all the way home.

HAVING A GOOD TIME

In the days before television, we flocked to the cinemas to be transported by the glamour and drama up on the screen. Despite such competition, the theatre held its own, while dance-halls throbbed to the beat of big bands. As the century progressed, a meal out at one of the growing choice of restaurants started to rival a night out at the pub.

Life was drab for many people in the 1930s. As one observer who lived through the decade recalled, 'to see the glamorous lives film stars seemed to lead was attractive … We all copied their clothes and hair styles and had film stars as pin-ups on our walls'. Or as the poet Louis MacNeice put it: 'The cinema gives the poor their Jacob's ladder / For Cinderellas to climb'.

Dream palace or fleapit, the cinema was the most popular destination for an evening's entertainment. More than 900 million tickets were sold in 1934: by 1939 the figure had risen to almost a billion – an average of almost 20 million people going to the cinema each week. It was one of the few public places where a respectable woman could go, on her own or with a friend, to enjoy a night out.

'SO, I SAID, MY DEAR'
Elderly ladies chat over tea and cake at the Ladies' Carlton Club in London in 1947. The club was established after the First World War as a meeting-place for Conservative women; it closed in 1958.

ALTOGETHER NOW
Customers enjoying a sing-song in a pub in Birmingham in 1961, their throats lubricated by pints of best bitter – or perhaps by the world's most famous stout, which even in the Thirties was claiming to be 'good for you', as in this advertisement which appeared in *The Illustrated London News* in 1932.

GUINNESS IS GOOD FOR YOU

Nothing takes its place

The unemployed would try to find the sixpence needed to buy a ticket and sit in the warm. Young women sent off to the film studios for autographed photographs of their favourite stars, whose clothes, hair and make-up they copied as best they could. 'In 1935 girls of all classes wear "Garbo"coats and wave their hair à la Norma Shearer or Lilian Harvey', one survey proclaimed.

Courting couples welcomed the dark of the cinema, while families enjoyed a weekly – or even twice weekly – night out, watching mostly American films such as Alexander Korda's *The Private Lives of Henry VIII*, or *Mutiny on the Bounty*, or Walt Disney's first full-length animated cartoon *Snow White and the Seven Dwarfs* which was seen by 28 million people when first released in 1937. British films were not much rated at the time – 'piffle' was a popular description. An initiative designed to stop US movies from flooding the British market badly misfired,

FILM FUN
Children in Cardiff queue for a free cinema show during the Christmas holidays in 1937. By 1939 there were around 700 Saturday morning children's cinema clubs in Britain, showing mainly cartoons and Westerns.

resulting in a stream of low-budget, generally unwatchable releases. But if the 1930s were far from the golden age of British film-making, they certainly were of cinema building.

Dream palaces

Although two-thirds of the nation's picture houses were small and outdated, known as 'fleapits' and smelling of Jeyes Fluid, the other third were newly built Odeons, Gaumonts and ABCs. And these truly were 'dream palaces', fantasies of escape and romance. The Trocadero at the Elephant and Castle, with its fabulous 'Renaissance' interior, opened in 1930 and was typical of this new breed of cinema. Comedy writer Denis Norden was a regular there as a child and recalled it 'providing three hours of luxury and comfort for the price of a sandwich'.

The Odeons were futurist constructions with soaring tiled exteriors, 'fin' towers and neon lights, while others were baroque whimsies taking inspiration from ancient Egyptian motifs and exotic architecture such as the palaces of Indian maharajahs, the Moorish Alhambra or Italianate villas. 'Egypto-Commercial-Renaissance-cum-Georgian', John Betjeman called them, but the patrons loved the plush seats, the soft lights, the cigarette-girls, the uniformed page boys, the big screen. Many had cafés attached and some had an organ — an elaborate, brightly-lit affair that

> *'You really were getting the only touch of glamour you could in those days.'*
>
> TV WRITER AND PRESENTER DENIS NORDEN WRITING OF THE 1930S

would rise up out of the floor in the interval. Soon most towns of any size had a cinema and many had more than one: with a population of 250,000, Bolton in Lancashire supported 29 cinemas by 1939, one seating nearly 2,000 and another 1,200. The Glasgow Odeon could accommodate 3,000 at a sitting.

The pictures in war-time and beyond

As soon as war was declared in September 1939, the government closed the cinemas. George Bernard Shaw was moved to write to *The Times* protesting this folly: 'What agent of Hitler has suggested we should all cower in darkness and terror for the duration?' Within days, most were opened again to provide much-needed morale-boosting entertainment. When an air raid was under way, patrons were given the opportunity of leaving the cinema to seek shelter. Most opted to stay in their seats enjoying the distraction provided by films such as Charlie Chaplin's *The Great Dictator*, MGM's blockbuster *Gone With the Wind*, starring Clark Gable and Vivien Leigh, Powell and Pressburger's *The Life and Death of Colonel Blimp*, Laurence Olivier's *Henry V*, or Noël Coward's paean to the Navy in wartime, *In Which We Serve*, which broke box-office records. It was common for people to go to the cinema two, three or even four times a week. Alan Bennett was one of those taking full advantage of the cinema riches on offer in 1940s Britain: 'Within a mile of so of where we lived in Armley in Leeds there were at least half a dozen cinemas … we always called them "the pictures", seldom "the cinema" and never "the movies" … To this day I don't find it easy to say "movies".'

After the war, film-going retained its popularity; the number of tickets sold in the mid 1950s equated to every person in the country going to the cinema 27 times a year. The 'flicks' still offered family entertainment but were also the destination of choice for a first date. And quality British films now joined Hollywood fare. A typical show included a Pathé newsreel and a secondary 'B' movie in addition to the main picture itself, starring James Dean perhaps, or Robert Mitchum, John Wayne, Marlon Brando, Audrey Hepburn or the bewitching Marilyn Monroe. Ealing comedies such as *The Lavender Hill Mob*, *The Ladykillers* and *Kind Hearts and Coronets* were popular, as were musicals such as *Singin' in the Rain* and *Oklahoma* and Westerns like *High Noon*. Classic dramas included the cult film *Rebel Without a Cause* and

PUTTING ON THE STYLE
By the mid 1950s, when these two young Teddy Boys were photographed outside the ABC at Elephant and Castle, south London, the glory days of cinema were coming to an end.

Alfred Hitchcock's *Vertigo* and *North by Northwest*. There was also a taste for realism in films such as *Blackboard Jungle* and *Room at the Top*, as well as for vehicles for 'MM' such as *The Seven Year Itch* and *Gentlemen Prefer Blondes*.

But change was coming. A night out was increasingly being replaced by a night in watching the 'tele'. The cinema fought back as best it could with 3D, Cinemascope and stereophonic sound. Another response to the growing appeal of the small screen was to make wide-screen epics with a cast of thousands, such as *Ben Hur* and *The Ten Commandments*. Another was to be more risqué than TV allowed: a long line of 'Carry On' films, the first of them *Carry On Sergeant*, would make household names of Sid James, Kenneth Williams, Barbara Windsor and many more British actors.

In an attempt to pull in the younger viewers who had flocked to see Bill Haley in *Rock Around the Clock* and Elvis Presley in *Jailhouse Rock* or *Love Me Tender*, British film-makers started to serve up a diet of films, usually mediocre ones, starring the latest pop singers such as Tommy Steele, Cliff Richard and Adam Faith. Cinema struck a richer vein with the glamour and thrills of James Bond. The first Bond film, *Dr No*, was released in 1962, followed by *From Russia With Love* and *Goldfinger*, all starring Sean Connery, the definitive on-screen 007. There were other spectacular cinema successes – such as David Lean's biopic *Lawrence of Arabia*, with Peter O'Toole in the title role, or his film adaptation of Pasternak's *Dr Zhivago* starring Julie Christie and Omar Sharif, and the all-time musical winner *The Sound of Music* showcasing the singing talent of Julie Andrews.

But cinema's heyday was over. As audiences waned, many of the cavernous picture palaces were turned into bingo halls. Bingo's popularity peaked in 1974, by which time row on row of mainly middle-aged and elderly women were 'eyes down', playing 'housey housey' for modest prizes. Yet for those of an intellectual persuasion, the cinema was revivified in the 1960s when the products of the French 'New Wave' reached the 'arthouse' cinemas, such as the Academy in Oxford Street, the Everyman in Hampstead and various 'bijou' venues up and down the country. The works of experimental directors like François Truffaut and Jean-Luc Godard alternated with the sombre films of Swedish director Ingmar Bergman.

SINGING THE BLUES
Excited female fans at a Tommy Steele concert in February,1957. Steele, who was born Thomas Hicks in Bermondsey, south London, in 1936, was Britain's first home-grown teen idol and rock'n'roll star. Like so many others, he would be eclipsed by The Beatles. The poster below is promoting the Fab Four's 1964 Christmas show at the Hammersmith Odeon, which also featured Freddie & The Dreamers, The Yardbirds, Elkie Brooks and Jimmy Savile.

A night at the theatre

Experimental theatre in the 1930s was largely confined to the politically committed. Those seeking a good night out were more likely to book seats for a Terence Rattigan play such as *French Without Tears*, which opened in 1934 and ran for more than a thousand performances, or one of Noël Coward's witty and sophisticated pieces such as *Private Lives* or *Design for Living*, or perhaps his ambitious historical extravaganza *Cavalcade*, written for C.B. Cochran. This was also the era of Ivor Novello's spectacular musicals, such as *Glamorous Nights* and *The Dancing Years*. For those wanting something more substantial, Shakespeare was a huge draw in the 1930s, as his plays continued to be throughout the Second

COMMANDING ATTENTION
Left: The crowd stands for the Queen Mother as she takes her seat for a Royal Gala Performance of Mozart's *Marriage of Figaro* at Covent Garden Opera House in May 1963.

DANCE CRAZE
Teenagers jitterbugging at the Rodney Youth Centre in Liverpool in March 1949.

World War – including screen versions. In 1930 there were three versions of *Hamlet* running concurrently in London; the 26-year-old John Gielgud was in the title role at the Old Vic, giving a performance that the actress Sybil Thorndike described as 'the Hamlet of my dreams'. Gielgud subsequently tackled the characters of Romeo, Richard II, Oberon, Hotspur, Antony, Macbeth and King Lear, the last when he was all of 27. The newly rebuilt Memorial Theatre at Stratford-upon-Avon also attracted a stellar cast of actors eager for roles in the bard's works, including Tyrone Guthrie, Laurence Olivier, Charles Laughton, Flora Robson, Sybil Thorndike and Peggy Ashcroft, acclaimed for her Juliet in 1934.

Any complacency to be found in the British theatre was blown away with the arrival of the 'angry young men', represented most powerfully by the writer John Osborne, whose *Look Back in Anger* opened at the Royal Court in 1956. 'Putrid' and 'juvenile', thought some critics, but Kenneth Tynan hailed Osborne as the saviour of the moribund British stage. Theatre-going would never be quite the same comfortable, complacent, chocolate-consuming treat again. Subsequent plays by Arnold Wesker, Samuel Beckett, Harold Pinter and others bought anger and complexity – and sometimes downright confusion – to the stage.

Dressed to impress

It was all but routine in the 1930s, and not unusual even into the 1970s, to wear full evening dress to the theatre or the opera. Night clubs too glowed with satin dresses and dark dinner suits as couples sipped cocktails – White Ladies (two parts gin, one part Cointreau, one part lemon juice with a twist of peel) and dry Martinis were thought particularly smart. Then they might venture onto a pocket-handkerchief-sized dance floor to gyrate sedately to the music of a small band, with perhaps a crooner like Al Bowlly adding to the atmosphere. The Embassy in Old Bond Street was popular, as was the Café de Paris in Leicester Square until it was bombed during the Blitz, killing 'Snakehips' Johnson who was performing at the time. Other night-spots included the Kit Kat and Number 43, whose owner, Mrs Kate Meyrick, kept getting arrested for serving drinks out of hours.

Evening dress would have looked out of place in a jazz club such as Ronnie Scott's, frequented by 'beatniks' wearing black polo-necks and jeans. Jazz fans of the 1950s had the choice between 'trad jazz', played by the likes of trumpeter Ken Colyer and clarinetists Cy Laurie and Acker Bilk, or more bluesy jazz associated with Chris Barber (with his singer Ottilie Patterson), George Melly (who sang with Mick Mulligan's Magnolia Jazz Band) and trumpeters Humphrey Lyttelton and John Chiltern, or modern jazz from saxophonist John Dankworth with his singer (soon to be wife) Cleo Laine, among others. Dancing was not what you did to jazz, but there were other opportunities. Annabel's opened in Berkeley

Square in 1963 as a smart nightclub where the wealthy could drink and dance after the gaming tables closed. Instead of live music it had a 'discotheque' with a disc jockey, or DJ, playing records. Similar, cheaper venues soon sprang up in imitation, luring the young to dance under glitter globes, then strobe lighting.

Dancing the night away

Discos took over from the dance halls that had been so popular in the 1930s, like the Hammersmith Palais, for example, which had opened in 1919 and was nightly packed to capacity with 7,000 dancers. The 'dance boom' of the Thirties spread across the country, bringing what had been largely an upper-class pastime to the masses. The Streatham Locarno was opened by Mecca in 1931, and by the end of the decade few towns were without somewhere for a light-footed night out – Glasgow was reckoned to have more dance halls per head of population than anywhere else in Britain. At a conservative estimate, 2 million people went dancing each week in 1938. By the end of the war the figure had risen to 3 million, and that was not even counting those 'cutting a rug' in town and village halls. The perennially popular waltz, the foxtrot – a First World War import – and the Charleston, which arrived in London in 1925, were joined by simpler fare devised for the new halls, such as the Palais Glide and the St Bernard's Waltz, as well as by novelty routines such as the Chestnut Tree, which even King George VI was seen to join in, and the Lambeth Walk.

'Everyone can do it, they don't have to learn it. There's never been an English dance success like it.'

MECCA DANCE INSTRUCTOR ADELE ENGLISH, ON THE LAMBETH WALK

PLAYGIRLS AT PLAYBOY
Croupiers dressed as 'bunnies', complete with 'ears' and a bob tail, serve tables in the main casino at London's Playboy Club in 1966. Victor Lowndes had opened this first British outpost of Hugh Hefner's empire the previous year.

Some took advantage of increasing car ownership to drive out to dance and dine in one of the 'road houses' that sprung up on the arterial roads out of London and other cities. Places such as the Ace of Spades on the Kingston by-pass brought a touch of US-style glamour to the suburbs, with a resident dance band, entertainers, cocktail bar and a swimming-pool for summer dips.

'No Jiving' notices were pinned up in some dance halls in the 1950s, but it was a Canute-like gesture. Jiving, be-bopping, then in the Sixties twisting were the future of dance for the young. 'Dance floor crowded, conversation not urgently necessary, often limited to a narrow range of remarks on the size of the crowd and the quality of the band' – a typical Saturday night 'hop' in the 1950s, this one in a South Wales Miners' Institute. As for the older generation, they continued to enjoy ballroom dancing – in the 1950s still second only to the cinema in popularity.

Going out to eat

Unless the venue was a high-class hotel or an expensive French restaurant, eating out was a pretty downbeat experience in Britain. The crime writer P.D. James recalls a typical meal in the late 1950s as consisting of Brown Windsor or oxtail soup, followed by lamb cutlets and tinned peas, rounded off with apple pie. Then Italian cooking burst on the scene. Britain had a large Italian population and friendly, family-run restaurants, with red check tablecloths, candles in chianti bottles, a mural of Sorrento on the walls, brought a taste of Italy by serving up spaghetti – but not on toast. This culinary delight was followed by pizza (the first Pizza Express opened in 1965) and elegant, white-tiled trattorias were soon opening up, offering a range of rustic dishes and favourite desserts such as zabaglioni and tiramisu, rounded off with a tiny strong espresso coffee.

On the high street, traditional eel and pie shops were being nudged out by new arrivals. By 1969 there were almost 500 Wimpy bars serving burgers in buns. David Acheson, Wimpey's managing director, believed they attracted 'people who weren't used to eating out. They liked seeing the food being cooked ... And having the menu in the window made it clear what it was going to cost.'

CULINARY OUTPOST
Chinese restaurants were still a rarity in Britain when this photograph of the Canton in London's Docklands, offering English and Chinese dishes, was taken in 1955. There was a large Chinese population in the neighbourhood. By 1970 there would be some 4,000 Chinese restaurants and takeaways as they opened up in practically every town in the country.

Immigrant cultures also brought new eating experiences. As washing machines made Chinese laundries redundant, their enterprising owners turned to opening restaurants and takeaways. Sweet and sour pork and chop suey soon became as familiar on the culinary map as haddock or cod and chips. So too did curry and tandoori. In 1950 there were just six Indian restaurants in Britain, catering mainly to the growing Indian and Bangladeshi communities; by 1970 there were 2,000 serving up chicken tikka massalas and fiery vindaloos. For many, it became almost a tradition to go for a curry to round off a Friday night spent in the pub.

The pub itself was changing so rapidly that in 1971 beer-lovers formed a new organisation to safeguard the traditional British pint – CAMRA, the Campaign for Real Ale. Dominic Sandbrook believes that beer-drinkers today owe them a debt: 'They were much mocked ... but it is only a slight exaggeration to say that whenever a modern Briton ... has a pint of proper beer after work, he ought to mutter a quiet thank you to those real-life Wombles of the early Seventies.'

PLAYING THE GAME

Taking part in – or at least watching – sport almost defines being British. The thwack of leather on willow in summer, the mud of the soccer or rugby match in winter, have forged an indelible mark on the national character. In the mid years of the 20th century being a 'good sport' was what people aimed to be and 'amateurism' – playing the game for the love of it, rather than winning – was prized.

Sport in Britain attracted more spectators than in any other country in the world. By the 1930s almost all children played some sport at school – the higher up the social scale they were, the more sport they were likely to play. Sport was considered to be good, healthy exercise and a better way of using time than 'sitting with your nose in a book'; it inculcated moral values of fairness, teaching players to be competitive yet at the same time 'good losers'. It was also socially calibrated. Cricket had its 'gentlemen' and its 'players', who for many years had separate entrances at Lords cricket ground even when playing for the same team; it was accepted that a 'player' would never captain the team.

SUNNY SPORT
The July meeting at Goodwood in Sussex, a four-day feast of horse-racing, was blessed with fine weather in 1947, the year that this photograph was taken. For spectators without hats a large clean handkerchief, knotted in the corners, served to keep off the sun.

Public-school boys played rugby, state pupils football; privileged girls played lacrosse, leaving hockey for the plebs. Besides the obvious draws of football, rugby, cricket, horse racing and greyhound racing, there were the TT (Tourist Trophy) trials on the Isle of Man, not forgetting gliding, fencing, boxing, pigeon racing, shooting, darts, baseball and table tennis. Speedway racing, introduced from Australia in 1928, proved immensely popular.

Having a flutter

If you neither played sport nor watched it, there was nothing to stop you betting on it. The middle classes had long enjoyed a 'flutter' on the horses. Off-course cash betting was illegal, but this was how most working-class punters placed their threepenny or sixpenny bets, through an army of unlicensed bookies operating in pubs or on street corners, with a look-out posted to spot the 'narks'.

THE BEAUTIFUL GAME
Billy Liddell, playing for Liverpool, takes a corner during a match against Burnley in April 1950.

Horse racing, once the sport of kings, had a loyal mass following in the 1930s. *Sporting Life* enjoyed a circulation of around 100,000; in London alone, half a million copies of the evening papers were sold daily, giving the results of the latest sporting fixtures. Most newspapers employed racing tipsters, and some suspected that the limited circulation of the *Daily Worker* would slip even further were it to drop its spot-on tipster column. In 1929 a 'Tote' (Horserace Totalisator Board) system had been introduced to control on-course betting – and to provide the government with a modest income. It made £4 million by 1936, but most punters still preferred to place their bets in the old, unregulated way.

The greyhound phenomenon

If the government was concerned about excessive betting on the horses, it was even more worried about greyhound racing. Men had always bet on greyhounds, whippets and lurchers, but when greyhound racing came into stadiums it was feared that the working classes might follow their supposedly feckless inclinations and bet the rent money on the dogs. In fact, greyhound racing was something of a 1930s phenomenon, the most popular spectator sport in Britain after football, and the huge crowds were by no means exclusively working class.

While women tended to flock to the cinema, men went to the dogs, although some women enjoyed greyhound racing too – one Glasgow track even provided a crèche. By 1932 there were 50 tracks around the country and more were being built. The White City stadium, built to house the 1908 Olympics, was converted into a venue for greyhound racing. Even Wembley, though let out for Cup Finals, was mainly used as a dog track. Most venues were full to capacity five or six nights a week, when the eyes of the crowd were glued to the spectacle of sleek and rapid

FOOTBALL EXCURSION
A Southern Railway poster advertising an excursion to Huddersfield to watch an FA Cup semi-final between Millwall and Sunderland in 1937. Both sets of supporters had to travel to the neutral venue.

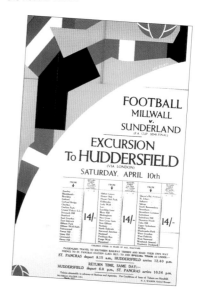

MUD FEST

Eton boys take a rest after competing in the school's annual cross-country run in February 1935. The first steeplechase was run in 1846.

FOLLOWING THE DOGS
Right: Spectators at the greyhound
track in Brighton in August 1939.

FOLLOWING THE DOGS
Right: Spectators at the greyhound
track in Brighton in August 1939.

dogs chasing an electric hare, first introduced in 1926 at Belle Vue in Manchester and advertised as offering 'All the skills and thrills of [hare] coursing without the cruelty'. Between races, there was just enough time to place a bet on the next one.

Family-friendly gambling

The most widespread form of 'armchair betting' was the football pools. By the 1930s it was reckoned that at least a quarter of the adult population of Britain did the pools every week. Dad would lick a pencil stub while the whole family conferred as to whether Blackburn Rovers were likely to beat Leyton Orient or lose, or would it be a draw? Then it was a matter of filling in the predictions with crosses in columns of tiny squares, posting off the form accompanied by a postal order, then gathering round the radio on Saturday afternoon – in later decades the TV – to listen anxiously to the results, ticking off the draws and hoping that this would be the week for a big win. Large amounts of money were involved. As John Hilton, a social affairs commentator, wrote in 1936: 'Fifty million pounds a season have been spent on the pools. You'll never suppress the pools … they will flourish because they are supplying a need. They are satisfying … the craving for the redistribution of wealth by irrational windfalls.'

As well as betting on football, a lot of men played it, as did women – there were more than 150 women's teams by the 1920s. Anyone who could find a patch of waste ground and a ball could rustle up an impromptu game. Factories often fielded football teams, and those who did not play might well end up watching. Hundreds of thousands did so each week at football grounds up and down the land, following the fortunes of their teams. Then, as now, soccer was a focus for local loyalties – fierce rivalries divided supporters of neighbouring teams.

It usually cost a shilling to get into the match, more if you wanted to sit under cover. Even so, the crowds were overwhelming. In 1932, when Scotland played England at Wembley, 52 special trains bought 23,000 spectators south. Some 93,000 watched Manchester City win the FA Cup, beating Portsmouth in the final at Wembley in 1932. Even Second Division games packed in the fans: in 1938, almost 50,000 turned out to watch Fulham play local rivals Millwall.

KEEPING FIT

REGIMES FOR HEALTH AND FITNESS
Left: Women war workers in Herne Hill in 1944
take a break from making life-saving devices for the
RAF to join in a spot of PT in the garden.
Top left: Sue Tulloh and her husband Bruce, a
5,000-metre runner, training together in their local
park in 1962, while their baby son, Clive, looks on
from his pram.
Above: Female office workers skipping on the roof
of Adelaide House in central London during a
lunch-hour slimming class in 1932.
Top right: Girls at Woodthorpe Elementary School
in Sheffield have a swimming lesson in their newly
completed pool in 1938.
Centre right: Working with weights in a gym at the
Covent Garden Sports centre in 1978.
Bottom right: A yoga evening class in a school
gymnasium in 1977.

**'Health can be as contagious as
disease'**, proclaimed one of the
doctors who founded the Pioneer
Health Centre, which opened in
Peckham, South London, in 1935.
The nation's 'will to fitness' had been
given a salutary boost when it was
found just how unfit many of the
volunteers were in the First World
War. That message was reinforced in
1936 when the Berlin Olympics
demonstrated the superior physical
condition of German youth over
British at a time when it was
becoming clear that Germany might
be a threat to peace. In response, the
government launched a 'National
Fitness Campaign' and provided the
funds to pay for playing fields, sports
facilities and swimming pools – or, as
the new outdoor 'urban beaches'
preferred to be called, 'lidos'.

Individuals and private
organisations did their bit to promote
the fitness cause, too. Originally
founded in 1906, the Health and
Strength League had 100,000
members by 1939. The Sunlight
League, established by Dr Caleb
Williams, an advocate of the health

benefits of heliotheraphy (exposure to sunlight), opened a number of clubs, some of them for 'naturists'. Mollie Bagehot Stack started the Health and Beauty League in 1930, teaching dance, calisthenics, remedial massage, slimming and rhythmical exercise to music, intended to make fitness available to all. By 1939 the League had 170,000 members in Britain and the Dominions, and put on displays of synchronised leg waving in Hyde Park and the Albert Hall.

Eileen Fowler was the fitness guru of the post-war years. Born in Hertfordshire in 1907, she initially trained and worked as an actress. In the 1930s, amid growing concerns about the level of obesity and lack of physical activity among the public, she made it her mission to counteract the trend by setting up exercise classes. By the mid 1950s she had an early-morning radio show, the first fitness programme on the BBC; before long it had half a million listeners. She later transferred to television, where she ran a 'dance disco' programme into the 1970s. In 1956 she launched the Keep-Fit Association and soon there were classes all across the nation urging women to try the 'rolling-pin swing' to keep them trim. By the 1970s, such village-hall activities had given way before the classes in aerobics, whose participants were urged to 'go for the burn', yoga and tai chi.

HOWZAT

Above: An archetypal local cricket match. This one is being played in the village of Blagdon in Somerset, but it could have been seen in almost any village in England and in any decade since the Thirties.

Below: West Indian supporters celebrate their team's victory over England at the Oval in the fifth and final Test of the series in 1963.

Like football, cricket could be played almost anywhere with an improvised bat and wicket. But as a spectator sport, the game was both rule-bound and class-bound. One sports journalist expressed the opinion that the 'football public is a cloth-capped, fried fish lot', while cricketing fans were 'altogether on a higher plane.' Yet the appeal of the game lay deep within the nation's soul. 'Cricket is far more than a game', wrote the music and sports commentator Neville Cardus, 'it comehow holds a mirror up to the English nation.' The cry of 'Howzat?' echoing round a village green, as men ran about in white flannels and women waited in the tea tent with sandwiches and cake, epitomised a country Saturday afternoon. Cricketers such as Jack Hobbs, Len Hutton and Dennis Compton (also an able footballer) were folk heroes. In 1939 the cotton town of Bolton had 155 cricket teams and 127 football teams playing at weekends. County cricket matches were usually played over three days midweek, so it was inconvenient for working people to attend, but when the Ashes were in dispute in a Test series against Australia, the crowds equalled those at football matches.

Unwanted interruptions

During the Second World War, the calendar of sporting events was necessarily interrupted. The Home Guard used the lawn tennis courts at Wimbledon for drill, football crowds were restricted in size to reduce the risk of mass casualties in case of air-raids, cricket pitches and golf courses were dug up for allotments, and the Kennington Oval was scheduled for use as a PoW camp. Many sporting fixtures were moved from the evening to the afternoon to avoid black-out restrictions, and there was pressure from more puritanical politicians to ban greyhound racing altogether in case workers were tempted to bunk off to attend day-time meetings, causing war production to suffer.

The return of peace released a huge, pent-up urge to restore the country's traditional sporting culture. Crowds at matches were larger than ever in the immediate post-war years: more than 41 million tickets were sold for Football League games in the 1948-9 season. In 1950 the average gate for Hull City home games was 32,000 and even small clubs like Grimsby could count on a crowd of around 15,000 every week.

Cricket experienced a golden age. The 1947 season became known as the 'Brylcreem Summer' after Dennis Compton, the face of the hair product's advertising, broke all batting records. And when the legendary Australian cricketer Donald Bradman came to Britain in 1948, his arrival created as much of a stir as the Olympic Games in London that year.

BATTLE OF THE BLUES – The Oxford and Cambridge University boat race

The annual Oxford and Cambridge boat race has been contested over a four-mile course on the River Thames, from Putney to Mortlake, since 1829, taking place at the end of March or beginning of April. Perhaps surprisingly, this battle of the oars between a privileged few gripped the capital every year. Each side of the river would be jammed solid with spectators – the crowds above are standing on barges, balconies and roof terraces as well as the tow path by Hammersmith Bridge to watch the race in 1934 – while street vendors sold ribbons and celluloid dolls dressed in appropriate colours (dark blue for Oxford, light blue for Cambridge). The BBC soon added the boat race to its outside radio broadcasts and practically the whole nation tuned in. A 1939 survey found that more than two thirds of those on a representative listeners' panel had heard the coverage of the event, compared to around half for boxing and football, and one third for the tennis at Wimbledon. From 1931 the commentary was provided by John Snagge, who made a classic commentator's gaffe in 1949 when he helpfully told his listeners, 'I can't see who's in the lead, but it's either Oxford or Cambridge'.

ENGLISH FOOTBALL'S FINEST HOUR
Bobby Charlton raises the Jules Rimet trophy in the air following England's 4-2 victory over West Germany in the World Cup Final at Wembley Stadium on 30 July, 1966. He is flanked by team captain Bobby Moore and Alan Ball; goalkeeper Gordon Banks is in the yellow jersey. The next day, the *Sunday Telegraph* reporter tried to convey the feelings of the crowd at Wembley: 'When 93,000 people are in the grip of that peculiar emotion somewhere between laughter and tears, there can be no mistaking the message. England had won and the crowd loved them.'

Spectating habits changed as television entered people's homes and the increase in car ownership allowed many families to go further afield for entertainment at weekends. Then, too, there was the erosion of the culture of 'separate spheres' for men and women: an increasing number of women started attending sporting events, but many men found they had other things than football to do on a Saturday afternoon. By the 1960s attendance at matches had fallen by a third; by 1980 the figure for the Football League season was down to around 20 million.

It was much the same story with cricket. Despite the pulling power of stars such as Peter May, Freddie Trueman and Geoffrey Boycott, attendance figures fell to a third of what they had been in the immediate post-war years. For a time, the sport came to be regarded as rather slow and old-fashioned, until rejuvenated by one-day games. Football lost its 'cloth-cap' image and attracted a wide spectrum of supporters, including the philosopher A.J. Ayer, a lifelong supporter of Tottenham Hotspur. The appeal of football was helped, at least in England, by the national team's triumph in the 1966 World Cup. The following year Celtic brought home the European Cup, the first of many victories for British teams in Europe.

Small screen stars

Television had a transforming effect on sport long before the advent of satellite broadcasting. In the 1950s Stanley Matthews, the star footballer of his day, earned around £20 a week, a wage comparable to that of a skilled industrial worker. By the 1970s, Manchester United's George Best was a national celebrity, the 'fifth Beatle' in many people's eyes, earning – and squandering – thousands. Watching television at home, or communally in the pub, enormously extended the audience for matches. *Match of the Day*, first broadcast on Saturday evenings in

1964, was soon an unmissable fixture for lads of all ages, with some 12 million viewers tuning in by the end of the decade. The Labour MP and cabinet minister Anthony Crosland was said never to miss it (his boss Harold Wilson was known to be a keen Huddersfield Town fan, while the Conservative leader Edward Heath had supported Arsenal since boyhood). In pre-television days, to help people follow a match on radio, the *Radio Times* printed a diagram of a football pitch divided into eight numbered squares: as one commentator described the action, another would interject with the number of the square where it was happening so listeners 'could get a mental photograph of what is taking place'. This was supposedly the source of the saying 'back to square one'.

By the 1970s a new class of sports commentator had emerged – Brian Moore and John Motson for football, John Arlott and Brian Johnson for cricket, David Coleman for athletics, Harry Carpenter for boxing, Henry Longhurst for golf, Dan Maskell for tennis, Eddie ('up and under') Waring for rugby league and Bill McLaren, the 'voice of rugby', for rugby union. Television succeeded in making some lesser-known sports compelling – snooker, bowls and darts all found loyal audiences, partly because of the advent of colour. Show jumping was first televised in 1950, and the Open Golf Championship arrived on screen at about the same time; in fact, the popularity of golf was growing as the game lost something of its exclusive aura. Television likewise brought new audiences for boxing, all-in wrestling, weight lifting, diving, skiing, athletics and even the Highland Games. One beneficiary was motor racing – Stirling Moss was the pin-up figure here, while his sister Pat became a champion rally driver.

OUR 'ENRY
Heavyweight boxer Henry Cooper warming up with a punch bag in 1966. Cooper, who fought Muhammad Ali (Cassius Clay) twice, remains the only British boxer to have won the Lonsdale Belt three times.

Broadening the field

The historian of sport Richard Holt has noted that the 1960s and 70s were a golden age for British sportswomen – not so much in traditional women's sports, such as netball and hockey, but in sports played by both sexes. In cycling Beryl Burton was a world champion, Mary Peters won Olympic gold in athletics, Rachel Heyhoe-Flint gained a high profile as captain of the England Women's Cricket team and Princess Anne became the only British royal to take part in the Olympic games, winning a silver medal in 1976. Britain might not have had a Wimbledon men's champion since Fred Perry pulled off his hat trick of titles in 1934, 1935 and 1936, but female players took the women's single title three times in the two decades – Angela Barrett in 1961, Ann Jones in 1969 and, most famously, Virginia Wade in 1977, the Queen's Silver Jubilee year.

The range of participatory sports was widening. Fishing remained immensely popular, with 2 million anglers, mainly men and teenage boys, spending their weekends on the banks of lakes, rivers and canals; over 100,000 of them regularly bought *Angling Times*. Now, though, men – and women – were taking up new activities, from jogging and wind-surfing to hang gliding and rock climbing. New sports were also imported from abroad, like baseball, softball and basketball. But large numbers of amateur teams, made up of friends and colleagues, would continue to turn out each weekend to play football or cricket in front of small but appreciative local audiences. And televised sport would become big business, as satellite channels overturned the broadcasting monopoly of the BBC and ITV.

THE LURE OF SPEED
A poster produced for London Midland & Scottish Railway (LMS) promoting a motor-sport event at Crystal Palace involving both cars and motorcycles in 1938.

THE AUSTERITY OLYMPICS

The entire budget for the Olympic games held in London in the summer of 1948 was just £760,000. At the time Britain was still in the grip of austerity, deeply in debt to the USA, with many items of food still rationed and a 'make do and mend' culture permeating the land. The opening ceremony of the games was performed by George VI in naval uniform, watched by a crowd of 85,000. The Olympic torch was carried by John Mark, a Cambridge blue who was also a doctor working in the NHS, which was just three weeks old at the time. A total of 4,000 athletes from 59 countries took part – neither Germany nor Japan were invited. India and Pakistan, newly independent from Britain and partitioned into two countries, sent separate teams.

Sponsors of the games included the manufacturers of Craven 'A'

'LET THE GAMES COMMENCE'
Top left: The Olympic torch is carried into Wembley Stadium by athlete John Mark during the opening ceremony on 29 July.
Bottom left: Army bands playing at the opening ceremony before the procession of national teams got under way. The weather was so hot that several people fainted.
Below: A workman sorts direction signs ready to be put up at the Olympic Centre in Richmond Park, Surrey, where 1,400 competitors stayed.
Right: The star of the games was Fanny Blankers-Koen, a 30-year-old Dutch mother of two, who won four track gold medals. Here she is on the winner's podium after the women's 200m final; Britain's Audrey Williamson won silver. Audrey Patterson, who took bronze for the USA, was the first African-American woman to win an Olympic medal.
Bottom far right: Temporary shops for the competitors set up in Richmond Park.
Top right: Tebbs Lloyd-Johnson from Leicestershire, who finished third in the 50km walk, became at the age of 48 the oldest ever winner of a track and field medal.

cigarettes, Coca-Cola, Guinness and Brylcreem. A gents outfitter donated a pair of 'Y-front' underpants to each male competitor, but generally all the athletes either had to buy their own kit or make it themselves. One Czech long-distance runner had to train in his army boots.

Accommodation was a major headache for the organisers. There was an acute housing shortage and thousands of civilians and demobbed service personnel were living in temporary homes. RAF camps, schools and colleges were fitted up as hostels for the competitors, and the Ministry of Supply provided beds, mattresses and crockery. Athletic competitions were staged on what was usually a greyhound track at Wembley stadium; a velodrome in south London hosted the cycling events; and the ice rink at the Empire Pool was melted for use as the swimming venue. Competitors were ferried to the stadium on old London buses or caught the tube.

The weather was the hottest London had known for 50 years, and the crowds turned out in force to cheer their support. The games actually made a profit of £29,000. 'You have really done your best' was the Swedish team's verdict.

Chapter Five | BRITAIN CELEBRATES

PARTIES FOR THE NATION

The empire, coronations and jubilees of kings and queens, the end of the war – such events formed the basis of Britain's landmark national celebrations in the 20th century. The festivities tended to take a familiar form: bunting in the streets, grand processions, cheering crowds and street parties where young and old had fun together.

At the turn of the century the Boer War dealt a blow to the country's confidence and prestige. In 1904, three years after the death of Queen Victoria (also Empress of India), Reginald Brabazon, 7th Earl of Meath, proposed an annual holiday to 'draw the attention of the next generation to imperial questions' – and thus bind the bonds of empire tighter. Empire Day won official recognition in 1916, by which time it was already being celebrated each year by many thousands of schoolchildren on 24 May – Victoria's birthday.

Ninety thousand people attended a thanksgiving service at Wembley Stadium as part of the Empire Exhibition in 1925, and throughout the 1930s Empire Day remained a red-letter occasion in the school calendar – aptly so, since classroom maps of the world were extensively shaded red (or pink) to show the overseas territories under Britain's imperial control. There would be a half-day holiday from school, with parades featuring children dressed in 'costumes of other nations', marching round the playground waving Union Jacks and singing *Rule Britannia* and *Land of Hope and Glory* at the top of their voices. Then would come the best bit – a tea featuring lemonade and sticky iced buns.

Such patriotism did not go entirely uncontested. In 1930 the mayor of Harrogate persuaded the local council to delete *Rule Britannia* and *Hearts of Oak* from the town's celebrations on the grounds that they were 'boastful war songs'. That same year, the communist *Daily Worker* called on its readers to form 'chalking parties' to scrawl anti-Empire slogans on walls to 'turn the flag-waving demonstration into a demonstration against the Empire and the slavery it stands for'. The campaign failed to muster much support, for Empire Day was popular even within socialist ranks. Louis Heren, a journalist with *The Times*, recalled that as a child he knew the words of the *Red Flag* and the

Internationale off by heart, but every year he 'rather enjoyed' Empire Day at school. In 1941 George VI became patron of the Empire Day movement, and on his death in 1952 his daughter Elizabeth II succeeded to the role, with Winston Churchill as vice-patron. Enthusiasm for it lingered on into the 1950s – boosted by Empire programmes at children's Saturday-morning cinema clubs. The poet laureate John Masefield wrote a poem to mark the event in 1955, but by then its popularity was on the wane. As the 'winds of change' began to blow through Britain's imperial possessions, the celebrations petered out and the BBC no longer mentioned the event in its news bulletins.

Silver jubilee for the 'Sailor King'

If the empire no longer stirred the hearts of the nation, the same could not be said for royal jubilees. There was great rejoicing for the silver jubilee of George V in May 1935 and a thanksgiving ceremony was held in St Paul's Cathedral. The King noted that he had never seen so many people in the streets before: 'Their enthusiasm was indeed most touching.' Bunting was strung across streets and from lampposts, flags fluttered from chimneys and porches, banners in the East End of London proclaimed 'Lousy But Loyal'. Buckingham Palace, the Houses of Parliament and St Paul's were lit by floodlights, and a chimpanzee at London Zoo was named 'Jubilee' in the King's honour. Children were given the day off from school, and shops and street traders did a brisk trade in royal knick-knacks. A special postage stamp was issued, a particularly fine one, since stamp collecting was one of George's passions. Less than a year later George V was dead.

'Nearly every door has a Union Jack ... When people who live in such abject poverty make such a show over royalty, one is brought to realise the superhuman task facing the communists.'

FRANK FORSTER, AN UNEMPLOYED LABOURER, WRITING ABOUT GEORGE V'S SILVER JUBILEE IN MAY 1935

The King is gone – long live the King

George's eldest son and heir – Edward Albert Christian George Andrew Patrick David, so called to emphasise the unity of the four kingdoms (he was always known simply as David at home) – briefly succeeded his father as Edward VIII. The coronation was set for May 1937, but in a radio broadcast to the nation on 11 December, 1936, Edward announced that he felt he had no option but to abdicate since a morganatic marriage with 'the woman I love' – Wallis Simpson, an American who had been married twice before – had been ruled out. He slipped out of Britain bound for France later that same night.

GOD BLESS GOOD KING GEORGE
Flags and bunting decorate a street in Stepney in London's East End to mark the silver jubilee of George V in 1935.

Thanks to a conspiracy of silence between the government and the press, the British people had known nothing of the constitutional crisis until the previous week. They were deeply shocked – 'the country is in a turmoil' wrote Madge Martin, an Oxford vicar's wife, on 6 December, 1936. Not only was Edward popular with the public, but there was doubt about the fitness of his younger brother Bertie to take his place on the throne. Indeed, Bertie was dubious about it himself: an undistinguished career in the navy and an incapacitating stammer did not augur well. But there was no choice: he would be crowned as George VI, and coronation mugs were duly emblazoned thus in place of 'Edward VIII'.

The coronation took place as originally scheduled in Westminster Abbey on 12 May, 1937. Edward, now Duke of Windsor, sat in exile in France, listening to what should have been his own ceremony broadcast on the radio. In a letter to her son after the abdication, Edward's mother Queen Mary left no doubt of her disapproval: 'It seems inconceivable to those who made such a sacrifice during the [First World] war that you, as their King, refused lesser sacrifice.'

Designed to blot out the stain of the abdication, the coronation was a splendid affair. Although a bus strike made transport difficult, special trains were laid on to get people to London — many arrived the night before to be sure of a good view. The streets were a tangle of patriotic bunting and window boxes all along the processional route sprouted red, white and blue flowers. Inside the Abbey was a glittering sea of diamond tiaras, satin dresses, fur stoles and bemedalled uniforms. The King acquitted himself well, though at times, he confessed, he had little clue of what was going on. Coached by an Australian speech therapist, he managed the necessary responses in a clear voice.

LOYAL SUBJECTS
Cheerful despite the rain, spectators watch the rehearsal for George VI's coronation in 1937 from a car roof. The label of the 'non-alcoholic champagne' below was specially prepared to mark the event.

A family affair – from father to daughter

A family was on the throne again. George VI and his wife Elizabeth would prove popular, the public's affection being cemented in the war years when the royal couple remained in London (although they repaired to Windsor Castle at night), regularly visiting neighbourhoods that had been blitzed. But George was not to achieve a silver jubilee as his father had — and as his daughter would do after him. He died in his sleep at Sandringham, aged 57, on 6 February, 1952. His body lay in state in Westminster Hall for four days as 300,000 people filed silently past to pay their last respects. The funeral took place in St George's Chapel at Windsor. The wreath from the Prime Minister, Winston Churchill, bore the simple legend 'For Valour'.

CROWNS AND CORONETS
Above: The residents of Swinbrook Street in Kensington, London, staged their own version of Elizabeth II's coronation in May 1953. Here, the local vicar places the crown on the head of the 14-year-old 'Queen' chosen to occupy the throne for the day.
Below: Peers of the realm, hurrying through the rain on their way to the real coronation ceremony on 2 June, lift up their robes to keep them off the wet ground.

'She is only a child', Churchill had said. But when she was crowned on 2 June, 1953, Elizabeth II was 27 years old, married to Prince Philip of Greece (who took the title Duke of Edinburgh) and already a mother of two children. The coronation took place 16 months after her accession. By 23 May, 1953, still more than a week before the event, more than a million visitors had arrived in London to admire the decorations. By 31 May, those who had not managed to secure a seat in the stands erected along the processional route had taken a pitch on the pavement to make sure of seeing the royal cavalcade go by. By nightfall on 1 June, half a million people were standing in the rain, waiting. The next morning the weather was still cold and wet, but there were warm cheers when news was received that the New Zealander Edmund Hillary and the Nepalese Tenzing Norgay, two members of a British expedition led by Sir John Hunt, had reached the summit of Mount Everest in the Himalayas, the world's highest peak. 'All this – and Everest too!' proclaimed the *Daily Express*.

Wearing a silk robe designed by Norman Hartnell, embroidered with emblems of the British Isles – a rose for England, a leek for Wales, a thistle for Scotland and a shamrock for Ireland – and of the Commonwealth, the Queen was crowned with St Edward's crown in front of 8,000 guests in Westminster Abbey, who rose to sing *Vivat! Regina!* as she entered and *God Save the Queen* as she left. Some 3 million people lined the streets and more than

20 million watched the coverage on television, with commentary by Richard Dimbleby. 'We all thought before it started that we could never sit solemnly throughout the whole procession and ceremony,' said one young Irish woman who watched it on television in London, 'but once it started we couldn't tear ourselves away from the set'. Apart from the new monarch, the star of the occasion was reckoned to be Queen Salote of Tonga, who rode bare-headed in an open carriage, smiling and waving through the rain.

In towns and villages all over the country, street parties were held for the children, with flags and bunting and a tea of iced cakes, jellies, ice cream and lemonade. Usually there was a present for each child to take home, and in some places a bonfire and fireworks to round off a memorable day. For the adults, the events were reminiscent of another unforgettable day some eight years before: Victory in Europe Day – 8 May, 1945 – known as VE Day.

'I'd say it cheers the country up. It's been a bit depressing since the war … A thing like this seems to work up the co-operation a bit.'

A 58-YEAR-OLD FULHAM WOMAN ON THE CORONATION OF ELIZABETH II

VE Day comes at last

There had been little time for planning, so people just drifted onto the streets, delighted that victory over Hitler was their's at last. Strangers linked arms, or clutched waists to dance the conga, wearing paper hats and waving Union Jacks. A red bus drove round Piccadilly Circus with the triumphant message 'Hitler Missed This Bus' chalked on its side. At three o'clock people stood quietly to listen to Winston Churchill addressing the House of Commons, his words relayed through loudspeakers to the crowds on the streets. 'The evil-doers lie prostrate before us,' he intoned. 'We may allow ourselves a brief period of rejoicing … Long live the cause of freedom.' The crowds cheered and a mighty roar of *God Save the King* echoed round Whitehall, followed by *For He's a Jolly Good Fellow*.

Later that afternoon the wartime leader appeared in public, first with his ministers, then on the balcony of Buckingham Palace with the royal family. That night there were celebratory bonfires, on some of which Hitler was burned in effigy. For many, it was an occasion to give thanks and pray. Sir Raymond Street, chairman of the Cotton Board, wrote of the service he attended: 'In that tiny country church we found the note we really had been seeking. Manchester businessmen and Cheshire farm labourers joined in a crowded service. References were made to those whose lives had gone in the purchase of victory.'

But as Churchill had made clear, the war was not yet over. It dragged on cruelly until August 1945, when the Japanese finally surrendered. The news was greeted with huge relief: at last the fighting was truly finished. The *Merthyr Express* reported:

OH HAPPY DAY
Joyful civilians walking arm-in-arm with servicemen as they celebrate the arrival of peace in Europe on 8 May, 1945, after almost six years of war. The conflict with Japan would not be over until August.

'All over South Wales colliery hooters, train whistles, detonators, fireworks and rattlers were used to swell the great chorus of celebration … Many bonfires were lit in the streets and on the mountain-sides, and shone out as symbols of peace and freedom.' The announcement came at midnight on 14 August, when most people were in bed, but many came out into the streets still in their dressing-gowns to cheer, dance and sing *God Save the King*.

As luck would have it, the following day – 15 August, 1945, now known as VJ Day – was also the day that had been chosen for that year's state opening of Parliament. The gold coach was not brought out for the event, and it drizzled for most of the morning as the King read out the policies – key among them nationalisation of the coal mines and the Bank of England – of Clement Attlee's Labour government, elected the previous month. By the afternoon the weather had cleared up and there were crowds in the streets, but even so, the festive air seemed strained and VJ Day lacked the animated high spirits of VE Day. 'I simply didn't know what to do', said one Glasgow woman, 'and the newspaper had no suggestions.' In war-ravaged Plymouth people made for the Hoe to dance and light a huge bonfire, recalling one lit as a beacon in the days of Francis Drake.

END-OF-WAR WORK
Factory workers in the East End of London photographed for the *Daily Herald* in April 1945, as they prepare flags and banners in anticipation of the victory in Europe. The flags depict the Allied leaders – Winston Churchill, US President Franklin D Roosevelt and Soviet leader Joseph Stalin. Roosevelt did not live to see the peace: he died on 12 April, less than a month before the German surrender.

They knew what to do in Liverpool, where the celebrations lasted for ten days; a highlight was an illuminated tram that drove along the promenade with a band on the open top deck. Such sights, not seen since George VI's coronation, made people feel that everything would soon be back to normal. But it wouldn't: despite 'the glorious knowledge that the killing is over' and the return of some prisoners of war from Japan, Britain would remain a dreary, austere place for years to come.

Saying farewell to Churchill

On 24 January, 1965, the man who had led Britain through the war, Winston Churchill, succumbed to a final stroke. He was 90 years old, his death was not unexpected, but the nation plunged deep into mourning. Flags were lowered to half mast, the lights were dimmed in Piccadilly Circus, and Prime Minister Harold Wilson announced that Churchill was to have a full state funeral in St Paul's Cathedral, the first commoner to do so since Gladstone in 1898.

Churchill's body lay in state in Westminster Hall for three days as more than 320,000 people filed past to pay their last respects. On Saturday, 30 January,

LAST FAREWELL
Right: The funeral cortège of Sir Winston Churchill, war leader and former Prime Minister, passes slowly down Whitehall on its way to St Paul's Cathedral on 30 January, 1965.

1965, the streets of the capital were lined with hundreds of thousands of people for whom Churchill had been an inspiring leader in Britain's darkest hours. A younger generation born in peacetime joined in too, watching in silence as the coffin was brought on a gun carriage from Westminster to St Paul's Cathedral, the ultimate symbol of Britain's wartime defiance. The escort was made up of men who had flown Spitfires and Hurricanes during the Battle of Britain in the summer of 1940, while RAF planes wheeled in a fly-past overhead. Eight guardsmen carried the coffin into

'This was an act of mourning for an imperial past [that] marked the final act of Britain's greatness.'

AN OBSERVER JOURNALIST, ON CHURCHILL'S FUNERAL

(continued on page 227)

THE FESTIVAL OF BRITAIN

Britain needed a 'pat on the back' after the long years of war and austerity, so in May 1951, a hundred years after the Great Exhibition of 1851, the Festival of Britain opened on a reclaimed bomb site near Waterloo station in London. The aim of the event, as the guidebook explained, was so that 'this country and the world could pause to review Britain's contribution to world civilisation in the arts of peace'.

That might sound rather worthy and dull, but the Festival was a triumph. In the words of the playwright Michael Frayn, it was 'a rainbow … a brilliant sign riding in the tail of the storm and promising fair weather'. The Festival's many attractions included pleasure gardens in Battersea Park complete with a fun fair, a travelling exhibition that toured the Midlands and the North, a Festival ship on the Thames and an 'Exhibition of Industrial Power' in Glasgow. But it was London's South

WELCOME TO THE FESTIVAL
Above: Looking out over the Thames from the 'Ships and Sea Pavilion' was a sculpture called 'The Islanders' by Siegfried Charoux, an Austrian artist who had settled in Britain.
Left: A promotion team with the travelling exhibition that took the festival around the country.

Bank that was the centrepiece of festivities. At the Dome of Discovery – then the largest in the world – an escalator took visitors up to a thrilling display of the solar system. There was the amazing Skylon, a futuristic 300-foot steel-and-aluminium structure suspended in the air with no visible means of support – 'just like Britain', as one wag joked. There was also the Royal Festival Hall, the only building that would remain when the rest of the festival structures were demolished.

Top designers, architects and artists were employed to create a series of

pavilions that narrated the story of 'the land and people of Britain'. There were piazzas, sculpture everywhere and open-air dancing . Everything was bright and colourful, in striking contrast to the drabness of post-war Britain.

George VI opened the Festival and Gracie Fields closed it five months later. In between, it had attracted 8.5 million visitors. Almost everyone agreed that it really had been, as the organisers intended, 'a tonic for the nation'.

ART AND FUN FOR ALL
The Festival served as a showcase for the best of British design.
Bottom left: Artist Victor Pasmore at work on the abstract designs for one of the restaurants.
Below: Edward Mills' multi-coloured 'Cocktail Cherry' screen, erected at the edge of the site to distract the eyes of visitors from neighbouring bomb sites.
Bottom right: The iconic steel Skylon, designed by the architects Moya and Powell.
Top right: A fairground ride in Battersea Park, where fun was the name of the game rather than education.

the cathedral, while ahead walked 12 pallbearers, comrades from the war years, among them three former prime ministers. The ceremony lasted half an hour, then the coffin was laid once more on the gun carriage and taken to Tower Bridge pier, where crowds pressed forward to see it transferred to a barge which would carry it upriver to Waterloo station. Bagpipes sounded a last lament, then as the coffin was lowered onto the barge, the strains of *Rule Britannia* burst forth. Dockers in the huge cranes that still lined the wharfs opposite lowered the jibs so they bowed 'like dinosaurs … in eerie civilian salute,' wrote one onlooker.

A wartime locomotive, the *Winston Churchill*, bore the coffin to Oxfordshire for burial. Churchill's final resting place was to be at Bladon parish church, close to his birthplace, Blenheim Palace. Dense crowds gathered at every station along the route and people lined the embankments as the train passed, bowing their heads in homage. Others stopped work in the fields or stood to attention in their gardens. An estimated 30 million people watched the funeral live on television. 'In the whole history of our land,' said Richard Dimbleby, the BBC commentator, 'there has not been a state funreal or an occasion which has touched the hearts of people quite as much as this one is doing today.'

Monarchy undimmed

Yet if Britain was no longer an imperial power, merely the junior partner in a 'special relationship' with the USA, there was still a monarch on the throne – a fact celebrated in style in June 1977. At the start of her reign Elizabeth II had symbolised youth and optimism, her accession hailed as the dawn of a new Elizabethan Age. Then, in the 1960s, for some she came to epitomise the stuffy Establishment. But ten years later the wheel had turned again and by 1977 she was being praised for standing as a beacon of uprightness and decency in an age of 'fluctuating fashions and considerable moral disintegration'. A poll that year found that just one in ten Britons thought the country would be better off without a monarchy, and the book *Majesty*, published for the jubilee, sold 200,000 copies.

HAPPY AND GLORIOUS
Smiling children waving flags on 7 June, 1977, the day of Elizabeth II's silver jubilee celebration holiday. The Queen undertook a royal tour of Britain and the Commonwealth to mark the occasion, enabling millions to see her in person. Street parties were held all over the country.

A public holiday was declared for the main jubilee celebrations on 7 June. The Queen and Prince Philip drove in an open carriage to St Paul's Cathedral for a service of thanksgiving. More than a million people lined the streets, and many of them craned to shake a royal hand as the royal couple walked from the cathedral to the Guildhall. Some 6,000 street parties were held in London alone, and around 2,000 in cities across the country. The *Daily Mirror* spoke of 'The People's Joy' as children in paper hats filled up on cakes and chocolate biscuits. Adults partied late under fluttering bunting and flags in a remarkable reprise of earlier royal occasions. It was a truly British celebration. Even the striking dustmen in the London borough of Hammersmith got the jubilee spirit, agreeing to clear up the detritus for just £10, rather than the £40 they originally demanded.

LIFE'S SPECIAL OCCASIONS

For most people, the biggest special occasion that will come their way in life is likely to be their wedding. For much of the 20th century, these were celebrated with a deep regard for tradition, but as the century wore on the marking of life's great rites of passage began to reflect the increasing diversity of our society.

'I met my husband-to-be, Dennis Whiteing, in a very conventional way, namely at a meeting of the local debating society', wrote Eileen Lawrence recalling middle-class life in Wallington, Surrey, in the 1930s. After a year's 'friendship' Miss Lawrence, who worked as an assistant editor in a local firm of publishers, and Mr Whiteing, who had a job in the local authority rating office, 'became engaged officially'. No doubt the engagement would have been announced in the local paper, and possibly the *Daily Telegraph* or *The Times* as well: 'Mr and Mrs Henry Lawrence are pleased to announce the engagement of their daughter, Eileen, to Mr Dennis Whiteing, son of ...'.

During the next 18 months the young couple 'saved very hard in order to fill the traditional "bottom drawer" and to buy the necessary furnishing and

SOCIETY WEDDING
Bridesmaids gather at the reception following the wedding of 18-year-old Raine McCorquodale – 'Deb of the Year' in 1947 – to Gerald Legge in July 1948. Raine was the daughter of the novelist Barbara Cartland and future stepmother of Princess Diana.

fittings for our future home. It was out of the question to start married life on secondhand bits and pieces …'. Eileen went on to keep a detailed account of her wedding, which like so many others followed the accepted pattern of such occasions, while also managing to feel uniquely special.

To honour and obey

The couple were married at Holy Trinity Church in Wallington on 'a day of brilliant sunshine and blue skies' in early April 1939. The bride wore 'a white lace dress, complete with a three-foot train made by a dressmaker in the Arcade, Sutton, for around £3, with hand-finished satin bindings and minute satin buttons, specially made'. The groom wore morning dress with white gloves; his best man and ushers were similarly attired. The service was 'fully choral, bells and all, and my four bridesmaids … looked delightful in their pale green organdie full-skirted dresses with lilies-of-the-valley in their hair'. The bride's bouquet of 'white roses, lilies and gardenias' had a 'glorious scent'.

The parents and guests were 'dressed to the hilt, dripping with picture hats, fur wraps and jewels'. Seventy four attended the reception in a local restaurant. 'The price for the upstairs hall was to be £1, and this included a sit down meal with waitress service, plus all crockery, glasses and flowers on the tables'. On the menu were 'sandwiches (various fillings), sausage rolls, lobster patties, fruit jellies or fruit salad, meringues and cream, coffee, lemonade, orangeade. Fancy cakes and tea to be served at the close. And all this for the unbelievable sum of three shillings per head!' The 'radiant couple' then changed out of their wedding finery into their 'going away' clothes and in a shower of confetti and cries of good will, left by train from East Croydon for a honeymoon in Eastbourne.

High society

Weddings were big business, whether relatively modest suburban affairs or showy society ones. The wedding of Jane McNeill, a fashion model for Norman Hartnell, and the Earl of Dalkeith was hailed as the 'union of two of Scotland's

BEST WISHES
Wedding guests shower newly-weds Mary Clegg and David Dallyn with confetti after their wedding in the church of St Mary, Our Lady of Pity, in Petworth, Sussex, in 1954.

'I still remember how thrilled and proud I was to be wearing my diamond ring for the first time.'

EILEEN LAWRENCE, ON BECOMING ENGAGED IN THE 1930s

(continued on page 232)

WARTIME WEDDINGS

When war was declared in September 1939 many courting couples, unsure about what the future might hold, decided to get married before conscription, evacuation or air raids could separate them. The number of weddings shot up from 409,000 in 1938 to 534,000 in 1940, as call-up reached its peak. There was a practical edge to this romantic haste. Wives of servicemen were entitled to a marriage allowance – and to a widow's pension if their husband was killed on duty.

Wartime weddings could be fraught affairs. Would the groom and the best man get leave in time? Would transport difficulties delay the guests? On a 48-hour leave pass, the couple would need to obtain a special licence and the honeymoon would have to be postponed indefinitely.

Wedding dresses were hard to come by and no extra clothing coupons were allowed. Some brides, lucky enough to get hold of some parachute silk, would run up their own; others borrowed a dress, either from a married friend or through a WVS (Women's Voluntary

Service) scheme to loan out donated dresses. Some brides married in smart day clothes and tried to do something fancy with a hat. Men often wore military uniform for the ceremony and women serving in the WRNS, the WAAF or the ATS increasingly did so too.

On the day, the couple would hope that the ceremony was not interrupted by an air raid warning. Although extra coupons could be obtained from the Food Office for a wedding party (as for a funeral), the amounts allowed were small, and in July 1940 the making or selling of iced cakes was forbidden. Bakers got round the problem by hiring out cardboard covers to slip over whatever cake was on offer, so that in the wedding photos the couple could be seen apparently cutting what looked like a traditional tiered cake.

WARTIME WEDDING DAYS

Top left: In the Berkshire village of Solhamstead, the bride looks on as her matron-of-honour puts the finishing touches to a young bridesmaid's outfit before the wedding party sets off for church in April 1942. The husband-to-be is a soldier, granted special leave in order to get married.

Bottom left: In November 1940 a bride steps out of her bomb-damaged home onto a carpet runner specially laid for her up the garden path. Her father stands ready to escort her to church.

Below: Jean, a Scottish bride, leaves the army base chapel with her American GI husband, Sergeant Nathan, following a service conducted by the US chaplain in September 1944. Earlier that day they had been married by a British registrar.

Bottom right: A young navy stoker gazes happily on his beaming bride after their marriage at St George's Church, Hanover Square, on 16 November, 1939.

Right: The lack of a wedding dress cannot dampen this bride's happiness on marrying her soldier sweetheart in London on 4 October, 1939.

ROYAL ICING

Above: The chief confectioner at the cake and biscuit manufacturer McVitie and Price puts the finishing touches to the four-tiered cake destined for Princess Elizabeth's wedding reception.

Left: Princess Elizabeth and Prince Philip of Greece walk back down the aisle of Westminster Abbey following their wedding on 20 November, 1947. Before a congregation of 2,000 guests, the woman who would one day be Queen had just promised to obey her new husband. In keeping with the austere post-war times, there was no public holiday for the event, but it was redolent of glamour and romance. The Princess was followed down the aisle by eight bridesmaids and her satin dress, designed by Norman Hartnell, was encrusted with pearls set in embroidered flower motifs.

most distinguished families'. The ceremony took place at St Giles Cathedral, Edinburgh, in January 1953, and despite the inclement weather more than 20,000 people lined the streets to watch the 1,600 guests arrive – including the Queen, Prince Philip and Princess Margaret – and see the bride get out of her car. She wore a dress of white French lace and a diamond tiara loaned by the Earl's mother, the Countess of Buccleuch, wife of one of Britain's most substantial landowners. The Queen's own wedding five years earlier had been in more austere times, and by royal standards was not a lavish affair.

THE FAIRYTALE WEDDING
Patriotically dressed young women camp out on the roadside, claiming a prime spot on the procession route, in the hope of catching a glimpse of Prince Charles and his pretty young bride, Princess Diana. The wedding took place in St Paul's Cathedral in the presence of 3,500 guests on 29 July, 1981.

Finding the perfect partner

A fairytale white wedding was not attainable by all. The First World War had left many women widowed or unmarried with little chance of finding a future husband. Boy babies were more likely to die in infancy than girls and more men emigrated to the colonies, so the 'surplus woman' – though not usually named as such in the 1930s – was a reality.

The age of marriage fell during the middle years of the century: in 1931 the average age for a first marriage for men was 27, for women 25 – figures little changed from a century before. But as the popularity of marriage peaked in 1971, the age at which a couple married dropped. In 1971 more than a third of men and approaching two thirds of women were married by their early 20s, compared to around a quarter in the 1930s; by their late 20s, almost nine out of ten were married. Before the war some 15 per cent of women and 8 per cent of men would never marry; by the 1970s, the number of lifelong spinsters was down to 5 per cent and permanent bachelors 7 per cent.

For that small number of singletons there was plenty of advice on the 'bachelor life' – male or female – but the single state was always assumed to be temporary. A wedding was presumed to be the dream of every young (and not so

FIFTY HAPPY YEARS
People raise their glasses to toast a golden wedding anniversary at a party in the Hope and Anchor pub in Brixton in 1969.

young) woman and man, and single siblings at their brother's or sister's wedding would have to fend off repeated questions of 'and when is it your turn?'.
On the whole the middle classes met their future husband or wife through family and friends, or through work, the church or the tennis club. The working classes were more likely to find love at the dance hall, a cycling club or at the 'monkey parade' of a summer evening or Sunday afternoon, when young men strutted their stuff in the hope of attracting a girlfriend.

There had been 'Lonely Hearts' advertisements in newspapers since the early 18th century and in the 1930s the *Matrimonial Times* carried many pleas along the lines of 'Spinster, 31, looks 25', 'Spinster, not painfully plain'. In April 1939 Britain's first marriage bureau opened in New Bond Street. It was run by two well-connected ex-debutantes, Heather Jenner and Mary Oliver, and it clearly fulfilled a need. On the first day there was a rush of 250 applicants – roughly half female and half male – from all walks of life. They ranged from tea planters and retired generals to teachers, nannies, shop assistants and widows; a plumber applied along with a master from Eton and an MP. Men were charged 5 guineas (£5.5s) to register, plus 20 guineas if a wedding resulted. Women were charged according to their means, which might be as little as 10 shillings.

The debutante season

The upper classes relied on trawling a network of family and friends and, of course, there was the 'season' designed expressly for the purpose of finding a future partner. A girl would 'come out' as a debutante in society when she was about 17, learn how to curtsey, be bought a wardrobe of suitable clothes and be presented at court – a tradition going back to the reign of George III – wearing a white dress to signify virginal purity. The deb's parents would host a dance for her at their town or country house – after the war more often at a smart hotel – and hope

SIKH WEDDING
Kuljeet Singh marrying Kaur Grewal at a hotel in Britain in July 1965. Sikh immigration to Britain was at its height in the 1950s and 60s; the Sikh population today stands at around 340,000.

that in the round of tea parties, pre-dance dinners, dances, theatre trips, Ascot and weekend house parties their daughter would meet her Mr Right (and not some bounder deemed Not Safe in Taxis). He would ask her father for her hand, an engagement photograph would appear in *Country Life*, then the wedding would take place somewhere fashionable – St Margaret's in Westminster, perhaps, where Winston Churchill had married Clementine Hozier, or maybe in the country church near the bride's home. She would be a vision of loveliness in lace or satin and tulle, and all would be set fair for a long, happy – and fruitful – union. At least that was how it happened in fairytales. Things were changing in real life. Fewer girls felt they needed to 'come out'. They might want to go to university or to art or drama school. And they could make their own circle of friends, thank you. In 1958 the tradition of presenting debs at court was dropped.

CHANGING ASPIRATIONS
Above: Wearing gowns and mortarboards, young women celebrate receiving their degrees at the University College of Cardiff in July 1936. Below: Seventeen-year-old Anna Massey dances with a 'deb's delight' at her coming-out ball, held in a pink-and-white-striped marquee decorated with '30 stag's heads and 89 yards of imitation pearls' at her family home in Highgate, London, in 1955. At the time Massey was making her debut as an actress in William Douglas-Home's play *The Reluctant Debutante*.

Calling time on tradition

Weddings continued to be remarkably traditional for most of the 20th century. The father of the bride was required to spend a small fortune on a wedding dress and reception, his reward the chance to walk proudly up the aisle, his daughter's arm in his, and give her away. On emerging the happy couple would be showered with confetti (unless the church had a policy against such littering), stand around

for a photographer who seemed to take forever, then move on to a reception in a hotel, village hall or marquee on the lawn. There would be a tiered-wedding cake, champagne – or at least a sherry – a sit-down meal and a slightly risqué speech by the best man, a friend of the groom. Then it was off on honeymoon. By the 1970s this was less likely to be by train to a seaside resort, as their parents had done, or by car with the regulation tin cans tied on the back to proclaim 'Just Married', than by plane to the Continent or even further afield.

But more couples were choosing to marry in a civil ceremony in a registry office, usually at the local town hall. The number of registry office weddings would exceed those in church in England and Wales by 1992. Some eschewed the floor-sweeping gown and invited just a handful of witnesses – and there was no 'giving away' of chattel daughters or promising to obey. The number of second marriages was increasing, which was one reason for the rise in civil ceremonies, as the church would not marry divorcees. In 1940 nine out of ten marriages were first time ones, but over the following decades the proportion fell to nearer 60 per cent, largely due to easier divorce. The Matrimonial Causes Act, piloted through parliament by the humorist and Independent MP, A.P. Herbert, was passed in 1938. Either partner could now petition for divorce after three years of marriage (less in certain circumstances) on

MARKING A NEW ARRIVAL – Christenings and names

A christening was traditionally a baby's first public appearance, when it was named and welcomed into the Christian church. The baby boy or girl had sponsors, the Godparents, who promised to guide it on the path of righteousness and stood by the font as the priest baptised the child with water. A silver rattle, a long white lawn christening gown and beautifully crocheted shawl, a white iced cake – these traditional accompaniments were still the order of the day at christening celebrations in the middle years of the 20th century. Even though regular church attendance had declined dramatically, people continued to enter their local church at least three times in their lives: for their christening, wedding and funeral.

A christening was a rite of passage, but there were other ways of marking a child's arrival. By the 1960s secular naming ceremonies were gaining ground, offering an alternative way of welcoming the fairly new-born child into the community. As christenings changed, so did the names bestowed. In 1930 the most popular boy's names included John, Peter, David, James, Robert, Richard, William, Frank, Raymond, Donald, Harold and Jack, while the favourites for girls were Mary, Betty, Dorothy, Helen, Barbara, Patricia, Doris, Shirley, Jean, Joan, Margaret, Virginia and Marilyn. By the 1950s Graham, Brian and Stephen were particularly popular for boys, Susan, Linda, Christine and Carol for girls. In the 1970s Richard and David were still holding their own, joined by Mark, Andrew, Daniel and Darren, while for girls Sarah, Rebecca and Emma made an appearance, along with Nicola, Karen and Claire. But there were still few 'celebrity names' in evidence and as yet no apparent desire to name an infant after a country (India, China) or a colour (Blue), or an object, such as Apple.

SPECIAL BIRTHDAY
The grand old age of 100 would be marked by a telegram from the Queen. Mrs Grace Caird of Stonehaven had already passed that milestone: this photograph shows her cutting her 105th birthday cake on 22 June, 1936. When Grace was born the railway age was in its infancy, Victoria had not yet come to the throne and slavery had yet to be abolished throughout the British Empire.

grounds of adultery, desertion, habitual drunkenness, or one of the parties being of 'an incurably unsound mind'. This was still a long way from the 'no fault' divorce enshrined in the 1969 Act, when irretrievable breakdown became the only grounds necessary, but at least it ended the farce of having to stage and prove adultery – often by staying in a hotel with someone paid for the purpose – even if both husband and wife wanted to end the marriage. By the 1970s, attitudes had changed to the extent that the odd progressive-minded couple would throw a 'divorce party' to demonstrate to friends that they were still on good terms, even if no longer married.

Living together

'After I had been going with her for two months, I tried to go all the way, but it wouldn't work', said one 20-year-old London man responding to a Mass-Observation survey in 1949. 'She wants a white wedding and marriage in a Church, and to be a virgin. I agree with her and don't try any more.' By the 1960s such attitudes were changing. More young people were setting up home together without the sanction of law and 'living in sin' no longer seemed an appropriate description of cohabitation. Some couples would marry after a few years, often when a first baby was expected. Others never did, which could cause problems in the event of a breakup as few rights over custody of children or ownership of property extended to unmarried couples. For same-sex couples a breakthrough and cause for celebration came in 1967, when it was finally made legal for consenting homosexual men over the age of 21 to be involved in a relationship.

Coming of age

The age of consent for marriage was 16 with parental consent, 18 without, but for voting it was 21 – the age of 'majority', the traditional entry into adulthood. Turning 21 was a significant life event, often marked by a substantial gift from parents – often a ring, although by the 1960s a record player had become a popular request. Cards sent by friends and relatives usually showed a silver 'key to the door' symbolising independence. This was a birthday that was almost always celebrated with a big party, with dancing, food and alcohol, since the former teenager was now an adult, able to enter into credit agreements as well as vote – though at 18 he had been able to fight and die for his country. In 1970 the voting age was lowered to 18 and this gradually became the 'new 21' for celebrations too, since that was when many young people reached the significant milestone of leaving school and going on to higher education or out to work.

Longer life before departing

In 1930 the average life expectancy for a man was 57, for a woman it was 60; by 1970 it had increased to 70 for men – the biblical three score years and ten – and 74 for women. And as death came later, it seemed to be marked less elaborately. In Victorian times a period of mourning, usually a year for widows, was obligatory for all who could afford the special black clothes. By the 1930s the visible mark of a death in the family had been reduced to a black armband on the sleeve of a coat, though people attending a funeral still dressed head to toe in black. The departed would be 'laid out' in the front parlour for a few days before the funeral so friends and neighbours could 'pay their respects' before the coffin was closed.

One major change in funeral practice in the 20th century was the shift from burial to cremation. The first official cremation in Britain took place in March 1885 and gradually what had been regarded as a pagan practice became accepted, in part through necessity given the shortage of space in churchyards and cemeteries. By the 1960s the remains of the departed were less likely to lie in a lead-lined casket beneath a headstone than to rest in an urn on the mantelpiece or be scattered somewhere of personal significance – a favourite holiday spot, a picturesque stretch of river or countryside, or even on the pitch of a football club.

Public figures were often given a memorial service some months after the funeral, with speeches of appreciation; lesser mortals would have a post-funeral wake with tea and memories. Few could match the send off that some notable East Enders were given – particularly local dignitaries such as pub landlord Charley Brown of Poplar in June 1932. The traditional cortège involved a Victorian glass hearse carrying the coffin, pulled by six black plumed horses, followed by a tail of Daimlers and 'Rollers' bearing the chief mourners.

THE FINAL SHOW
The highly traditional funeral procession of Jim Lloyd, a Battersea street trader, wends its way to Wandsworth Cemetery in 1949. The horse-drawn hearse is piled high with wreaths and flowers. The approach to dying and funerals was about to go through significant change. As one Norfolk funeral director has commented: 'Before the 1950s the vast majority of people would die at home. They'd stay in the house, in the front room the curtains would be drawn … advertising that there's been a death. And neighbours would come round, the children would be there, and they would see it as being very much a real part of life … that disappeared in the 1950s, 60s and 70s. Instead people came to the chapel of rest … [and] most people died in hospital rather than at home.'

A CALENDAR OF TRADITION

Festivals, customs, rites — nearly all have their origins in the seasons of the year, the rhythms of country life and the great festivals of the Christian tradition. As the years went by, increasing cultural diversity, the revival of ancient customs and the invention of new ones added yet more variety to our national calendar.

The list of festivals and customs in Britain is rich, varied and all but endless. Some are truly ancient, their origins lost in the past — like the Derbyshire Well Dressing ceremonies in May, said to descend from pagan rites to the gods of water. Others with a long lineage began as local customs, like the Dunmow Flitch Trials where, for the prize of a flitch of bacon, married couples try to convince a judge and jury that for 'twelve-month and a day' they have never 'wished themselves unmarried'. Traced back to 1104, the Dunmow custom was revived in Victorian days and is now held every leap year. Others are modern, like the Mad Maldon Mud Race where, since the mid 1970s, contestants squelch across the River Blackwater and back at low tide. What they all have in common is a link with a particular season — late spring, summer and midwinter respectively.

Certain festivals have always been celebrated in summer, when the sun should shine; others were expressly held to leaven the long dark days of winter. Most fall on or around a fixed day or days each year and together add up to a calendar that, from year to year, signposts continuity with the past. And as it is a calendar, the start has to be New Year, which for celebration means New Year's Eve.

'The man I saw pressing flower petals into damp clay back in 1974 was a giant ... it was hard to believe he could handle those fragile flower petals with such delicacy. But when he stepped away and showed the crowd the results of his efforts... there was a warm buzz of admiration.'

JOHN RAVENSCROFT, RECALLING A DERBYSHIRE WELL DRESSING CEREMONY

Marking the New Year

New Year is the gateway to fresh possibilities, the turning over of a new leaf, a time to make resolutions. At New Year's Eve parties up and down the land, people join hands at midnight to sing a poem by Robert Burns, written in 1788 and set to the tune of a traditional folk song: 'Should old acquaintance be forgot and never brought to mind ... We'll take a cup of kindness yet for the sake of auld lang syne' (roughly, 'for the sake of old times'). Londoners who lived near the river would hear the sound of hooting from the boats on the Thames

FIRE FESTIVAL
Shetlanders surround an elected member of the Lerwick 'Up Helly-Aa' committee, dressed in full Nordic costume, as he takes a photograph of the event. Held on the last Tuesday in January, the celebration commemorates the Norse invasion of the Shetland Isles in the 9th century. It culminates in a torchlight procession and the burning of a replica Viking longship.

RINGING OUT THE OLD
Left: New Year revellers celebrating as the chimes of midnight rang out on 31 December, 1969, in Albert Square, Manchester.

at the stroke of midnight. In Liverpool an eerie chorus would float up through the fog from the boats on the Mersey as the year turned. Several places in Britain have kept alive ancient fire festivals – some with roots going back to Celtic times – that mark the changing of the year, ceremonies that once seen are not soon forgotten. At Comrie, Biggar and Wick in Scotland, processions of flaming torches end with bonfires to 'burn out the old year'. In the fishing port of Stonehaven, kilt-clad men swing fire-balls round their heads and march through the town to the sound of pipes and drums, ending at the harbour where they fling the flaming balls out to sea. The Allendale Tar Barrel Parade has men in fancy dress carrying blazing half-barrels around the town, the strains of pipes replaced by a brass band. At the first stroke of midnight the fiery barrels are slung onto the bonfire, lighting a fire that toasts the cheeks of the crowd and blisters the paint on pubs and shops around the town square. Traditions like these survived even through the black-out years of the Second World War, reduced to candles or embers in a bucket.

In Scotland housewives would 'reddy' (make ready) their homes for New Year in a frenzy of mopping, scrubbing, dusting and polishing, all to make sure that they were as clean as the proverbial pin to welcome the New Year in through the front door as the Old Year slipped out the back. It was supposed to be bad luck to start the New Year in debt, so if possible the tallyman would have been paid off – not so easy during the Depression of the 1930s. The first person to cross the threshold brings luck for the coming year: ideally, the first-footer should be a

'A MAN'S A MAN FOR A' THAT'
Piping in the haggis at a Burns Night dinner at the Savoy Hotel, London, on 25 January, 1959. A piper leads the way, followed by the chef carrying the haggis and a waiter bearing bottles of whisky to help the poetry flow. This annual celebration of Robbie Burns, one of Scotland's most famous sons, is held on the poet's birthday.

PRIZE POOCH
Anxious owners parade wire-haired fox terriers before the judges at Crufts dog show in April 1948. The show, held each year in spring, has been running since 1886.

dark stranger bringing with them a lump of coal, bread or whisky, to symbolise the coming of the New Year. Audrey Butler's family in Yorkshire had light complexions and fair hair, so setting aside the bit about a stranger, she recalls how 'my mother blacked up my father's face and he wore black gloves: the New Year was officially let in and all was well'.

The first day of the year has not always been on 1 January: it was legally decreed as such in 1600 in Scotland and in 1752 in England and Wales, where New Year's Day did not become an official bank holiday until 1974. It was pragmatic to make it so, since New Year's Eve parties usually ensured that few turned up for work the next day. In Scotland, in recognition of all-night Hogmanay partying, 2 January became a holiday too.

On 6 January is the Epiphany, commemorating the arrival of the Magi bearing gifts for the infant Jesus. This is now remembered mainly for being Twelfth Night, marking the end of Christmas festivities when wassail (punch) was drunk, the Lord of Misrule banished and merrymaking ensued. All that lingered by the mid 20th century was that it was the day to undeck the halls – if the tree and other decorations were not taken down, this was supposed to bring bad luck.

An alternative New Year in the dark days of February

Festivities for the Chinese New Year – the most important holiday in Chinese tradition, which falls between 21 January and 21 February – started to be noticed from around 1973. From small beginnings, they grew into immensely colourful and lively occasions lasting up to a week in 'Chinatown' in London, in Liverpool and in other cities with a large Chinese community. There would be dragon and lion dances, Chinese lanterns lighting up the streets, music, firecrackers and special menus on offer in the restaurants and cafés. At the end of the festivities, the year would have handed over from one animal to the next in the rota of twelve creatures that represent the Chinese astrological calendar.

Candlemass on 2 February was a festival of light when priests blessed the altar candles. It marked the purification of Mary 40 days after the birth of Jesus, but was remembered more for predicting the weather, similar to St Swithun's Day on 14 July: 'If Candlemass day be dry and fair/The half of the winter is to come and mair/If Candlemass Day be wet and foul/The half of the winter is gone at yule'. Badgers supposedly poked their noses out of their dens on this day to see if it was time to come out of hibernation.

Valentine's Day on 14 February does not celebrate St Valentine, an early Christian martyr, but the exchange of love tokens. It has been documented in letters since the 15th century, but it was not until the early 19th that cards were produced commercially and not until after the Second World War that it started to become big business. Unlike most customs, Valentine's has increased rather than decreased in popularity in the 20th century, with cards or gifts exchanged between sweethearts and the sending of unsigned cards to an object of secret passion. Ash Wednesday signals the start of Lent, which for Christians in much earlier ages meant 40 days (excluding Sundays) of fasting, penance and piety recalling Christ's 40 days in the wilderness. Lent ends on Easter Saturday but the start is moveable between 4 February and 11 March. Ash Wednesday gets its name from the burning of the previous year's palm crosses and marking the foreheads of penitent worshippers with the ash. By the 20th century Lent had become a test of self-restraint, as people gave up alcohol, chocolate or some other pleasure for the duration. Immediately before the start of Lent was a last feast on Shrove Tuesday, better known as Pancake Day when people used up their milk, eggs and fat before the fasting began. In 1948 the vicar of Olney revived the old tradition of a pancake race for the women of the village. Since 1950, the women of Olney have competed with the women of Liberal, a town in Kansas, for the world title.

The scent of spring

Spring is a time for nesting, the human form of which has been celebrated annually at the *Daily Mail Ideal Home Exhibition* since 1908. The houses, furnishing and gadgets on display are an evolving barometer of British domestic tastes and aspirations, which the catalogues perfectly bring to mind. Spring is also the time of all but one of the saints' days commemorated in the constituent parts of the United Kingdom – St Andrew's Day, for the patron saint of Scotland, is

WOMEN ON A MISSION
The runners in the pancake race at Olney, Buckinghamshire, in 1955. The custom dates back to 1445, although the race had not been run for many years until revived in 1948. The race takes place every Shrove Tuesday and is open to any woman of the village over 18 years of age. Each competitor has to flip her pancake at least twice during the 415-yard race, then once more on the finish line.

GIVING THANKS
A Jewish mother in Whitechapel in London lights the Sabbath candles on 12 April, 1952, at the climax of the Passover feast which commemorates the Exodus from Egypt.

HOUSE OF THE RISING SUN
Spectators gather to watch Druids conduct the Dawn Ceremony at Stonehenge on the summer solstice – the longest day of the year – 21 June, 1956. The structure on Salisbury Plain is Britain's most famous prehistoric monument.

the odd one out on 30 November. St David's Day is 1 March, marked by wearing leeks and daffodils and parades of the Welsh Guards and Welsh Regiment to commemorate the death of the patron saint in AD 589. The 20th century saw St Patrick's Day, 17 March, evolve from a purely Roman Catholic feast day into an exuberant secular celebration of Irish culture and music. Shamrocks abound at St Patrick's Day parties, with celebrations particularly notable in Liverpool and at the Cheltenham Gold Cup. The Cheltenham race meeting is a sort of dress rehearsal for the Grand National at Aintree on 29 March, a race that attracts more office and 'housewife' bets than any other.

St George's Day, 23 April, is named for a patron saint who (if he existed) slayed a dragon but never set foot in England – his story was brought home by the Crusaders. Shakespeare gave the battle cry 'God for Harry, England and St George' to his Henry V. England's greatest bard is also linked to its patron saint by his birth and death, the former said to have been on St George's Day in 1564, the latter known to have been in 1616. By the 1960s the English did little to mark the occasion, apart from the occasional red rose in a buttonhole and a ceremony in the Chapel of St George at Windsor Castle.

From Mother's Day to Easter Day

Mothering Sunday on the fourth Sunday in Lent was traditionally the day when those working away from home, usually in service, could go back to visit their mothers, taking flowers or a small gift. The fast of Lent was sometimes relaxed to allow for the eating of simnel cake. Mothering Sunday continued to be celebrated in church services, but its offshoot, Mother's Day, overtook it in a flurry of commercially produced cards and gifts. Father's Day, a more recent import from the USA, entered the British calendar on the third Sunday in June but struggled to be taken seriously.

All Fool's, or April Fool's, on 1 April was for playing practical jokes. Anyone who fell for a joke before noon was an 'April Fool', but after noon the tables were turned and the joker became the fool. The BBC enjoyed getting into the spirit, memorably with a spoof *Panorama* report on the failure of Italy's spaghetti harvest in 1957.

On Maundy Thursday, the day before Good Friday, the Archbishop of Canterbury distributed small silver coins known as 'Maundy Money' to the poor on behalf of the sovereign, though the Queen is often present herself. The number of recipients equals her age, so in 1957, for example, when she was 31 years of age, she gave Maundy alms to 31 men and 31 women who had given service to the church or the community that year.

Good Friday (probably a corruption of God's Friday) is the day when Christians remember Christ's crucifixion. In a more

A SPRING IN THEIR STEP
Above: Children in the 1950s dance round a maypole at Cheriton village school near Wincanton, Somerset, to celebrate May Day. Below: Festival-goers gather at the second Glastonbury Festival, also in Somerset, in June 1971. This was the first year that the famous pyramid stage – now a permanent feature – was used for acts that included David Bowie and Joan Baez.

religious era, it was a solemn day of penance, but the eating of spicy hot cross buns is the most persistent custom that survives in a more secular age. Christ's resurrection on Easter Sunday was represented by an egg, the symbol of birth and of the stone being rolled away from the entrance to the empty tomb. This led to lots of customs involving eggs – dyeing or painting them, rolling them down banks, hiding them in the garden for a children's treasure hunt – and in particular every child's favourite part of Easter: the giving and eating of chocolate eggs, as the end of Lent sees chocolate restored.

Easter Monday marks the start of the season, when travelling funfairs return to the road, summer sports take to the fields (whatever the weather), stately homes open to the public and innumerable local festivals begin the year's fund-raising for local causes. Troops of Morris dancers on village greens are a tradition particularly associated with Easter Monday and with Whitsun, once a moveable feast but since May 1971 a spring bank holiday on the last Monday of May.

LADIES DAY
Mrs Gertrude Shilling making an entrance at Ascot Races in June 1969. Even by the eccentric hat standards of Ascot, the enormous feather-trimmed cartwheel creation, designed by her milliner son David, is flamboyant. Ascot is just one of a veritable feast of horseracing festivals in the British summer calendar. The Derby at Epsom is also in June, followed by 'Glorious Goodwood' in July and ending with the St Leger at Doncaster in September.

May Day

The first day in May is celebrated as the first day of summer – even though the weather can feel far from summery. At dawn the choir of Magdalen College, Oxford, climb to the top of the 144-foot college tower to sing the Latin anthem *Te Deum Patrem Colimus*, watched by students and now by growing numbers of tourists. The Celts danced round a living tree, remembered in the custom of dancing round the maypole. In 1952, on a housing estate in Shrewsbury, four modern maypoles were constructed out of pram wheels stuck on a pole. Another tradition to survive is the crowning of the May Queen and in some places – notably Minehead in Somerset and Padstow in Cornwall – a decorated hobby horse is brought 'out of hibernation' and paraded through the streets full of singing and dancing crowds.

Since 1891 May Day has been recognised as an annual event for workers and trade unionists. In 1904, at a meeting in Amsterdam, the Internationalist Socialist Conference called for it to be 'mandatory upon the proletarian organisations of all countries to stop work on 1 May, wherever it is possible without injury to the workers'. In Britain it was a day for trade union marches, rallies and speeches. The long campaign for recognition of May Day as an official bank holiday bore fruit in 1977 – but it is once more under threat.

The most famous of the trade union celebrations is held not on May Day but in July. The Durham Miners' Gala (or 'The Big Meeting') was first held in 1871 in Wharton Park, Durham, and apart from the Second World War and during major strikes it has been an annual event ever since; at its peak it attracted more than 300,000 people. Miners marched from their collieries, accompanied by brass bands and drums. Their large banners depicted leading union figures – miners' leaders for the most part, though the banner from Chopwell depicted Marx and Lenin; it was taken on a tour of the Soviet Union in 1935. A banner draped in black signified that there had been a death in the pit during the previous year. The day culminated in speeches, a picnic on Durham race course and a service at Durham Cathedral. 'In its heyday', writes Raymond Chesterfield, 'the Durham Miners' Gala was a sight to behold.' Traditions have been kept even after pits closed, with banners still unfurled at the march, but can it survive, Chesterfield wonders, 'now all the pits in Durham have closed. There are no working miners left anymore. As ex-miners gaze into the past, they are only left with memories.'

Music and more

In 1934 Mozart's *Marriage of Figaro* was the first opera staged at the recently restored Glyndebourne house in Sussex. The opera festival has since become an annual event, with visitors arriving in evening dress to watch the performance,

THE ANNUAL GARDEN FÊTE
A home-made fairground game at the vicarage fête in Chislet, Kent, in August 1939. The scene was typical of summer fairs in villages up and down the land. The contestant lucky enough to have hooked a bottle is Sir William Wayland, the Conservative MP for Canterbury.

armed with well-stocked hampers for a picnic in the grounds. The 'Proms', the now familiar season of mainly classical music, began in London in 1895; they were first broadcast from the Albert Hall by the BBC in 1942.

On a very different note, the day after Jimi Hendrix died in September 1970 the first Glastonbury Festival opened in a field in Somerset on a farm belonging to Michael Eavis. Entry was £1, including free milk supplied from the farm, and Marc Bolan topped the bill. The following year the date of the festival was moved to the summer solstice and by 1980 it was attracting thousands, with the profits going to the Campaign for Nuclear Disarmament. It inspired an ever increasing rash of music festivals all over Britain throughout the summer.

Bards and musicians gather each year in August for the week long Royal National Eisteddfod, a celebration of culture in Wales conducted entirely in Welsh. The winning poem is awarded the Bardic Crown, presented to a woman for the first time in 1953.

In the grim world of postwar austerity, the Edinburgh Festival was launched in 1947 to provide 'a platform for the human spirit'. It has grown into the largest cultural festival in the world, offering a varied agenda of theatre, music and dance. The 'Edinburgh Fringe', staged in small spaces all over the Scottish capital, started the same year. The Edinburgh Tattoo began in 1950, showcasing British and Commonwealth forces; by the mid 1950s it was drawing around 160,000 spectators each year.

Summer's end

Fairs and garden fêtes were a particular feature of a British summer, as practically every village put on its own little party, open to all. Often they were arranged by the local church or school, with simple pleasures such as cake stalls, tombolas and perhaps donkey rides for the children. In some places they could be more ambitious affairs. Kathleen Stirzaker grew up in Exeter in the 1930s, the eldest of eight children, and had fond memories of the annual Bank Holiday fair: 'They had a greasy pole, the men tried to climb up to get the leg of pork tied to the top. There were races for the children in the morning, and in the afternoon for grown-ups; egg and spoon races, sack races, three-legged races for all ages … They had coconut shies and roll penny booths. They had a band playing most of the day and there was a large marquee selling teas of strawberries and cream.'

'Every year we had an August Bank Holiday Fair … All the people from miles around came to join in the fun …'

KATHLEEN STIRZAKER, RECALLING HER CHILDHOOD IN EXETER IN THE 1930S

The Anglo-Caribbean community has held an annual carnival on August Bank Holiday weekend in Notting Hill in London since 1964. Set up largely under the auspices of the Trinidadian and Tobagonian ('Trini') British population, who started to settle here in the 1950s, it was from the start a vibrant celebration of Caribbean music, dance and pageant – and it soon grew. By 1976 some 150,000 people were turning out to enjoy the steel bands, exotic costumes and spicy foods.

Harvests and bonfires

The beginning of autumn, season of mists and fruitfulness, was the time for communities to hold the annual harvest festival. Chapels and churches were filled with flowers, vegetables and sheaves of corn for a service to give thanks for crops safely gathered in. This was followed in the evening by the harvest supper, a meal with its origins in the end-of-harvest feast a farmer would supply for his workers.

Hallowe'en on 31 October derives from old Christian festivals to honour the dead and before the custom of 'trick or treat' was imported from the USA, it was marked in a very different way to now. With hands behind backs, children would try to eat apples hanging on strings; or 'bob' for them in a bowl of water, trying to catch one using only their mouths – if a girl was successful she might try to peel it in one strip, then toss the peel over her shoulder to divine the initial of her future husband's name. The evening would end listening to ghost stories by firelight, with a peeled grape passed round as a witch's eyeball, peanuts as her teeth.

HIGHLAND GAMES
A wrestling match at the Braemar Games in Aberdeenshire in September 1952. Other traditional events at the games included tossing the caber, highland dancing and throwing the 'weight', a metal ball weighing in at around 25kg.

For most children, the biggest event by far in autumn was bonfire night, held to celebrate the overthrow of a Catholic plot in 1605 to blow up Parliament and King James I: 'Remember, remember, the fifth of November/ Gunpowder, treason and plot.' In some places, notably Lewes in Sussex, the occasion remained redolent of religious and political conflict, but for the most part by the mid 20th century, it had become an evening of fun.

Preparations began weeks in advance with children sewing together old clothes and stuffing them with straw to make a 'guy'. The finishing touch was drawing on a mask, then it was out into the streets to beg 'a penny for the guy'. The pennies went to buy fireworks for the night itself – sparklers, jumping jacks, Catherine wheels, Roman candles. Weeks were spent collecting wood, cardboard and anything burnable to build bonfires in back gardens or on waste ground. On the night itself the guy was perched precariously on the top before the bonfire was lit. Fathers took the role of 'firework-lighter-in-chief', nailing Catherine wheels onto gate posts (they rarely spun as they should) and placing rockets in milk bottles, before proceeding to 'light the blue touch paper and retire'. Bonfire fare usually included potatoes baked in the embers, sausages, gingerbread and homemade toffee so hard that a hammer was needed to break it. But the day of the back-garden bonfire was doomed as health and safety rules and regulations encroached. Increasingly, civic bonfires and firework displays held in parks or recreation grounds took their place, a local authority employee ousting dads from their traditional role.

By the late 1970s Diwali, a five-day 'festival of light' involving large displays of candles, lamps and fireworks, was increasingly celebrated by Sikh and Hindu communities in Britain. Falling between mid October and mid November, it sometimes naturally merged with the bonfires and fireworks of Guy Fawkes night.

A sombre occasion of remembrance has been held every year since 1919 on the Sunday nearest to 11 November, commemorating the moment in 1918 when the guns of the First World War fell silent on the Western Front. In 1945 the names of the dead from the Second World War were added to war memorials, and later those who died in Korea and other conflicts. All are remembered in the laying of wreaths and the wearing of British Legion red poppies.

It's Christmas

Until the advent of bank holidays in 1871, Good Friday and Christmas Day were the only holidays that workers could expect. Christmas was a time to look forward to, as Audrey Butler recalled from her childhood in 1930s Yorkshire: 'Around the end of November we began thinking of Christmas … we invariably had the first snows and frosts. We loved the snow and built snowmen and went sledging …' Even the most agnostic seemed to rejoice in singing or listening to carols and sending cards. At this time of year, many families would move into their sitting

REMEMBER, REMEMBER
Boys building a bonfire on the South Downs near Lewes in Sussex in preparation for Guy Fawkes night on 5 November, 1961. The world-famous Lewes Bonfires commemorate not only the Gunpowder Plot of 1605, but also the memory of 17 Protestant martyrs burned for their faith during persecutions in the reign of Mary I between 1553 and 1558.

THE WONDER OF CHRISTMAS
Right: Visitors gaze at the pine Christmas tree erected in St Paul's Cathedral in London in 1953. Crowned with a representation of the Star of Bethlehem, the tree traditionally remains in the Cathedral until Twelfth Night (6 January).

room, kept for special occasions, where bright concertina streamers were strung from wall to wall, or perhaps paper chains made by the children with liberal use of the glue pot. Children helped to decorate the tree – with baubles made from milk bottle tops in wartime – finishing off with a fairy at the very top.

Thousands who never normally went to church would go to Midnight Mass – some straight from the pub. Or to a morning service on Christmas Day, as Sidney Chave and his wife did in their local church in London in 1940: 'It was a wartime service, the choir was smaller than usual and the congregation included many uniforms. However, we sang old carols with great vigour – and enjoyed them too. The vicar preached a short sermon – and a good one. He emphasised our prayer for peace, but said there could never be peace until there was goodwill between men'.

Presents great and small

Children hung a stocking at the end of their bed, having briefed Father Christmas by letter or on a visit to his 'grotto'. As Christmas morning dawned, they rushed to see if he had got it right. Presents were not lavish. Children would expect to find an orange and some nuts in their stocking, perhaps a chocolate coin wrapped in gold or silver foil, a puzzle or other small toy. Then by the tree there would be one main present – a train set, a doll's pram or tricycle were the acme of desire. For grown-ups gifts were usually practical – a scarf, gloves, handkerchiefs, or perhaps a 'coffret' containing talc and bath salts for a woman, a shaving stick for a man.

The focus of the day, for adults at least, was Christmas dinner. The younger ones were often more interested in other food on offer: 'The great thing about Christmas was eating. The big boxes and tins of Cadbury's Roses, Quality Street, that you didn't have much of during the rest of the year. And the nuts, and the oranges', was one recollection of Christmas in the 1950s. Christmas was not the extended holiday it would become by the end of the century. Most people would stop work only a little earlier than usual on Christmas Eve and unless Christmas fell over a weekend they would be back at work on Boxing Day. It was all over for another year.

'One Christmas I had a pair of roller-skates and we took turns playing on them. Another Christmas I had a scooter ...'

AUDREY BUTLER, RECALLING CHRISTMAS IN HER CHILDHOOD IN YORKSHIRE IN THE 1930s

INDEX

Page numbers in *italic* refer to the captions.

A

'A' levels 28, 33
Abdication Crisis 218-19
Aberfan 71
abortion 105
Advisory, Conciliation and
    Arbitration Service
    (ACAS) 96
agriculture 56-65
    agribusiness 61
    agricultural depression 56,
        57
    arable farming 56, 61
    dairy farming 57, 58, 61
    diversification 65
    electrification 57-8
    hop picking 62-3
    labourers *56*, 57, 60
    market gardening 57
    marketing boards 57
    mechanisation 60-1
    monocultures 61
    sheep farming 57, *58*,
        65
    subsidies 58, 61
    wartime 58, 60
Air Raid Precautions (ARP)
    81, 82, 83, *83*
air travel *92*, 172, *173*, 176,
    189
aircraft industry 81
Aldermaston marches *49*, 50
allotments *136*, 141, *143*
Anderson shelters 140-1,
    141
apprenticeships 45, 48, 73
April Fool's Day 244
The Archers 133, 134
art schools 50, 51, 52
asbestos 58, *73*
Ascot *246*
au pairs 88
Automobile Association
    (AA) 173
Auxiliary Fire Service
    (AFS) 82

B

baby shows *16*
babygros 15
Baden-Powell, Robert 36-7,
    39
Bailey, David 53
Band of Hope 41
bank holidays 53, 176, 177,
    246, 248
Barclaycard 158
barristers *100*, 102
bathrooms 123
battery farming 65
BBC 86, 128, 130, 131,
    134, 209, 244 *see also*
    radio broadcasting;
    television
beat generation 50

Beatles 52, 53, *197*
beatniks 198
Beeching, Richard 117, 166
Belisha beacons 173, *173*
Betjeman, John 114, 126,
    194
betting 203, 205
Bevan, Aneurin 104
Beveridge Report 104
Bevin, Ernest 71, 94, 127
Bevin Boys 71, *71*
Biba 52, 157
bicycling *168*, 169, *169*
bingo 197
birth control 10
Blackpool 86, 177, 178, *178*,
    179, 182-3
blacksmiths *59*, 65
Blitz 82, 125, 156, 219
    see also Second World War
Blue Peter 35, *35*
Bluebird 153, 164
boardgames 132, *132*
boarding houses 178, 179,
    181, *182*
boarding schools 31, 33
Bob a Job week 37-8
Bonfire Night 250, *250*
Boots the Chemist 155
boutiques 52-3, 157, *158*
Bowlly, Al 130, 198
boxing *41*, 211, *211*
Boy Scouts 36-8, *37*, 39,
    41
Boys' Brigades 39, *39*, 41
The Brains Trust 129
breathalysers 173
Brown, Louise 13
Brownies 39, *39*
bubble cars 171
Bucknell, Barry 127
Burns Night *242*
buses 167-8, *168*
Butlin's 184, *184*, *185*, 188

C

Café Royal *200*
Campaign for Nuclear
    Disarmament (CND)
    49, 50, 248
Campbell, Malcolm 153,
    164
camper vans *175*
camping *37*, *186*
CAMRA 201
Candlemas 242
caravans 185-7, *187*
Carlton Club *192*
Carnaby Street 52
cars
    car industry 57, 77,
        85-6, *87*
    cost of 169, 171
    MOT tests 171
    ownership 69, 85, 169,
        171, 173, 187
    secondhand 171
    streamlining 164
CentreParcs 184
chain stores 152
charladies 85, 127
Chelsea Flower Show 142,
    175

childbirth 10-15
    antenatal class *10*
    bottle feeding 15, *15*
    fathers' role *10*, 13, 15
    home births 10, 11, *11*,
        12, 13
    hospital births 11, 13
    maternal mortality 10, 11
    medicalisation of 10
    natural childbirth 11-12
    premature babies *11*
    test tube babies 13
    see also infant care
childminders 88
children
    child development
        milestones 17
    childbirth 10-15
    education *see* education
    infant care 15-17, 87-8
    part-time work 45
    pre-school care 20-1,
        24-5
    social organisations 36-9,
        41
    toys and games 22-3, *26*,
        110, 120-1, *121*
    TV and radio for 34-5,
        128
    wartime 42-3, 83
Children's Hour 34, 128
Chinese New Year 242
Chinese restaurants and
    takeaways 201, *201*
christenings 237
Christmas 160-1, 176, 242,
    250-1
churches *101*, 117, 237
Churchill, Winston 94, 95,
    128, 217, 219, 220,
    221, 222-3, *222*, 227,
    236
Cider with Rosie 56, 57
cinema and film 47, 49, 75,
    96, 105-6, 192-5, *194*,
    195, 197
the City 98-100
Civil Defence 46, 79, 80,
    82-3, *83*, 89
Civil Service 86, 91, 98,
    101
classical music 130, *247*,
    247-8
clerical work 90
clergymen 100, *101*
closed shops 96
clothes rationing 156
co-education 30
Co-operative Society 148
coach services 166, 185
coal mining and miners *56*,
    66, 70-1, 94, 96, *96*,
    101, 222, 247
cohabitation 238
collective bargaining 94-5
comedy entertainment 132,
    135
comics *130*
coming of age 238
commuter belts 119
comprehensive schools 30,
    30
conscientious objectors 80
conscription 47, 71, 79

construction work 76, 84
    house building 110,
        112-13, 119
    housing boom (1930s) 76
    school building boom
        (1960s) 26
    'spec' building 76, 112
consumer society 85, 93,
    127, 158
convenience foods 151
cooks and cooking *63*, 144,
    144, *146*, 148, 150,
    151, *151*
corner shops 148, *148*, 151
coronations 35, 134, 219,
    219, 220-1, *220*
cotton industry *see* textile
    industries
Cradock, Fanny 150
credit cards 158
cremation 239
cricket 202, 208, *208*, 210
Crimplene 39
Crufts dog show *242*
Cubs 38

D

dance halls 199-200
dancing *40*, 198-200, *198*,
    216
day trippers 179, 190-1
Daz *124*
death and funerals 239,
    239
debutantes 235-6, *236*
decor and furnishings 122-7,
    158
department stores 89-90,
    92, 152, 153-4, *153*,
    156, 157
Depression (1930s) 33, 66,
    77, 160
Diana, Princess of Wales
    233
Dick-Read, Grantly 11-12
Dickins & Jones 156, 157
Dig for Victory campaign 43,
    58, 140
dinner parties *135*, 151
discos 199
divorce 236, 238
Diwali 250
DIY 127
dockers 69
doctors 10, 104, 105-6,
    106, 113
domestic service 45, 75, *75*,
    77, 85
dormitory towns 117
Dr Who 34, 35
drink-driving laws 173
driving tests 173
drugs 53
Druids *244*
Durham Miners' Gala *96*,
    247

E

E-Type Jaguar 171
Easter 243, 244, 246
Eavis, Michael 65, 248
Edinburgh Festival 248

education
    child-centred learning 26
    co-education 30
    elementary system 25-6,
        28
    11-plus examination
        28-9, 30
    General Certificate of
        Education (GCE) 28
    higher education 33, *46*,
        48, 50-1, 98, *236*
    pre-school education 20,
        24-5
    primary education 25-7,
        25, *26*, *27*
    public schools 31, *31*, 33
    school leaving age 27, 28,
        46
    secondary education
        27-33, 98
    wartime 43
educational toys 23
Edward VIII 218-19
Eisteddfod 248
electricity grid 56, 57, 85
Elizabeth II 217, 227, *227*
    coronation of 35, 134,
        220-1, *220*
    wedding 232, *232*
Elizabeth, the Queen Mother
    118, *138*, *197*, 219
Empire Day 216-17, *216*,
    217
employment
    children 45
    equal pay 66, 91
    holidays with pay 94, 176,
        177
    home-working movement
        118
    marriage bar 86-7, 95
    mechanisation 73, 75, 100
    national minimum wage
        96
    part-time 87, 89
    professional classes
        98-107
    reserved occupations in
        wartime 60, 79, 80
    skills shortage 73
    unemployment 66, 69, 72,
        94, 144
    wartime 60, 78-83
    women 86-91, 99, 100,
        101, 105
    working conditions and
        practices 73
    young people 46
    see also specific industries and
        occupations
engineering profession 100,
    101
entertainment 132, 192-201
    see also cinema and film;
        holidays; radio
        broadcasting; television
espresso bars 50, *200*
European Union 96
Everest, conquest of 220

F

farming *see* agriculture
farm shops 65

fashion 51-3, *154*
  beat generation 50
  boutiques 52-3, 157
  Teddy Boys 46
Festival of Britain (1951) *100*, 126, 159, 224-5
festivals and customs 240-51
financial services industry 93, 98-100
fire festivals 241
fireworks 250
fishing *59*, 77, 211
flats, high-rise 84, *85*, 118-19, *118*
flower and vegetable shows 142, *142*
folk music *46*
food 144-51
  convenience foods 151
  eating out 200-1, *200*
  food shopping 147
  meals and mealtimes 144, 146-7, 151
  rationing 48, 147-8, *148*
  takeaways *51*, 201
football 203, *203*, 205, 208, 210-11, *210*
football pools 205
Formica 127
Friendly Societies 104
Froebel, Friedrich 20, 23
fur coats *153*
furniture and furnishings 122-7
furniture manufacture 125

G

gang violence 47, 53
garden centres 143
garden city movement 112
garden fêtes 248, *248*
gardens 114, 119, 136-43, 153-4
General Certificate of Education (GCE) 28
General Strike (1926) 70-1, 94
George V 217-18
George VI 219, 222
Girl Guides 38-9, *38*
Glastonbury Festival 65, *245*, 248
Glyndebourne 247-8, *247*
golf 211
Good Friday 244, 246
The Goons 34, 132
Gorbals, Glasgow *18-19*, *84-5*
GPs 105, 106
grammar schools 28, 29, 30, *30*, 33, 98, 100
Grange Hill 35
Gresford pit disaster 71
greyhound racing 203, 205, *205*
Grunwick strike 96
Guy Fawkes night 250

H

Habitat 158
hairdressing salons *91*
hairstyles 53

Hallowe'en 249
Harben, Philip 150, *151*
Hargreaves, John 41
Harrod's 156
harvests and harvest festivals *57*, *60*, 61, 62-3, 249
heliotherapy *15*, 207
herring lassies *77*
high street stores 154-5, 158-9
Highland Games *249*
Highway Code 173
hippies *52*
hire-purchase (HP) 85, 124, 171
hiring fairs 56
hobbies 132, *133*
holiday camps 184-5, *184*, *185*, 187-8
holidays 172, 176-91
home-working movement 118
homelessness 118, 134
hop picking 62-3
horse-power *60*, *60*, 61, 69, 166, *166*
horse-racing *202*, 203, *246*
hospital consultants 105-6
hospitals 11, 13, 104, *106*, *107*
household appliances 85, *90*, 125, 127, 144, 151
housing 110-19
  decor and furnishings 122-7, 158
  estates 112-13, *114*, 119
  flats 84, *85*, 118-19, *118*
  home ownership 113
  local authority housing 110, 112, 113, 122, 138
  prefabs *117*, 118, *138*
  recommended building standards 112
  rented 110
  second homes 115
  slum clearance 76, 110
  suburban 110, *110*, 112
Hulanicki, Barbara 52, 157
hunger marches *94*

I

Ideal Home Exhibition *127*, 243
immigrants 27, 151, 201, *235*
incomes 49, 52, 57, 60, 63, 86, 113, 177, 210
Indian restaurants 201
industrial accidents 73
industrial relations 96
  see also strikes
infant care 15-16
  baby-centred approaches *17*
  bottle feeding 15, *15*
  breastfeeding 15
  childminders 88
  father's role *16*
  nannies 16, 17, *17*
  nappies 12, 15
  potty training 17-19, *19*
  Truby King regime 15-16, *17*

inner cities 119
IVF 13

J

Jarrow March 69
jazz 50, 53, 130, 198
Jekyll, Gertrude 137
Jewish communities 98-9, *244*
John Lewis 156
Jolly, Hugh 17
journalism *102*
Joyce, William ('Lord Haw Haw') 129

K

keep fit movement 206-7
Kibbo Kift Kindred 41
Kinks 52
kitchens 123, *123*, 124
  farmhouse *146*
Knole *126*
Korean War 48, 49

L

Labour Exchanges *77*
Lake District *65*
Laker, Freddie 189
Lambrettas 169
Lancaster, Osbert 113
land prices 117
land speed records 153, 164
landscape architects 137
laundry 124, *124*, 127
Laura Ashley 52, 157
Leach, Penelope 17
Lee, Laurie 56, 57
Legal Aid scheme 103
legal profession *100*, 101-3
Lego 23, *23*
Lewes 250, *250*
Lewis and Harris *115*
life expectancy *238*, 239
light industries 72-3, 77, 117
linoleum 123
Listen With Mother 34
local authority housing 110, 112, 113, 122, 138
loft living 119
London Underground 114, 168
Lonely Hearts advertisements 235
Longleat 190-1
'Lord Haw Haw' 129
luncheon vouchers 90
Lyon's Corner Houses *93*

M

Maclaren buggies 15
Macmillan, Harold 85, 119
Magdalen College, Oxford 246
managerial class 100
manual workers 66
  see also semi-skilled workers; skilled workers; unskilled workers
Margaret, Princess *104*

market gardening 57
Marks & Spencer 153, 155, *156*
marriage and weddings 52, 228-33, 238
marriage bar 86-7, 95
marriage bureaux 235
Mass Observation project 138, 238
Maundy Money 244
May Day *245*, 246-7
Means Test 69
mental health services 105
Midnight Mass 251
midwives 10, *11*
milk
  dairy farming 57, 58, 61
  for babies and children *15*, *15*
  free school milk 26
Mini 171
model villages 117-18
modernism 118
Mods 53, *53*, *190*
Monopoly 132, *132*
Montessori nurseries 25
Moon landing 135
Morris dancing *216*, 246
mortgages 113, 119
MOT tests 171
Mothercare 15
Mothering Sunday 244
motor racing 211
motor shows *171*, 185
motorcycles and sidecars 169, *169*, 173
motorways 56
MPs 101
munitions industry *79*, 80, 81
music *36*, 50, 52
  classical 130, *247*, 247-8
  folk *46*
  jazz 50, 53, 130, 198
  radio 130, 131, 132
  rock'n'roll 47, 53, *197*
musicals 197

N

names, popular 237
nannies 16, 17, *17*
nappies 12, 15
  disposable 12, 15
national celebrations 216-27
National Childbirth Trust (NCT) 12, 13
National Garden Scheme (NGS) 142-3
National Health Service (NHS) 10, 13, 104-7
National Insurance 46, 69
national minimum wage 96
National Service 47-9, *48*, 50
National Trust *126*, 143, 191
nationalisation 66, 71, 101, 222
new towns 29
New Year customs 240-2
night clubs 198-9
Notting Hill Carnival 249

nurseries, day *19*, 20
nursery schools 20, 24-5
nursing profession 106-7, *106*, *107*

O

Olympic Games, 1948 212-13
opera 247-8, *247*
Orwell, George 76, *112*
Oxford and Cambridge boat race 209
Oxo cubes *151*

P

package holidays 176, 187, 189
Pancake Day 243, *243*
parking meters 173
Passover *244*
Patten, Marguerite 150
Paul, Leslie 41
Peabody Trust 110
pedestrian precincts 158-9
penicillin 11
picnics 174-5
Pioneer Corps *81*
pirate radio 131
Pizza Express 200
Playboy Club *199*
playgroups 25
plywood 125
polytechnics 51
Poor Law 11, 69, 104
pop concerts and festivals 52, 65, *245*, 248
postmen 65, *140-1*
pot noodles 151
Poundbury 118
prams 15, *18*
prefabs *117*, 118, *138*
prep schools 31, 33
Priestley, J.B. 66, 178
primary school 24, 25-7, 176
prisoners-of-war 60, *60*, *117*
professional classes 98-107
Promenade Concerts 130, 248
Public Assistance Committee 69
public schools 31, *31*, 33, 203
public sector employment 100
public transport 113
  air travel *92*, 172, *173*, 176, 189
  buses 167-8, *168*
  coach services *166*, 185
  trams 167, *167*
  see also railways
pubs 113, *193*, 201
Punch & Judy 182

Q

Quant, Mary 51-2, 157, *158*
Queen Mary 68, *68*

R

radio broadcasting 128-33, 133-4
  children's programmes 34, 128
  gardening programmes 138, 143
  light entertainment 128, 129, 132
  music 130, 131, 132
  news broadcasts 128, 130
  outside broadcasts 209
  pirate radio 131
  wartime 129, 130
radiograms 131-2
radios 85, 128, 131, 132
railway posters 66, 69, 72, 112, 164, 177, 179, 181, 184, 185, 187, 189, 203, 211
railways 72, 73, 101, 112, 114, 117, 164-6
  Beeching closures 117, 166
  diesel, conversion to 166
  electrification 119, 164, 168
  London Underground 114, 168
  nationalisation 165
  privatisation 166
  speed records 164-5
  steam locomotives 72, 164-5, 165
rationing
  clothes 156
  food 48, 147-8, 148
Ready Steady Go 53
record players 131, 131
Redcoats 184
registry office weddings 236
Reith, Sir John 128, 130, 134
Remembrance Sunday 250
Retail Price Maintenance 151
retail trades 88-90
Richard, Cliff 50, 197
road houses 200
road safety 173
rock gardens 142
Rockers 53
rock'n'roll 47, 53, 197
Rolling Stones 52, 52
Ronan Point collapse 119
Ronnie Scott's 50, 198
roof gardens 153-4
Royal Academy Summer Exhibition 246-7
Royal Automobile Club (RAC) 173, 190
royal jubilees 217-18, 218, 227, 227
rural life 56-65
  depopulation 57, 65, 115, 117
  rural crafts 59, 65
  rural idyll 56
  see also agriculture

S

Sackville-West, Vita 80, 137
safari parks 190-1, 190

safety belts 173
Sainsbury's 148
saints' days 243-4
Salvation Army 114
same-sex couples 238
Sandhurst Military Academy 104
satire 135
Savile, Jimmy 34
school leaving age 27, 28, 46
schools
  boarding 31, 33
  building boom 26
  class sizes 27
  comprehensive 30, 30
  grammar 28, 29, 30, 30, 33
  immigrant pupils 27
  middle 30
  nursery 20, 24-5
  prep 31, 33
  primary 25-7, 25, 26, 27
  public 31, 31, 33, 203
  secondary moderns 29, 29, 30
  sport 27, 28, 33, 202, 203, 204
  technical 29
Scouts see Boy Scouts
seaside resorts 178-83, 178, 179, 183
Second World War
  agriculture 58, 60
  bomb damage 78-9, 118, 156, 168
  child evacuation programme 42-3
  civil defence volunteers 82-3
  conscientious objectors 80
  conscription 71, 79
  employment 60, 78-83
  Phoney War 82
  VE and VJ Day 221-2, 221
  wartime sporting fixtures 208
  wartime weddings 230-1
secondary modern schools 29, 29, 30
secondary picketing 96
secret ballots 96
self-service retailing 90, 148, 148
Selfridges 89-90, 153, 157, 157
semi-skilled workers 66, 72, 77
service industries 92-3
sex discrimination 91
sheep farming 57, 58, 65
Shelter 134
shipbuilding 66, 68-9, 68, 69, 81
shopping 147, 147, 152-61
shopping centres and malls 159
Shrimpton, Jean 53
Simpson's of Piccadilly 153
Sissinghurst 137, 191
Sitwell, Osbert 137
the Sixties 19, 23, 45, 52-3

skilled workers 66, 72, 73, 80, 98, 113
skills shortage 73
skinheads 45
sliced bread 151
slum clearance 76, 110
Smith, Delia 150, 151
smogs 167, 168
smoking 167
social mobility 98
solicitors 101-2, 103
space exploration 127, 135
'spec' building 76, 112
speed limits 173
speed records 164, 165
Spock, Benjamin 17, 18-19, 20, 24
sport 202-13
  see also individual sports
  school sports day 27
stately homes 117, 126, 191
steel industry 66, 96, 101
Steele, Tommy 50, 197, 197
sterling devaluation 96
Stock Exchange 99-100
stockbroking 98, 99, 99-100
Stonehenge 244
Stopes, Marie 10
strikes 94, 96, 107
suburbs 76, 110, 110, 112, 112, 113, 113-14, 138
summer houses 142
summer solstice 244, 248
supermarkets 90, 148, 148, 151
synthetic fabrics 126

T

teaching profession 101, 105 see also education; schools
technical schools 29
Teddy Boys 46-7, 195
teenagers see young people
telephones 85, 123
television 35, 102, 129, 132-5, 221
  BBC 134
  children's programmes 34-5
  colour television 35, 135
  cookery 150, 151
  DIY 127
  gardening 142, 143
  ITV 134-5
  soaps 134, 135
  sport 210-11
Territorial Army (TA) 79
Tesco 148
test tube babies 13
textile industries 66, 74, 75, 75, 115
Thamesmead 119
Thatcher, Margaret 26, 71, 96
thatching 65
theatre 197-8
Thrower, Percy 142, 143
Timber Corps 81

tourism 93, 188, 189
  see also holidays
town planning 103
toys and games 22-3, 26, 110, 120-1
trade unions 66, 69, 70, 94-6, 246, 247
traffic wardens 173
trams 167, 167
transistor radios 131, 132
trolley buses 167
Truby King, Frederick 15-16, 17
Tudorbethan style 115
Tunnard, Christopher 137
Tupperware 134
Twiggy 53, 158
typing pools 90, 90

U

unemployment 66, 69, 72, 76-7, 94, 144
universities 33, 46, 48, 50-1, 98, 236, 246
unskilled workers 76, 77
Up Helly-Aa festival 241
utility furniture 125-6

V

Valentine's Day 242-3
VE and VJ Day 221-2, 221, 222
vegetable gardening 138, 140-1, 141
Vespa scooters 53, 169
Victoriana 127
villages 116, 117, 118
voting age 52, 238

W

Wakes Week 177-8
wallpapers 122-3, 126
washing day 124
Watch With Mother 34, 35
Wheatcroft, Harry 142
white collar workers 86, 93, 95, 113
The Who 52, 53
wildlife gardening 143
Wilson, Harold 36, 211, 222
Wimbledon 211
Wimpy bars 200
wine 151
Woburn Abbey 191
women
  employment 45, 66, 75, 75, 77, 86-91, 95, 99-100, 101, 105
  housewives 85, 86, 135, 144
  marriage 52, 86-7, 228-33, 238
  military service 80, 87
  sportswomen 211
  trade union membership 95
  war work 20, 60, 78-9, 80-1, 80
Women's Institute 129, 141
Women's Land Army 60, 80, 81

Women's Voluntary Service (WVS) 82, 83, 230-1
Woodcraft Folk 41
Woolworths 89, 155-6, 156, 161, 182
work see employment
working hours 73
World Cup Final 1966 210, 210

Y

young people 44-53
  anarchism 50
  employment 46
  music 50, 52
  National Service 47-9, 48, 50
  spending power 52
  students 50-1
youth culture 50-3, 52
youth hostels 185

BIBLIOGRAPHY

Akhtar, Miriam, and Humphries, Steve, *The Fifties and Sixties: A Lifestyle Revolution* (Boxtree, 2001)

    Some Liked it Hot: The British on Holiday at Home and Abroad (Virgin Publishing, 2000)

Beckett, Andy, *When the Lights Went Out: What Really Happened to Britain in the Seventies* (Faber & Faber, 2009)

Gardiner, Juliet, *From the Bomb to the Beatles: The Changing Face of Post-war Britain* (Collins & Brown, 1999)

    Wartime: Britain 1939-1945 (Headline, 2004)

    The Children's War (Portrait, in association with the IWM, 2007)

    The Thirties: An Intimate History (Harper Press, 2010)

    The Blitz: The British Under Attack (Harper Press, 2010)

Graves, Robert, and Hodge, Alan, *The Long Weekend: A Social History of Great Britain, 1918-1939* (1940; Cardinal, 1985)

Hardyment, Christina, *Dream Babies: Child Care from Locke to Spock* (Jonathan Cape, 1983)

Holdsworth, Angela, *Out of the Doll's House: The Story of Women in the Twentieth Century* (BBC Books, 1988)

Horn, Pamela, *Behind the Counter: Shop Lives from Market Stall to Supermarket* (Sutton Publishing, 2006)

Horseman, Grace, *Growing Up in the Thirties* (Cottage Publishing, 1994)

Humphries, Steve, *Labour of Love: The Experience of Parenthood in Britain 1900-1950* (Sidgwick & Jackson, 1993)

Kynaston, David, *Austerity Britain 1945-1951* (Bloomsbury, 2007)

    Family Britain 1951-1957 (Bloomsbury, 2009)

Lawson, John, and Silver, Harold, *A Social History of Education in England* (Methuen, 1973)

Pressley, Alison, *The Best of Times: Growing Up in the 1950s* (Michael O'Mara Books, 1999)

Roud, Steve, *The English Year* (Penguin Books, 2006)

Rowley, Trevor, *The English Landscape in the Twentieth Century* (Hambledon, 2006)

Sandbrook, Dominic, *Never Had It So Good: A History of Britain from Suez to the Beatles* (Little, Brown, 2005)

    White Heat: A History of Britain in the Swinging Sixties (Little, Brown, 2006)

    State of Emergency: The Way We Were, Britain 1970-1974 (Allen Lane, 2010)

Stevenson, John, *The Penguin Social History of Britain: British Society 1914-45* (Allen Lane, 1984)

Walton, John K, *The British Seaside: Holidays and Resorts in the Twentieth Century* (Manchester University Press, 2000)

Weight, Richard, *Patriots: National Identity in Britain, 1940-2000* (Macmillan, 2002)

PICTURE CREDITS AND ACKNOWLEDGEMENTS

Abbreviations: t = top; m = middle; b = bottom; r = right; c = centre; l = left

All images in this book are courtesy of Getty Images, including the following which have additional attributions:

Apic: 171

John Bulmer: 54-55, 114, 124t, 162-163

Romano Cagnoni: 51

The Conservative Party Archives: 119t

Gerti Deutsch: 16b

Epics: 149t

Tim Graham: 226

Imagno: 36

Keystone-France: 148, 213br, 251

Steve Lewis: 159

National Geographic: 24, 40b, 121br

New York Times: 71t

Popperfoto: 2, 11b, 22r, 29t, 30t, 32, 35r, 87t, 88t, 93, 102b, 104, 123, 139, 142b, 144t, 147b, 156t, 157, 158t, 170, 174t, 175br, 180, 191l, 195, 206b, 213l, 218, 219b, 224m, 231br

Princess Diana Archive: 233

Redferns: 44, 197b

SSPL: 15b, 21, 26, 30b, 43t, 53b, 62r, 66, 69b, 72b, 87b, 89m, 97, 106t, 110, 112b, 128, 134, 154b, 164, 165, 172b, 177b, 179t, 181, 184t, 185b, 187b, 189b, 203b, 204, 211b, 219t, 220t, 222, 240

John Tarlton: 214-215

Time & Life Pictures: 126, 140t, 179b, 199, 228, 231l

Display quotation on page 240 © 2006 John Ravenscroft (http://www.johnravenscroft.co.uk), taken from TimeTravel-Britain.com

Quotations on the Durham Miners' Gala in the text on page 247 © 2003 Raymond Chesterfield, taken from the Durham Miner project website © 2011 Durham County Council

PICTURES WITHOUT CAPTIONS

FRONT COVER: East End boys photographed by John Chillingworth at a coronation party in Morpeth Street, London, in 1953.

BACK COVER: A family at the beach in 1950, photographed by Norman Vigars.

TITLE PAGE: A fairground scene somewhere in Britain in 1949.

MEMORIES OF BRITAIN PAST

Published in 2011 in the United Kingdom by Vivat Direct Limited (t/a Reader's Digest), 157 Edgware Road, London W2 2HR, in association with Getty Images. Picture research and layout for Vivat Direct Limited by Endeavour London Limited.

Written by
Juliet Gardiner

For Vivat Direct
Project editor: Christine Noble
Senior art editor: Conorde Clarke
Freelance editor: Tony Allan
Indexer: Marie Lorimer
Proofreader: Ron Pankhurst

For Endeavour
Publisher: Charles Merullo
Designer: Tea Aganovic
Picture editor: Jennifer Jeffrey
Production: Mary Osborne

Editorial director: Julian Browne
Art director: Anne-Marie Bulat
Managing editor: Nina Hathway
Picture resource manager: Sarah Stewart-Richardson
Pre-press technical manager: Dean Russell
Product production manager: Claudette Bramble
Senior production controller: Jan Bucil

We are committed both to the quality of our products and the service we provide to our customers. We value your comments, so please do contact us on 0871 3511000 or via our website at www.readersdigest.co.uk

If you have any comments or suggestions about the content of our books, email us at: gbeditorial@readersdigest.co.uk

Colour origination by Chroma Graphics Ltd, Singapore
Printed and bound in Europe

CONCEPT CODE: UK 2746L-OP
BOOK CODE: 400-500 UP0000-1
ISBN: 978 0 276 44663 4